CONTENTS

ACKNOWLEDGEMENTS

Illustrations from 'Tarot of the Spirit' reproduced by permission of U.S. Games Systems, Inc. Stamford, CT 06902 USA, Copyright ☐ 1996 by U.S. Games Systems, Inc. Further reproduction prohibited.

Reproductions from Robin Wood by kind permission of Robin Wood. I am very grateful to Ms Wood for permitting me to use illustrations from her fine deck, copies of which are obtainable from Llewellyn Publications, St. Paul, Minnesota, 55164-0383, USA. You may contact Robin Wood through her website at www.RobinWood.com

I am also very grateful to Pamela Eakins for her permission to use the 'Tarot of the Spirit' and for her kind comments. Copies of this deck are available from the address above.

DEDICATION

For Dakota,

May your quest ever be full of:

The wonder of the Fool
The achievement of the Magician
The sensitivity of the High Priestess
The love of the Empress
The cleverness of the Emperor
The belief of the Hierophant
The clarity of the Lovers
The force of the Chariot
The courage of Strength
The wisdom of the Hermit
The luck of the Wheel of Fortune
The truth of Justice
The service of the Hanged Man
The liberation of Death
The serenity of Temperance
The realisation of the Devil
The safety of the Tower
The hope of the Star
The intuition of the Moon
The joy of the Sun
The freedom of Judgement
The unity of the World.

All these I offer you, little one
May you use them wisely.

THE SPIRIT OF THE TAROT

Etheric essence, unseen, unheard
The trunk of this particular tree
Blend of seventy-eight symbols in one
As life always was you ever shall be

The visualisation of the concept complete
The dramatisation of the silent scene
The encapsulation of all poignant principle
You are alpha, omega and all points in between

Proud sentinel of truth esoteric
Preserver of knowledge and mysteries known
Guardian of (pre) Atlantean tradition
You bring the breath of all life to truth carved in stone

As rivers of water fill the cups of your blood
The strength of the soil forms the rock of your bones
The rays of the Sun, fiery rods of your soul
Cuts the air of your breath clear as the sword flows

In combination blessed serene unity
Being Divine formed long aeons ago
Time beyond time, interpretation sublime
Humanity's Guide, the Spirit of Tarot

FOREWORD

A cursory glance at the Bibliography of this book will confirm that the Tarot is a subject about which a great deal has been written. Why then, have I seen a need to add to the collection?

Like all esoteric subjects, that Tarot can be seen as a living thing, with an indomitable spirit that has continually evolved since its mysterious origins, a little like humanity itself. Esotericists agree that there is a life force or energy that pervades all things. For example, the Native Americans believe that so-called inanimate objects such as rocks and stones have a life of their own, a distinct consciousness. This attitude or belief is called animism - the idea of this energy animating, or giving life to, all things.

We shall see through the course of the three volumes of this book that the energy or power of the Tarot lies in the symbols which constitute its holistic identity. These symbols can also be viewed as having a life force of their own. This is because many of them, like the Tarot itself, have been in existence for thousands of years. When a symbol becomes widely recognised and accepted as such, it attracts an energy to and around it, congealed from the countless thought forms and mental energy patterns directed at it, as people across the world and over the years study and work with it. We will examine this process in more detail when we look at how the Tarot works, but for now it is enough to recognise that the energy around an object is affected, in however small a way, by all it comes into contact with.

There are many such parallels the Tarot has with humanity, echoed throughout this book, which here serve to illustrate for us something of the understanding of the human condition which the Tarot depicts and explains. When viewed in this way, the experienced consultant has much to offer the client of a therapeutic nature by its use.

4

The same is true of the Tarot as a whole. Each book written about the Tarot and indeed each new deck created, offers its own particular and individual energy or power to the spirit of the Tarot, as in some small way, does each person that consults it. It is this rich diversity and eclectic approach that the Tarot welcomes and is uniquely suited to, that not only allows, but embraces, such a number of interpretations, views, opinions, studies, images . . . and books.

At this particular time in the history of humanity we find ourselves on the threshold of the Aquarian Age. Again, a great deal has been written about this and from the writings on offer we learn that this can be the beginning of a 'golden age' of peace and plenty for humanity as a whole. However, when we look at the condition of the world which humanity has brought about, this does not seem very likely. It serves no purpose to catalogue the violence, exploitation, cruelty, poverty, injustice, greed and so on that exists across the world today, but such things do serve to point out that we have much to achieve if we wish to see this golden age occur. In the naive and pure spirit of the Fool of the Tarot, I believe that this is a possibility and can become reality - for all peoples of the Earth. Clearly however, we will need much guidance to make it happen. The Tarot, having been around, in some form, since well before the beginning of the passing Piscean Age, is perfectly placed to offer us its knowledge and wisdom, culled from this vast experience.

To maximise the potential of this experience, it becomes necessary for the Tarot to adapt its position on the axis of the two Ages, shifting its view to that of a forward looking guide and teacher, having the benefit of hindsight. Humanity must also learn to do this and as such, can come to view the Tarot as a helper on two levels.

For a global golden age to come to birth individuals must discover what it is they are lacking in themselves, what prevents them from fulfilling their potential and reaching wholeness. Only when this has been done, in a 'critical mass' of people the world over, can the Aquarian Age be truly said to have arrived, as it was always intended to be. For this wholeness to be found in enough people there must exist a body of teaching and guidance that transcends the limits of individual or even global belief, as it occurs in the different religions of the world, something that teaches sacredness and that accepts your particular beliefs, whatever they may be. With adaptation for this stage in our development, the Tarot can be one such entity or at the least a part of one.

In this we can celebrate the differences of our spiritual beliefs and practises, without letting them divide us to the point of war. Rather, we can find the similarities in our doctrines and the meeting points in our devotions. It is my experience that the Tarot is capable of showing us, at both this individual and collective level, the sacredness that is so clearly lacking in so many people today. Given the correct approach, the Tarot can reveal to us once again, from its wizened position of embodying ancient wisdom for all, the therapy we all need.

In turn, to achieve this therapeutic view of the Tarot, we must view it differently, taking a deeper look into the eyes of the Fool and letting the wisdom of his innocent folly guide us. Having seen an esoteric place and perhaps necessity for more offerings concerning the Tarot, we must bring that higher level down to Earth and see how we can apply its knowledge in ourselves and lives, as we must all spiritual teaching. Therapy is needed at all four levels of the human individual, physical, emotional, mental and spiritual and as we shall see, the Tarot is ideally suited to produce this, in the hands of a capable and professional therapist.

The purpose of these volumes is to explore the therapeutic nature of the Tarot as one that can guide us to the sacredness we seek in our soul and that ultimately can unite us as we turn the card to welcome the dawn of a new era in our history. It is hoped that this will also begin to restore the Tarot to its rightful place of honour as a sacred method of healing.

INTRODUCTION

This book will attempt to investigate the Tarot as a therapeutic method of healing. This means healing in its widest sense, being that which brings or returns the patient, or client, to a state of wholeness. We will come to identify exactly what this wholeness is when we undertake the Seekers Quest, accompanying the Fool on his journey through the cards of the Major Arcana. We will come to see through this book that the Tarot can be a powerful and vital tool to have by your side, as we each journey through our lives on our own particular quest for wholeness.

This does not mean that we must be on some conscious quest for spiritual enlightenment or wisdom. Whilst the Tarot is undoubtedly and eminently suited to acting as a worthy guide toward such lofty goals, we will discover that its truths apply in the everyday world in which we live out our lives. It is at this level that therapy or healing must be applied.

It is perhaps this that has led the Tarot to where we find it now, occupying a stall in the market place that is but a dim reflection of the hallowed status of office it once held. When mention is made of the Tarot in conversation, the talk is of fortune-telling and predicting the future. This may seem a strange thing to question, such is the limited view that most hold of the Tarot at present, including many of those who profess to be practitioners of its art. These people may well be expert in the use of the Tarot for divination, as is the correct term for future prediction. However, we are extolling here an alternative interpretation of this term.

The Collins English Dictionary defines divination as 'the art or practice of discovering future events or unknown things, as though by supernatural powers'. Whilst we will not debate the ambiguity of the use of the phrase 'as though', we will focus on the term 'supernatural power', using this to put forth our proposition for what divination truly is. Most, if not all, who use the Tarot, in whatever way, will agree that there is some higher power in existence, whatever that form may be viewed as and whether it is viewed as the power behind the accuracy of the Tarot's ability to predict future events or not. The term divination therefore implies to consult or interact with, the Divine, whatever we conceive this to be.

If by using the Tarot, we are having some kind of communication with a Divine being, does it not follow that the questions submitted, as well as the answers given, are likely to be of a rather deeper, more serious or meaningful nature than the typical questions posed by many when encountering the Tarot at the ubiquitous 'Psychic Fayre'. This is where we find the Tarot in use in its modern and accepted method, that of fortune telling.

This commercial use of the Tarot is certainly a successful one and we can see this as a symbol of the Piscean Age, particularly in the last two hundred years, when primarily since the Industrial Revolution, first the Western and now the Eastern world has become motivated by the work ethic initially, which then grew to become consumed by profit and is now satiated only by excess. Perhaps fortunately, we are leaving behind the Piscean Age and so, in time, all it has come to represent, following the commercial traps capitalism has laid for each of us. Now, we must look forward to the Aquarian Age and a different set of motives and ambitions. Equally our use of the Tarot must also change from being driven by the amount we pay per minute for our 'reading' to a healing consultation in a sacred environment.

It should be made clear at this stage that fortune telling is not wrong and that it has its place, both via use of the Tarot and the myriad other options available, such as Runes, Crystal Ball, Tea Leaves, palm and so on. The popularity of the psychic fayre (why, I wonder is it not spelt fair?) attests to this. However over the years that I have worked with it, I have come to view the Tarot in a rather different light than that of a tool that is able to tell who and when we will marry and so on.

This light is a sacred one, as for I and I know for many others who use or consult it, the Tarot depicts a body of ancient wisdom that is still relevant today as we attempt to unravel the mysteries of our life and its purpose and meaning. Though it shows us much of the spiritual world it also tells us a great deal about the material world in which we live, move and have our being. When viewed in this light, the Tarot serves to remind us that we are all on a sacred or spiritual quest, the difference being whether we are aware or accepting of this or not.

For those that are not, they may deny the existence of such spirituality and that indeed is their prerogative. These noble folk we will leave to their lives, wondering where their motivation comes from and applauding their ability to remain optimistic and cheerful amidst the tragedy of human existence.

For those able to accept the existence of some form of divine being we come to see that the Tarot can act as a guide along our life's path to atonement. If we accept that life is a spiritual quest it follows that our individual quests, wherever we may be on Earth and whatever religion or belief we subscribe to, must eventually meet up with this one Divine being. The aim of such lives is therefore atonement with the Divine.

In keeping with our method of interpretation of the word divination, we can see atonement as meaning 'at-one-ment', or a state of oneness with, the Divine. When this has been achieved, we can consider ourselves truly whole, since it is from this Divine that we once came, as the Tarot itself shows, which we will also see through the Seeker's Quest. When we realise we are indeed on this quest simply because we are alive, there takes place a spiritual awakening in the body, heart, mind and spirit of that lucky person. After this, much is needed.

Chief among these needs is a guide that can show us the way, someone who has been this way before, knows the pitfalls, dangers and traps, but can also encourage us with the promise of the rewards to come. The spiritual life, however it is lived, is one that shapes a radically different goal and objective from that of the purely material. Its goals are equally different, being unconcerned with the acquisition of goods or the climbing of the corporate ladder and so on. The guide for such worldly matters can be the province of the fortune tellers and there we shall leave them

The spiritual life is fraught with uncertainty, worry and even potential disaster. One who would aspire to be a guide to those travelling this rocky road must therefore be experienced, sure of themselves, even self-sacrificial if necessary, since their previous journey has shown them that 'the needs of the one outweighs the needs of the few, or the many'. The spiritual guide must be one whose essence is pure, untainted by the lower motivation of profit or material gain, driven instead by a desire to serve and to unite, to heal and make whole that which has been separated. Our guide must be able to keep us keeping on, as we stumble blindly through the wasteland that is life on Earth, lifting our eyes above the bullshit of human existence, focusing instead on the glory and wonder of creation, all the while determined in our resolution to find our way (back) to the Divine. In short, our guide must in some way reflect something of our own image of the Divine.

When we examine the Tarot in the glare of this sacred light, we find it is all these things and a great deal more besides. As such, it is able to function as a loyal friend for even the most ardent and puritanical of seekers. Viewed in this way, we realise that those who aspire to use it in this therapeutic light have a very tall order to meet.

We cannot hope that all those who use the Tarot as a therapy will be perfect reflections of the Divine; far from it, but we can at least strive for the best we are able to achieve. Anything less is nothing short of an insult, both to us and the Creator of this wonderful place. The times of abuse and degradation must end and they must end first with those who are prepared to live the spiritual life to the best of their ability, at whatever cost. For them, the rewards are great, but they cannot be measured in worldly terms, nor will or should they ever be seen as such. It is to such people this book is addressed, in the hope that they may be able to use the Tarot as a means to guide firstly themselves and subsequently others on their quest.

We have seen that the therapy spoken of in this book is first and foremost a spiritual one. However, just as the material life must eventually and inevitably lead to that spiritual life, so the therapeutic use of the Tarot can first apply in our daily lives. When we are seeking to make ourselves whole, we need to address our needs on the four levels of existence that are the physical, emotional, mental and spiritual. The Tarot, as we shall see when we investigate its structure, is perfectly suited to address these needs, thereby becoming the method of healing we desire at both a practical and spiritual level. When interpreted in such a manner, the Tarot becomes the perfect therapeutic guide, able at once to bring the sacred to the mundane, thereby bridging the gap that covers the chasm in modern life. It is in this way that the Tarot is so much more than the prediction of a 'tall, dark stranger crossing your path'. It is an ancient and sacred body of knowledge which can address the deepest needs, bringing light and healing.

There is currently developing a much needed and welcome, increasing acceptance of the so-called 'complementary therapies' into the mainstream, medical field. This includes such therapies as aromatherapy, reflexology and healing, in its many forms. With this integration comes the necessity for the therapists that administer the procedures to be practising to accepted, professional standards and to be affiliated to bodies that regulate and award these standards, having studied an approved curriculum to demonstrate their ability in their chosen therapy.

Whilst, as previously mentioned, this integration into the mainstream is welcomed and is indeed, a natural consequence of the progression of medicine, it also brings with it developing therapies that begin on the fringe of the healing field, before they too, in time, make their way into the centre of that field. This is the present place of the Tarot and other esoteric therapies, when used in this way.

One of the many benefits that widespread acceptance of complementary therapies brings is the fundamental view of the human being as body, mind and spirit. In choosing which therapy to treat yourself with, there are many available, some perhaps more accessible than others. Each aims to treat the client with the above, holistic view. The majority of these therapies do however, focus on the body as the means of healing the dis-ease presented. Healing of the mind and spirit are often seen as coming from the healing of the body, the result of focussing primarily on the physical need.

There are many aspects that the complementary therapies have in common, perhaps the strongest 'common denominator' being the acknowledgement of both the existence and use of energy, in both the client, 'healer' and the treatment itself. Indeed, it is becoming another widely accepted principle in the fringe field of healing that the medicine of the future is that of 'vibrational medicine', being the manipulation of this energy to bring about a return to balance and wholeness in the client, which precipitates the 'healing' of the physical manifestation of this state of 'dis-ease'.

The Esoteric, or spiritual, view of the nature of things is that all things come from and exist of, energy, or life-force. This is the same life-force that complementary practitioners acknowledge and that scientists are now beginning to accept. The esoteric healer or therapist works from the standpoint that physical dis-ease and indeed all physical nature is the end result or manifestation of energy in a particular form. In the case of human health, a physical dis-ease is the result of a blockage or imbalance in the clients' energy. As the physical body and its health or dis-ease is but one part of the energy matrix that is a human being, it follows that treatment, of whatever form, must occur at this energy level to have a lasting and profound effect. This is not to say of course, that the complementary therapies are invalidated; far from it, for they simply work from the physical to the energy level. The Esoteric therapist works from, with and in the energy level of the client, bringing about a shift or movement here, that precipitates change and a restoration of balance at the other levels of the client, these being the mental, emotional and physical respectively. In this way, the medicine of the future and of the Aquarian Age, is born.

Esotericists have long accepted and worked with this all-pervading life force or energy, seeing it as existing in all things and at all levels of life. The exciting field of quantum physics is giving us new insights and understanding into our very natures. It has been stated that when we fully understand the nature of the Universe in which we live, at the quantum level, we will understand the mind of God. Whilst this is a sweeping statement open to much debate, it does indicate the level at which we must approach the human being, if we are to continue to develop and progress through the 21st Century. This includes the awareness of the life-force energy and the conscious knowledge that all things exist in and of this state.

In the many years I have been involved with and studied esoteric and healing matters, these principles are for me, nowhere better illustrated and expounded than in the Tarot. This vast body of work and knowledge explains, in symbolic and pictorial format, the nature and outworking of energy, showing the place of the human being at the earthly level of ourselves and lives, as the physical level of our being in the wider Universe and context. As such the Tarot is perfectly placed to offer knowledge and guidance and, in the hands of a suitable 'Tarot Therapist', precipitate healing to the client.

This requires, of course, the Tarot to be seen in this 'new' (actually, very old!) light. For this to occur, on a wide scale, much work needs to be done, initially on a local level. In the case of the above named, accepted complementary therapies, the necessary curriculum and professional administering bodies have been in existence for some time and the required standards are being met. In the public eye and therefore at the vital archetypal level where fundamental change must occur, the Tarot languishes sadly at the end of the pier and in the fortune-telling booth.

For the Tarot to be restored to its rightful place as a sacred healing method/tool, it must be seen and accepted as such. For this to occur professional standards must be introduced that we see have brought the other complementary and natural therapies into the mainstream of medicine and healing, from the fringes where they began. Affiliation to regulatory bodies must be aimed for, codes of practice and conduct must be introduced and adhered to, basic standards must be set and examinations implemented. Only then can the Tarot begin to reclaim its standing as the great and powerful sacred therapy it is.

In observing the move to central acceptance of complementary therapies that is taking place, I have noticed that they are being promoted and utilised by the nurses, rather than the surgeons and consultants. For change to be effective, it must take place within and such is the case here. It is not from the top down that natural therapies are being used in the NHS, but from the inside out. In my work through the Consultations I offer and through the lectures, workshops, and courses I teach, and now through the medium of this book, I am applying this principle to the Community.

In this book I have focussed on the Tarot as the principle method of esoteric therapy that I apply. This is because, as stated above, it has always been the spine around which my work gains its flexibility and adaptability. It should be stressed however that this is only one aspect of the consultations I work with and that I use the Tarot with a specific therapeutic intention, taking it a long way away from the use of fortune-telling to which it is usually put.

By combining the Tarot with meditation and inner work, shamanic journeying, smudging, drumming, healing and so on, as seems appropriate for the client, healing, as a restoration of balance and well-being is brought about. The Tarot has the ability to illustrate the nature of the dis-ease or imbalance and techniques such as those named above are then utilised to effect the cure. I view this not as a weakness, but a strength of the Tarot, since it has continually demonstrated to me an ability to explain the different philosophies and belief systems I have explored and adapted itself to them. Here it shows an ability to work perfectly alongside many other therapies, such as those mentioned throughout this introduction.

It should also be stressed that when used in a therapeutic way the Tarot alone is often enough to bring about the energy shift or movement required to precipitate the healing required in the client. The power of the realisation that the sensitive Tarot Therapist can effect within the client is easily enough to cause energy to flow, adhering to the powerful esoteric law that 'energy follows thought'. This causes a healing brought about at the mental level of the client, facilitating the holistic healing required for it to be true. Whatever its point of origin, therapy or healing, must occur at the energetic level of the patient or client as we shall refer to them, to be truly effective, lasting and bring about the state of balance and wholeness required.

It is acknowledged however, that perhaps the most effective therapy is that which effects its cure at all four levels of the client: physical, emotional, mental and spiritual. Neither should be underestimated or seen as more important than the other. Healing can be seen as the ability to restore a state of balance in the client. This balance requires at the very least an acknowledgement of the needs of these levels in the client. The Tarot automatically achieves this minimum requirement since, by its very nature, it consists of those four levels itself, in the suits of the Minor Arcana. This ability is made all the more powerful as it goes on to combine these four levels in the body of the Major Arcana, enabling therapy or healing to be addressed at the whole person, at their deepest or highest level. The Tarot is perfectly placed as a therapy and astonishingly powerful and effective when combined with other such natural tools for cure.

This is not a promise of some instant, miracle cure of course, for such things are rare indeed. The nature of energy is to flow and move, in the case of the human being, in accordance with the nature of the individual personality it exists within. The existence of freewill means that we can choose what we do with this energy. In the case of a Tarot Therapy Consultation, this may be to accept or reject the energy flow brought about through it.

As we live our lives in the hectic, pressured and polluted world we have created for ourselves we find that we each have occasions where we need external assistance to restore our balance, health and well-being, reminding us of our sacred nature and purpose of our existence. In short, we do not need to wait until some physical manifestation of an energetic imbalance occurs to seek therapy. In other word, you do not have to be ill to have healing. It is always a privilege and honour to work with clients in this way and a wonderful experience to be involved in.

For this to happen the Tarot practitioner, or consultant, must view the cards in this light and learn of their healing ways for themselves, before they are able to pass this energy on to their clients. Because of this,. I have included exercises, meditations and suggestions to facilitate this process. As such this book can also be used as a course of instruction in learning how to use the Tarot for therapy, or healing.

By such processes, of which this is of course only one, the Tarot can begin its long journey back to owning the place it deserves as the embodiment of ancient wisdom. The essence of the Tarot has never changed since its inception, for this ancient wisdom is also timeless, for it is simple truth. It is, veritably, as good today as it has always been. This is because it is truth and truth is beyond time, above all reason and argument and comes from a place of peace.

This peace is to be found in the Divine of course and also in every human. It is our birth right to feel it and retain an awareness of its presence throughout our life, full and conscious. It is only that we have forgotten, or lost, that awareness in our human state. By incarnating as human, we leave behind something of the fullest perception of our reflection of the Divine. By such practices as meditation and ritual we can regain it, but as we live out our daily, practical lives, we lose all sense of the presence of the Divine within us. The Tarot acknowledges this and goes on to show us how we can recapture the peace and comfort of the Divine, thereby being naturally therapeutic on both a mundane and spiritual level. The bridge between the two is that which the Tarot built so long ago and which still stands firm today, ready and able to support all those who dare to cross. The bridge is that of truth.

Such truth can only come from a higher level than our human existence. There is every indication that we are in dire need of this information at this time in our history and we have been granted the Tarot as one method by which we can learn 'the truth'. Let us embrace the energy of this truth by utilising the therapeutic nature of the Tarot and help both ourselves and others in so doing. I hope that this book helps you to do this.

CHAPTER 1 - FALLING OFF THE CLIFF

This book will take as its theme the therapeutic ability and use of the Tarot, with due regard to its sacred nature, which in turn stems from its subject matter; that of ancient and established spiritual wisdom and truth. These factors will be borne in mind throughout the book, requiring every aspect of the Tarot to be examined in this light. Consequently, the book will include some aspects of the Tarot given scant, or no regard elsewhere. Equally, it may not mention some areas of consulting the Tarot common and accepted in other places. By way of example of this, an emphasis will be placed on the ability of the reader to listen to their intuition and inner voice, as the means of interpretation of the cards, as opposed to meanings given for you to use in your consultations. Reasons for this, together with methods to achieve it will be explained in due course.

VARIETIES OF TAROT

Included here and to begin with, is one largely ignored subject, that of the varieties of pack now available and how to choose your first pack of Tarot. The adjective 'first' is included deliberately since Tarot seems to have an unnerving ability to become addictive. With the advent in recent years of so many different packs being designed and becoming available, many beautiful and all with something to offer, the era of the Tarot card collector comes upon us. Here I must stand and declare myself a member of the 'T.A.' - 'Taroics Anonymous', saying a little guiltily but also proudly that 'I am a Tarot addict'!

When the applause to this admission fades, I meekly offer the following warning. The Tarot depicts the journey through life, as a spiritual path, that all of us must someday travel, in this or some other life. It therefore has the ability, at some point in its 78 cards, to identify with where we are at any given moment. At this point we cry 'Eureka' and from this moment on, the danger of addiction rises. When we identify with something in our inner being, it is very easy to form an attachment to the source of that identification, whatever it may be. It is a very comforting thought to have; that you are not alone in the Universe, that out there is someone or something that 'knows', that expresses something of what you feel at the core of yourself and that you may have even been only vaguely aware of yourself, until now.

A natural reaction to this pleasurable vice, as with any other, is to seek more of it. I therefore take this time to warn that you that when you have the 'Tarot Eureka' experience, you may well find yourself scouring shops that sell Tarot packs in search of a pack that more closely resembles the Universe you, as an individual, feel and envision that you live in. I would also say here, that if you do not have this experience at some stage whilst reading this book, it is likely that the Tarot, at this therapeutic level, is not for you.

In truth what has happened to you to bring about your addiction is an initiation, an entry into the world of the Fool, who will henceforth be your guide, mentor and teacher as you try to find your way out of the maze you have crossed the threshold of, as the Tarot can seem on entry. You have inhaled of the perfume of the rose the Fool carries, become intoxicated by its scent and lost all sense of reason and objectivity. With the Fool by your side, you have plunged over the edge of the cliff he patrols, looking for likely candidates and found yourself in the strange and magical world of the Tarot.

As stated above, every pack has something to offer. This perfectly illustrates the power of the Tarot, lying as it does in its ability to be all things to all people. This brings me to my favourite saying regarding the cards:

'The Tarot teaches you about life and life teaches you about Tarot'.

An emphasis is to be placed on the word 'you'. It is how you relate to each and every card, through your own experience and knowledge that will set you apart from merely regurgitating routine, mass produced, book meanings of the cards. It is this ability, arrived at through much hard work, study and application which lifts your use of the cards above that of fortune telling and into therapy. By relating this, following the prompting and guidance of your intuition, to your client, then listening to them and discussing the issues raised between you, the Tarot is enabled to do the work is was truly intended to do, for those who come humbly to it. There is a great deal more that can be added to this, such as the ascription of herbs, essential oils, meditations, chakra workings and so on, but this will be discovered in due course.

It is perhaps because the Tarot reflects life and life reflects the Tarot that allows for the wide variety of packs now printed. We now have available Tarot packs based on almost every conceivable theme. To act as an aid in familiarising yourself with the Tarot and what it is, I have listed in Appendix 1, some of the central themes which different designers have focused on when creating their respective packs. These fall into the broad categories given. This documentation can also act as an aid when choosing the kind of pack you wish to work with and may help to carry you some way across this particular minefield.

It is true to say that the standard reference work for Tarot decks produced in the 20th Century has been the Rider Waite, produced in 1911. This has established the Tarot in its pictorial format and has been invaluable in this. The majority of packs produced since then have been based on the symbolism of the Rider Waite deck, expressed to the view of the particular artist. It is my belief however that, with due high regard to this deck that its time has ended. In the new millennium and with the benefit of new technology that allows for ever more intricate and effective techniques, cards produced now can show a great deal more detail than with previous ones. Equally important is the need for a different style and expression of the symbolism of the cards that reflects the Aquarian age principles outlined in these books and facilitates the therapeutic use of the Tarot here proposed.

THE TAROT OF THE SPIRIT

The three volumes that constitute the work of 'Tarot Therapy' are illustrated with the Tarot of the Spirit, by Pamela Eakins. This unique pack among the many produced recently is perfectly suited to Tarot Therapy work, for it shows, in beautiful detail, the energies of the cards, as they apply to the client consulting them. It is my belief that it is time for some aspects of the traditional designs for the Tarot to make way for those more related the principles of the Aquarian Age which our methods of healing and therapy must adopt. The Tarot of the Spirit achieves this in a most beautiful, clever and effective manner, adding power to the message of the cards. Whilst the reproductions in the book serve to illustrate the card energies perfectly, it is best to obtain a pack of cards and see them in colour for full effect and understanding.

THE ROBIN WOOD TAROT

There are also illustrations of some of the cards of the Robin Wood Tarot. This deck, created by the lady of the same name, is an excellent example of a modern pack that is faithful to original designs. I have chosen this pack specifically for the clarity of its designs and because it serves perfectly to illustrate the core symbolism of the modern Tarot deck, used in the books where needed, thereby allowing for the explanations needed to bring about the therapeutic use of the Tarot.

BUYING A PACK

From the very partial list given in Appendix 1, it is possible to see that the purchase of one's first Tarot pack is a minefield of potentially wasted money, time and energy. It is hoped that the list will go some way to preventing this, by offering the reader some clues as to what each pack contains. To further this goal, I have set out here some guidelines regarding the purchase of a pack of Tarot.

I have been asked the question 'which pack should I choose' many times and the only true answer to this is to pick the one that you like the most. In this way is the Tarot allowed to begin to speak to its owner, right from the outset. We shall discover that the Tarot is a language of symbols and it is these symbols that are able to speak directly to our intuitive self. If we allow ourselves to simply choose the pack that appeals most, for whatever reason, we will be responding at a deeper level to what the designs of the cards, via the symbols that are their component parts, say to us. What they say is not important, but the fact that they say something is. If a pack cannot speak to you in some instinctive form, even at this stage, it is not the correct pack for you.

This presents us with an occupational hazard. What we are looking for when selecting our Tarot pack is some response in our heart and/or mind that says we identify with the picture on the card. This will not be every card of the pack necessarily, but a majority should do something for us if we are to use them for our therapeutic work. This response may be a marvelling at its artwork, an identification with its theme, curiosity or just a positive impulse within our being.

To find this, it is desirable to look at the complete pack. However, very few shops will have an opened pack for potential buyers to examine. The reason for this is that manufacturers' supply packs sealed in cellophane in order to preserve their purity so that another's 'vibration' or energy imprint is not upon them when we first use them, and to keep them unspoiled of course. I would point out here that it is likely that at least one person from the manufacturers will have touched them at some point and that artificial cellophane and indeed the cardboard or plastic box cards are packaged in, will not prevent such energies from seeping through to the cards themselves.

A pack of Tarot cards is 78 pieces of laminated card or plastic, nothing more. It is what is on those cards that is alive, once we learn to interact with their energy. In time, our cards certainly need to become a sacred object, as a reflection of our regard to their wisdom, not the actual physical cards themselves. It is for this reason instructions are included shortly regarding their care. To start with, it is necessary for us to sanctify our cards, to make them a fit vehicle for interaction with the Divine, such will be their use when we use them for Tarot Therapy. For this, please see the Ceremony in the Exercises at the end of this Chapter.

Some publishers, in an effort to negotiate this impasse, supply a selection of cards in a folder which buyers can browse through. If we are not able to look through a friends cards or examine the whole pack in some other way, this is our next best option. One further option to consider is that there may be a book available which contains illustrations of the cards, even though these may be in black and white (the cost of colour reproduction being very expensive). These can also be examined and the content of the book searched for its usefulness. The standard form of packaging for Tarot has become a box set, with cards and a small book. Such books are usually useful for explaining the content of the cards and their particular symbolism, but little else.

When examining cards and book as best you are able, give yourself time, alone, to pause for that all important inner response. If this does not happen with any of the packs available, wait and return another time, perhaps to examine different packs. If you feel that more than one pack 'speaks' to you, it is simply a matter of choice. In this situation, I would recommend choosing that which you like emotionally the most, if for no other reason than to please yourself.

A small, further point to mention here is not to be guided or pushed by cost. With the tendency to package cards complete with a book, costs have inevitably risen and publishers are notoriously reticent about producing packs at all, for little profit is in fact given to them and to the seller themselves (and probably less to the designer!). However, this does not really matter to you when buying your cards. If you cannot afford them, they are not the pack for you. If your heart is set upon a particular pack, wait and save until you can afford them, asking the Universe to supply the funds in exchange for your energy in some way in the meantime. Equally, do shop around as prices vary greatly from place to place.

I have utilised several different packs in my consultations over the years as I have learnt more about the Tarot, my tastes have changed and new packs become available. It is still a pleasure to read with my very first (and beautifully dog-eared) pack at times, but the challenge of adapting to new packs pushes you to evolve your knowledge and use of the Tarot, which is essential for therapeutic work. Of the many packs I own, there are four that I use regularly in my consultations, but many that are close to my heart.

Lastly here, it is necessary to expound one of the many myths that surround the Tarot. It is often said that you should not purchase your own Tarot pack, but that it should be given to you, preferably passed down the family line. Many Tarot students have hinted at this to me, explaining in hushed tones of reverence that they have been given their cards, as if they have magically manifested like an apport from the Spirit world!

Whilst it is very nice to be given a present such as this and indeed it can be a symbolic gift, it is certainly not incorrect or even harmful as some believe, to buy your own cards. The tradition of passing cards down comes from the Gypsy way, in which many such heirlooms and principally knowledge were and are shared with ones family members. There is great value in this, and we would do well to remember the wisdom of our elders in wider society too. Perhaps it is that the passing down of one's Tarot pack brings with it access to the ingrained knowledge of those cards, lying like buried treasure for the devoted and serious seeker to discover. For the rest of us, it is a trip to the local booksellers.

CARE OF THE CARDS

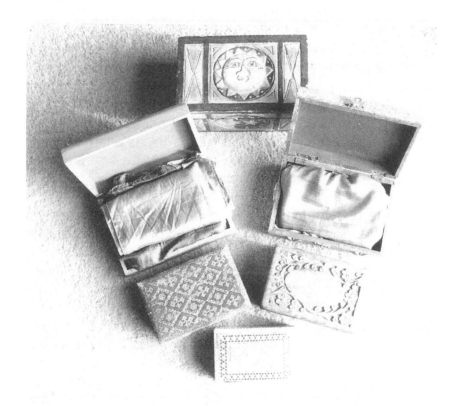

Having purchased our cards we must now concern ourselves with their care. This is both in the physical sense and the deeper level of the unseen energy that surrounds and permeates all things.

As mentioned, the majority of Tarot packs are presented either in a cardboard or plastic box. With the level of use required and hoped for therapeutic work, this will soon fall apart, so an alternative is required for long term storage and preservation of the cards. For this a wooden box is recommended, both for its robust nature and its ability to protect against the aforementioned vibrational imprint.

With regard to this energy protection, it should be explained that it is the regard towards the Tarot cards themselves, as the manifestation of sacred knowledge and the embodiment of spiritual wisdom that requires their being set apart from the mundane, encased within something that will keep them special. All things have energy, be they thoughts, feelings, objects or people. As different forms of these things come into contact with your cards, particularly clients and their associated problems and conditions, some of this will inevitably rub off on your cards. It is not necessary to explain the mechanics of how this happens, for this is a large and complex subject in itself, but we do need to be aware that it does and adjust our actions accordingly.

It therefore becomes necessary to protect them and ensure that they are not 'infected' with anything of a negative nature. If nothing else, this good practice ensures that your regard towards your cards is of the highest nature it can and indeed should be. Wood is a natural material that is known to absorb the energy emanating from all things and as such acts like a sponge, soaking up that which we wish to keep apart from our cards. With their sanctity intact, the cards are preserved as a holy or sacred object, ensuring that each time you unwrap and use them, you do so with a purity of intent equal to the cards themselves. The choice of style and design of box is of course up to you and they can be purchased cheaply from many craft outlets. One small tip here is to check the hinges closely as many tend to be loose or ill fitting.

As with all things magical, the most effective tools are those that are made by your own hand. If you are able to carve or chisel your own, this is ideal, but for the majority of us, we can find a compromise in purchasing a ready-made box of untreated wood from a good craft or hobby shop. This can be painted in a design of our choice, varnished and displayed proudly on our consulting table. Such practices do add to the individuality of your use of the cards, which, it has already been mentioned, is all important when it comes to Tarot therapy. This also psychologically demonstrates, to ourselves and others, that we have a special regard for our cards, which they are more than worthy of.

Many people also choose to wrap their cards in a piece of silk, also being a naturally protective material. That this must be black is a myth, which like all myths, has its basis in fact. Black, as the darkest colour (or a non-colour if you will) is therefore absorbent of all but the densest energy flows and is ideal for protective any sacred object and particularly a pack of cards. However, any colour will do, if you feel its qualities blend with the particular cards. The silk does serve to provide a buffer keeping the edges of your cards from becoming 'dog-eared' so quickly, as they are bound to do, whilst minimising damage from accidental spillages and so on.

This silk should not be confused with the different piece of cloth kept apart on which to read your cards. Being usually very thin, it will slip on your table and catch the edges of your cards. It is good therefore to construct your own unique square of cloth to lay out on your table or surface for when you wish to spread the cards. Again using the principle of imbuing magical objects you make yourself, it is preferable to sew and decorate your cloth yourself, though some packs do come with their own offering if you prefer. A beautiful and effective cloth can easily be stitched and added to with your own choice of design, using embroidery or fabric pens. This can serve to set your cards off wonderfully, giving an eye catching display to your consultations to be proud of.

EXERCISES

Consider the kind of artwork you like and if you have any preference as to a particular style. Look around your house at the pictures you have and see if this guides you as to the kind of pack of Tarot you feel you would like best. It is this pack that you will be able to respond to most deeply and effectively. Seek out pictures of cards in books in your local library and look at the sample cards available in good shops before you buy. Let yourself respond inwardly to what you see and follow your instincts in choosing a pack.

Once you have purchased a pack of Tarot, find a suitable box or solid container to keep them in. Try to find ways to decorate this, to make it individual and personal and make it a suitable place to keep a cherished and sacred object. Purchase a square of silk or suitably coloured material to wrap your cards in. Remove them from any cardboard box they may have been in first. Find or create a special place to keep your box.

Examine your newly purchased cards. Make sure the correct number of cards are there (78) and that you have identified which suit is which and which cards are Major and Minor Arcana. Practise shuffling them while you are watching television or otherwise unoccupied. Try to lose the 'factory feel' and stickiness of the cards. This will soon wear off with repeated use, but this is a good way of personalising your cards and becoming familiar with their feel, as well as getting you adept at shuffling without dropping them everywhere!

Examine your pack in detail, letting your eyes wander over the images and noting down any immediate responses you may have as you look at them. If any one card strikes you as particularly potent at this time, discover a little more about this response by seeing how it might by applying to you and your life. Make notes about the cards that strike you as being particularly strong at this time, writing down what your reaction to the image is as you look at it.

CHAPTER 2 - THE EVOLUTION OF THE TAROT

To enable the Tarot therapist to use the cards as such, it is necessary for them to understand the inner workings of the pack. This requires an inner acceptance of the concept of the cards and something of their philosophy. For this to be complete, a knowledge of the suggested origins of the Tarot and the development of its history are at the very least helpful and at most essential. For those not of such a mind however, you may safely skip this Chapter. For the remainder of us we will discover the complex and fascinating progression of the Tarot and discover the evolutionary ability it has to adapt to the circumstances in which it finds itself, creating a mirroring effect between the cards and humanity.

The history and development of the Tarot spans the world, emphasising its global nature and demonstrating its ability to speak a universal language, which as we have seen, is that of symbols. However, the actual origins of the Tarot are shrouded in mystery, suspicion, rumour and secrecy. Out of these mists a clear picture emerges of the Tarot as a volume of esoteric and ageless wisdom, applicable in any place and at any time.

That we do not know with any certainty where and in what form the Tarot began is in keeping with its esoteric nature. To those who have no knowledge of this inner meaning of the cards and the pack as a whole, they are merely able to predict what may or may not happen in their future. Though this may be beneficial for these people, they have encountered only the exoteric or outer nature of the cards. This does not change the truth that the Tarot also has an inner, or esoteric truth too, and this realm or level of the cards must become familiar and accepted by the Tarot therapist. One may wonder why, if such spiritual wisdom is indeed true and applicable for all time, it is not common knowledge, to assist humanity in its development. Here enters freewill and the need for each individual, as a manifestation of that truth and wisdom, or the potential for it, to choose of themselves, to follow this path in life. When humanity has a 'critical mass' of people following their own true path of sacredness, in whatever religion or belief system, humanity can finally begin to realise its potential. The same is true of those coming to understand the Tarot and aspire to its therapeutic use.

It is perhaps for this same reason that the beginnings of the Tarot are indefinite. Such ancient and powerful knowledge as the Tarot portrays needs not to be abused, lest its potency become diluted to a shadowy reflection of its true nature. Remembering that the subject matter is that of indisputable spiritual truth, it is essential that this is preserved as such, for the future guidance of those who willingly come to it, to absorb and apply in their lives. In this way does this truth guide and assist humanity and so it is with the Tarot as the depiction of this truth. Should it be fully understood by the minds of those who decry and reject the way of the spirit in the mundane world, the Tarot would be fully labelled as the stuff of cranks and charlatans. Though this is partly the case today, those who come to it with a true heart of respect and humility, not for the Tarot but for the sacred spirit within them, discover still the ancient truth in wonder and splendour that the Tarot eternally portrays.

In considering the origins and history of the Tarot we must therefore be mindful of the fact of 'true' history being only that which is written down. In this we can helpfully recall the view of Henry Ford that 'History is bunk'! Since the subject matter of the Tarot concerns abstract ideas and maxims, we must enlarge our scope to that of myth, story and belief, mindful that all myths have their origins in fact! What is presented below is a distillation from many Tarot authors and experts for each readers to decide on their level of agreement.

In keeping with the scientific and logical approach to history we now have, we find that earliest written reference to cards, of any kind, occurs in the 11th Century in China, in the form of paper money. This form of cards is thought to have evolved during the Tang dynasty, between 618 and 908 CE. This follows the Chinese practice of engraving designs on to copper and silver plates, which were then copied on to paper, giving a set of cards. This evolved into the symbolic game of chess, when the principles of Yin and Yang were added to the cards in the form of black and white colouring. Chess is intended to be a representation of the game of life, requiring the same skills for its success as the passage through life. It is also possible that the Court cards of the pack originated in some of the chess pieces. In this we have an immediate association of the Tarot with the nature of life itself.

The majority of references to the early origins of the Tarot that we have speak of it existing first as a pack of four suits, to which the Major Arcana as we know it today, was added later. The amalgamation of the two packs is often attributed to an heretical Christian sect known as the Waldenses, in the 11th Century, using the cards to teach converts. This group is only one of a number of similar organisations that become linked with the Tarot throughout its history, including those in modern times. It is from these four suits that the later playing cards were derived, at the end of the 14th Century, presumably in the more simplified form that they are so as to make cards the widely popular pastime they became. The four suits we know today have been in existence since the 'paper money' packs of Southern China. Throughout medieval times particularly, games were widespread and the Tarot too was adapted to the form of a game called Tarocchi, with decks being created specifically for this purpose . For those wishing to explore the rules and structure of this, I refer you to Michael Dummet's 'Twelve Tarot Games'. It is at this stage that the Tarot seems to have become widely used in its context of fortune-telling, as a source of amusement in the Courts, to relieve boredom.

There are many and diverse theories and propositions pur forward as the origin of the Tarot, both in time and place. Northern Italy seems a great favourite amongst recent scholars for a variety of reasons. At the time of the Renaissance this region was the centre of activity in developing thought and its creative expression, so the Tarot fitted nicely and indeed there is documentary evidence to confirm the existence of the Tarot here, which we shall cover later. However, such spiritual truth the Renaissance period craved and which the Tarot depicts has been around a great deal longer than a few hundred years.

Another theory as to the cards origins takes us to India, seeing them as a representation of the Hindu god of love and light, Vishnu. He is depicted with a lotus, conch, mace and discus and these are likened to the symbols of the four suits of the Minor Arcana in a different form. Another Indian deity, Ardhanarisvara, a combination of male and female power, is shown with a cup, sceptre, sword and ring. The four castes of Hinduism have been seen as the origin of the four Tarot suits,, with cups belonging to the Brahman (priests), swords to the warrior Kshatriyas, coins to the merchant Vaisyas and wands to the serf Sudras.

Links have been made with the Buddhist tradition, with the Fool being likened to the traditional 'wandering monk' figure, like that portrayed by David Carradine in the popular 'Kung Fu' television series of the 1970's. Other Major Arcana images reflect characters important to the Buddhist mythos.

From Asia, we can sail the Indian Ocean and Red Sea to Egypt, where the original Gypsies are said to have possessed, or indeed, 'invented' the Tarot, in the land of Khem. Certainly these proud and nomadic folk utilised fortune-telling and still do, and were widespread through Europe in the 15th Century, when their principal fortune-telling art was that of palmistry, not the Tarot. The Hungarian Gypsy word 'tar' does though mean a pack of cards. Further weight is lent to the Egyptian corner in the form of the word

'Ta-rosh', meaning 'royal way', certainly an apt description of the Major Arcana and the Fool's journey. It is thought that the spread of cards from the East was due to merchants, using the port of Venice as a trading post. Others say however that it was Arabs bringing the cards to our continent as they spread through Africa and Asia, then Spain, Italy and France in the 7th and 8th Centuries. Already we have travelled through Africa, Asia and Europe in our quest, giving, if nothing else, a further emphasis on the global nature of the cards.

In the 11th Century the Norman invasion facilitated the popularisation of Celtic beliefs and interest that have remained to this day. The 'matter of Britain' has been the subject of much work and investigation, chief among the matter being the legend and search for the Holy Grail. In these legends, there are four symbols, treasures or Hallows of Britain that suggest a link with the Tarot. These are the grail, sword, lance and platter, familiar in the Tarot as the symbols of the four suits in one form or another. In turn, these can be traced to the cauldron, sword, spear, and stone of the Tuatha de Danaan, the faery people of the Goddess who were the original inhabitants of Ireland. Tracing the origins of the Arthurian tales and figures, a vital part of the 'matter of Britain', back, allows us to theorise, in line with popular modern thinking, as to the beginnings of the ancient wisdom we have at our disposal, to which we shall address ourselves shortly.

During the 12th and 13th Century another sect, the Cathars (from the Greek for 'pure') have been linked to the Tarot, the suggestion being they produced the cards as a means of depicting their doctrine of belief to those unable to read them. This order operated mostly in Southern France and Northern Italy. Tarot designs do not however, show a clear reflection of the Cathars beliefs, which follow the theory of dualism, that the Universe is an eternal battle between good and evil. In their illustration of the journey of an individual spirit, as an aspect of God or the Divine, the Major Arcana blends well with the Gnostic theme of redemption by evolution, and since God is within us, the Divine nature too. Gnosticism itself mixed together Indian, Chaldean, Persian, Egyptian, Greek and Hebrew belief and philosophy. Fittingly, the word 'Gnostic' means a 'wise one' or 'wizard'. Gnostic teachers such as Basilides and Valentinus, even in the 2nd Century, turned more to Pagan, nature religion and symbolism in their quest for wisdom and it is to these that we are turning today, finding the origin of the Tarot not in history, but in the world and Universe around us and of which we are a part. Puritanical Christianity was rife at this time and so the Tarot had the added advantage of being suitable for the use of the earlier, Bardic practise of mnemonic memory. By this method of visualisation, entry to the sub conscious mind and recall when required, the knowledge that the Tarot represents, could and indeed can, be committed to memory easily, particularly from the 22 Major Arcana cards. This practise was the major factor in the survival of Gnosticism through this period, aspects of their teachings being found in the Masonic and Rosicrucian lodges. By this time however, the popular Tarot had been reduced to the fore-runner of its modern fortune-telling status.

Consequently, the Tarot as we know it today includes influences from many and diverse cultures and beliefs systems that span the globe. We see Egyptian, Indian, Celtic, Christian, Buddhist, Jewish, Norse and a great many others in our cards that illustrate so beautifully the ability of the Tarot to express humanity's search for truth, redemption, enlightenment and healing. It is for this reason that we can turn to so many mythological stories and characters to decode the meaning of the cards.

Possibly the earliest written reference to cards in the Western world that we have occurs in 1377, with a description of a card game, Ludas Cartarum, given by a German monk, Brother Johannes of Brefeld, from a Swiss monastery. Such was the popularity of cards that a year later their use is banned by the Council of Regensberg in Germany. The following year they are also banned in Paris. John 1, King of Castille (Spain), bans the use of cards in 1387. Through the following two hundred years or so, there are numerous records of monks and authority figures giving sermons and speeches warning the people of the dangers of cards. This demonstrates the first links with the suspicion and mistrust some still hold of the Tarot. Their banning is also evidence of a power inherent in the cards that those in officialdom did not trust. There is evidence that at this time cards were however, also in use in France, Switzerland and Belgium, completing their domination of Europe.

The origins of the Tarot have been attributed to another of the slightly mysterious Orders, both military and esoteric that have exited through history. The Order of the Knights Templar have been the subject of much recent written material. They were founded in 1118 by Hugh de Payens and eight other Knights, to protect Christian pilgrims. Following the accumulation of much position and prosperity, they were the subject of a torturous inquisition and were eradicated in 1314. There is however, no clear evidence to connect them with the Tarot.

It is in 1392 that the first written and so historical record of the Tarot occurs. Charles V1 of France, known as 'Charles the Mad', was given a pack by his Queen, Odette, the payment to artist Jacquemin Gringoneur being recorded by the Kings accountant, Charles Poupart. The request was made by the Queen seeking a cure for the King's madness or boredom, having three packs made "in gold and diverse colours, ornamented with many devices". It is perhaps significant that Gringoneur was also a qabalist, suggesting an esoteric ability, or at the very least message, in the cards. It is here that the 'Court' cards gain their name, as they featured figures prominent in Charles' court of the time. They had been previously known as 'coat' cards as the figures were shown in long, rich coats. It is then said that the Queen gained the idea of her gift to the King when a Gypsy read her fortune. An enterprising soldier then had a pack made, depicting the military splendour of France and its King and soon everyone wanted a pack!

In 1415 there is record of a pack being made for the Duke of Milan, one Filippo Maria Visconti. It was the nobility only who could afford such luxuries, since all cards were then handmade and painted. These were painted by Bonifacio Bembo and a pack that closely resembles these exists still, with some of the oldest cards in existence being held in the Bibliotheque Nationale in Paris. Interestingly, in Northern Italy the River Taro, a tributary of the Po, runs through the Plains, giving some the conclusion that the cards were named after this place. However, there are other place names that can lay equal claim, including a village named Tarot in Upper Burma and a lake Tarok Tso in Tibet.

In London, the British Museum also holds many early Tarot packs, which they will show on request. Through the 15th Century the popularity and availability of Tarot spread, with packs beginning to be made from woodcuts. The IJJ 'Swiss' Tarot, available today, serves as an example of these packs as they are based on these early wood cut designs. Some Court cards in existence dating from 1440 are the earliest made from woodcuts.

By 1462 the Tarot had crossed the Channel as we read that Edward V1 forbade the import of foreign cards, in order to protect the home market. By the reign of Elizabeth 1, the Tarot was in use to advise military and political strategy. The Queens interest in the esoteric is well documented, particularly through her advisor, the astrologer and magician John Dee. In these Renaissance times there was a deep interest and exploration of the nature of the Universe and nature itself. We have already seen how the Tarot is able to combine these into an explanation of both.

By the 16th Century we have written record that the Major Arcana cards were is use in a document entitled the

'Sermones de Ludo Cum Allis'. The first non-Italian Tarot pack, the Catelin de Geoffrey deck, appears in 1557, though these are copied from a set designed by the engraver Virgil Solis in 1544. The standard form for modern Tarot emerged in 1631, when the manufacturers of the Marseilles Tarot received a royal edict for their cards. The earliest surviving copy of these card dates from 1717. This established them as the accepted pack to use, although cards are being manufactured in Rouen, Lyons, Paris and Nancy, throughout France. At this stage many historical packs in existence today were created, often with a differing order to the Major Arcana cards and with different numbers to the total in the pack. For those with a mind to study such things further, I would refer readers to 'The Encyclopaedia of Tarot' where the most complete records of such decks exists.

One of the most famous characters associated with the development of the Tarot, Antoine Court de Gebelin, published a new theory as to the origins of the cards in 1781. In the eighth of his nine-volume work, 'Le Monde Primitif' '(The Primitive World') this French occultist and archaeologist stated that the cards are the remains of the Book of Thoth, the ancient Egyptian book of spiritual truth and wisdom. de Gebelin was a member of the Rosicrucian Order of the Philalethes, so it is possible the ideas he put forward were also the work of other members of the Order. This idea was later developed by the work of the infamous Aleister Crowley, to whom we shall return. de Gebelin, a Freemason, said that the sacred Egyptian texts had been burnt, but that a portion of them, the Book of Thoth, remained in the Romany's possession. This idea was expounded in 1980 by Frederic Lionel in his work 'The Magic Tarot' in which he details 108 'golden foils' being engraved to preserve the ancient wisdom with which we have come to associate the Tarot. 30 of these foils are lost, the remaining 78 comprising the Tarot as we know it today. This gives further links with the Gypsies and the Tarot, added weight being given in their language being known to be a pure form of the sacred Indian language of Sanskrit. The Egyptian

42

origins of the Romany is further suggested by the existence in Southern France of a chapel reserved for Gypsies containing a shrine to Saint Sara of Egypt, their 'patron saint', in the Church of Les Saintes Maries de la Mer. Saint Sara has been likened to the Egyptian deity Sarapis, the god of the dead. de Gebelin also tells us that the Tarot came from the Egyptians to Rome then to Avignon from where it spread throughout Provence. An addendum to the 'Le Monde Primitif' by an unknown author tells us the Tarot came to Europe through Spain with Muslims and was taken to Germany by the troops of the conqueror Charlemagne. It is also explained here that the word Tarot means the doctrine or science of Thoth.

The Book of Thoth was written by the god Thoth, the Egyptian god of wisdom. He equates to the Roman Hermes Trimegistus, (thrice great Hermes), later Mercury, said to be the inventor of writing and who presided over the writing of the Book of Thoth shortly after the Biblical Flood. From this tradition we have the origins of Tarot as being painted on leaves of gold on the walls of an initiation chamber in Memphis. These were viewed only by the highest initiates, the key being held by the High Priest. This pictorial beginning to the art of the Tarot is utilised today in the Greenwood Tarot (see Bibliography) which is based on pre-Celtic European shamanic cave art. The symbolism found here dates back to 30,000 BC allowing us to link the knowledge and wisdom contained in the Tarot, if not the actual cards, to at least this period. The people of this time took their symbolism directly from nature and the animals around them. It is for this reason that the excellent Greenwood Tarot depicts the Court cards as animals and uses overly natural images.

This early writing took the form of Hieroglyphics, famously adorning walls of chambers in Egyptian pyramids. Until recent discoveries such as the Rosetta Stone's in 1799, explaining some of their meaning, many differing interpretation of the hieroglyphics found have been given, much like interpretations of the cards.

The publication of de Gebelin's book popularised the Tarot and this was further enhanced by a Parisian barber or wigmaker and claimed professor of Algebra, Alliette, writing under the backwards name of Etteilla, He gave instructions for fortune-telling with the cards and this period also saw the establishment of some noted clairvoyants using cards, among them Marie-Anne Lenormand who included amongst her clientele the Empress Josephine, famous partner to Napoleon. Alliette also made a number of significant alterations to the earlier versions of Tarot he worked with, such as first inverting the Hanged Man, calling him Prudence, the idea first occurring from a printing error in a Belgium pack.

It was in 1855 and for the following decade that the esoteric nature of the Tarot was publicly explored, through the writings of Alphonse Louis Constant, writing under the Hebrew version of his name, Eliphas Levi.. He said that the Tarot came from the Biblical son of Cain Enoch, long before Moses. The connection with Moses comes from his receiving the two tablets of instruction from God, one being the exoteric, suitable as rules for all and the other esoteric, suitable only for initiates. Levi also published four books that linked the 22 cards of the Major Arcana with the 22 letters of the Hebrew alphabet and the mystical system known as the 'yoga of the West', the Qaballah. The Qaballah is said to have originated with the Biblical Moses, who was educated in Egypt and is viewed as a powerful magician which can be viewed as a method of structuring the data of the Universe. The word means 'tradition' and it is seen as being the secret or inner, esoteric meaning of the law as given to Moses. Further Hebrew links are suggested by the Torah, the Hebrew book of the law, read from right to left in the Hebrew fashion, the word becomes Tora, similar to the Tarot.

Especially worthy of note and of relevance to our therapeutic studies is the quote from Levi that 'The oracles of the Tarot give answers as exact as mathematics and as measured as the harmonics of Nature. By the aid of these signs and their infinite combinations, it is possible to arrive at the natural and mathematical revelation of all the secrets of Nature".

The Qaballah depicts 10 spheres, known as Sephiroth that equate to the numbered cards of the Minor Arcana. These are linked by 22 paths which are likened to the Major Arcana cards. These are commonly depicted as a glyph which shows the progression of Divine energy to physical manifestation. This follows the idea of Paracelsus, who gave us 21 solar agencies, that resonated forth from the Sun, who told us 'man's spirit is from the Stars, his soul from the planets and his body from the elements'. The Qaballah, the 'ladder of the heavens', is the principal subject connected with the Tarot not covered in this book for its subject is entirely esoteric and requires at least one volume of its own, which has already been achieved by those far more worthy than I (see Bibliography for such works).

Further Egyptian links with the Tarot were suggested in 'A History of Magic', published in 1870 by Paul Christian, the pseudonym of Jean-Baptiste, a pupil of de Gebelin's. This told of an initiation chamber under the pyramids, with 78 steps leading to a hall in which hung the Major Arcana cards. This may not be historically true but it does add further weight to the inner and esoteric side of the nature and matter of the cards, requiring some kind of training, study and initiation to reveal and understand.

The exploration of the Tarot via publications continued in subsequent years with a notable booklet on divination from Samuel MacGregor Mathers in 1888. Mathers was also one of the founders of the Hermetic Order of the Golden Dawn, a mystery school that sought its answers in linking the esoteric systems of the East and West. The Tarot played a major part in this and received much publicity thanks to the Golden

Dawn counting amongst its members many famous literary and other figures.. It was the Golden Dawn who also connected the Major Arcana with the 12 zodiacal signs and 10 planets of astrology and made links between the Tarot and the Chinese I-Ching. 1888 also saw the publication of an astrological work by Eugene Jacob, under the name Ely Star in which 50 pages are devoted to the structure of the Tarot.

The following year Oswald Wirth painted and published his own card designs showing the Hebrew letter correspondences. Also in 1889 Dr Gerald Encausse, under his name given by the Rosicrucian Order to which he belonged, Papus, published a work entitled 'The Tarot of the Bohemians' which is still in print today and was the first work solely concerning the Tarot. The book used both the Marseilles and Oswald Wirth decks as illustrations of the cards. This complicated book details, for the patient, a method of interpretation of the cards based on a numerical system linking the four suits and much else besides with the meaning and interpretation of the four syllabled Tetragrammaton, or Holy Name of God. The links between numerology, the study of 'sacred mathematics', Egypt and the Tarot are deepened by Pythagorus, who we are told was initiated into the esoteric centres of Egypt to introduce his 'philosophy of numbers' to the West. Numbers are seen in this context as depicting the essence and power of all things and as the link between the word, as the sacred breath of God and its manifestation into physicality. It is this Universal nature that causes the numbers of the Tarot cards to be as important and significant as they are.

Shortly after the turn of the century, in 1910, came what remains perhaps the most widely recognised and utilised Tarot pack, known now as the Rider-Waite deck. Arthur Edward Waite, working with the artist Pamela Coleman-Smith, created his pack of cards and published them along with a book entitled 'The Key to the Tarot'. These were the first cards to feature scenic picture interpretations for the Minor Arcana and contained what is widely regarded as the most complete esoteric symbolism on the Major Arcana cards. Waite also gave us English translations of the books by Papus and Levi and founded the Order of the True Rosy Cross, following spells in the Golden Dawn.

Aleister Crowley added to the links between the Tarot and Qaballah with his publication which he entitled 'The Book of Thoth' and by creating his powerful 'Thoth' cards, with the artist Lady Frieda Harris. At the end of the 1930's, Isreal Regardie produced the original system of cards used by the Golden Dawn , subsequently made available to the public in 1977, working with Robert Wang.

Under the auspices of the American esoteric group known as the Builders of the Adytum', Paul Foster Case published his work, 'The Tarot' in 1927 and four years later cards that were the first to be printed with just black and white outline, intended for the user to colour their own cards according to their choice of symbolism, a practice followed by others since. Case's work was notable for the suggestion that the Tarot originated in Morocco, around 1200 as a system of communication, designed for bridging the gap created by the Babel-like confusion of languages caused by Fez acting then as the trade capital of the world. A more likely link with Fez comes from the idea of the cards as the key to the secrets of the ancient mysteries. The Moroccan link comes via tales of adepts of the ancient mystery schools spiriting away the manuscripts detailing the knowledge preserved in the Great Library of Alexandria and the Temple of Jupiter Serapis when fanatical Christians began to pillage and burn them. In order to preserve this knowledge in the face of adversity, these Adepts are said to have devised the Tarot, in some way an attempt at encapsulating all the knowledge of the Universe, as later tried by Francis Bacon.

Following the publishing boom of the 1960's and since, there have been hundreds of Tarot card designs created, each offering something a little different, new or untried before. Cards of all sizes and even shapes have emerged, decks following specific themes, myths, cultures and traditions. Significant among these have been the cards created by the esoteric order The Servants of the Light, headed by Dolores Ashcroft-Nowicki, works by Alfred Douglas, Gareth Knight, and recently Rachel Pollack and Caitlin & John Matthews. The Tarot has continued throughout modern history to influence artists and a range of creative souls as diverse as Dali and James Bond!

From this rich and colourful history a development of the Tarot can be traced which influences many aspects of human life, society and behaviour. Exactly where the Tarot began, in something resembling the form we know it today, is still unknown. What we do know however and what the attention given the Tarot by so many gifted people shows, is that what it represents cannot be dated, is beyond date and time itself. Clearly the Tarot encapsulates the highest spiritual wisdom and knowledge in the possession of humanity. This cannot be given a place and time of origin for its very nature is eternal, its essence timeless. This knowledge is alive of itself, and is in a continual state of degeneration and rebirth, like the wheel of the Tarot itself. It is not limited by history as written data, perhaps because it cannot be written down and codified in words. It expresses something which each individual can only experience for themselves in their own way. Perhaps this is ultimately what has led to so many interpretations of the Tarot in its development.

By turning to this wisdom and knowledge we must also open ourselves to that range of information and inspiration known as myth, for in these rich and colourful tales of the world we find the basis of our known, logical fact. Our myths are there to teach and guide us and each must judge them according to his senses. We can only do this with both an open heart and mind. It is in this humble manner that we approach the shores of Atlantis.

Long forgotten and sadly neglected, Atlantis lay off the Western shore of the Gibraltan peninsula. Its well known destruction is thought to have taken place around 9500 BC. Prior to this and for an unknown period of time, Atlantis was a magical place that signified so much more than a land of peace and paradise, as is usually assumed. In his fascinating essay, 'Atlantis, An Interpretation', Manly P. Hall, writing for the Philosophical Research Society, explain how Atlantis was a land that encapsulated in and of itself, the process of human creation from energy, as we know it today. The land and its inhabitants, like the later King Arthur, were one. The maker of Atlantis, the god of the sea and distribution of nature, Poseidon created a paradise of islands on which were to live his ten male children, by his chosen partner Cleito, each with their own island. Hall, in his essay, explains how this is an allegory for the creation of the human form and physical matter and that the resultant Atlanteans lived in a realm where the astral forms that became the demons, dragons, serpents and faery folk characters of our myths. From these divine beginnings the human shape was formed, with an inherent portion of divinity. This divine nature faded over a great many years, the lesser and grosser human nature won precedence and the Atlanteans found themselves seduced by the astral glamour we see once more today.

There are many clues to this image of the beginnings of humanity, not least the ten islands for Poseidon's sons. Each of these ten, Hall tells us, is a different world in the sages of creation of physical matter. These can be expressed as numbers with their accompanying principles. These ten are divided into three, for the "conditions of matter" and seven, for the forms they evolve by, the significance for our purposes, of which we shall see in the next Chapter. Those given dominion over these lands are some of the major characters, in some of the major places, of subsequent myths across the world, including the Native American, Norse, Celtic, Egyptian and Mayan. The beginnings of Atlantis are the beginnings of humanity as we know it. Its construction was the construction of matter itself, each island relating to the planets and the energies which they radiate. This descent into matter from stellar form sowed the seeds for its destruction, for the memory of what they once were was lost to the Atlanteans, so that, in the due course of time the lower nature asserted itself over the higher and the path to disaster was begun.

During their time the Atlanteans had, as their natural and instinctive condition, knowledge of magic and powers now lost to us. As some of the initiated priesthood began to foresee the pending destruction and downfall of their land, they sought a means by which they could ensure the survival of the knowledge of their origins and the significance and nature of their form and Universe. As the tides swelled about them, the Atlantean priesthood set sail in four directions. From here they founded the great spiritual, mythical, magical and tribal societies of the world. Thus did Atlantean wisdom find a home in the Druidry of the British Isles, the methods and practices of the Native Americans, and the pyramid structures of the Mayans and Egyptians, amongst others. The aforementioned Great Library and Temple of Jupiter Serapis, was founded around 300 BC in Alexandria by

Ptolemy 1. This contained all the relevant knowledge of both Atlantean and Egyptian and Greek thought, giving victory to the intentions of the original Atlantean priests.

In AD 391 however,, following the assertion of Christianity, the Great Library, and its knowledge, were looted and burnt, under the edicts of the Roman Emperor Theodosius. The purity of the knowledge and wisdom of Atlantis was rejected by the new 'civilised' age of Christianity and humanity had turned its back on the world of natural power, magic and imagination. Some however, remained determined to preserve such jewels and the keys to this knowledge were taken to Fez in Morocco. From here, the Tarot seems to have adopted a strong Egyptian influence as it spread across the world.

At some stage in this sequence of events it seems highly likely that the Tarot was given its structure and form, from which are descended the cards we have today. This establishes the Tarot as the oldest and most pure form of divine knowledge available to humanity. In its keys lie the mystery of creation and the nature of matter. When we look at the many and seemingly varied esoteric philosophies and practices of the societies mentioned above, we find Astrology, the Qaballah, Egyptian hieroglyphics, the British wheel of the year and others. Inherent in each and all of these is the Tarot. The Tarot is the modern expression of the truth of our divine nature and spiritual existence and as such, is the best guide and basis on which to live our lives we can have.

It does not matter therefore, where and when the Tarot began, only that it did. For the genuine and determined, patient, true seeker, the wisdom and knowledge of the Tarot is still available. By such means as this can we find that which we have lost, the key to the certain knowledge of our spiritual inheritance and nature. As humanity seeks to survive another millennium, the Tarot stands poised, ready, able and willing to serve us as a guide. We have travelled many miles away from the realms of future prediction now, indeed this practice exhibits many of the hall marks of the aforementioned astral glamour that wrought so much Atlantean havoc, that the true use and purpose of the Tarot must be restored.

The continued popularity and fascination with the cards testifies to its relevance to modern times and life and it is certain that as humanity uncovers more of its true nature and purpose, so will more be revealed of the Tarot. It is fascinating and exhilarating to speculate what secrets will be unlocked as we discover more of our ancient history and even the land of Atlantis itself. At this dawn of a new millennium it is exciting to speculate and wonder what secrets, wisdom and guidance the Tarot will offer to all those who come to it with an open and humble heart.

At the beginning of the Aquarian Age, the Tarot can act as the ultimate guide, on the path to human wholeness and completion. The goal of all complementary and natural therapies is to restore the individual to a state of wholeness. This must also be the goal of humanity on a collective level, as we repeatedly wobble dangerously close to our destruction by war and natural disaster brought about by our mismanagement of the planet. This wholeness and completion must be established in the heart and minds of a great many people, spanning all corners of the globe, in whatever way is appropriate for them. In the Western world we have the body of the Tarot that can act, in the hands of one filled with its knowledge, a desire to serve and the compassion that accompanies it, as the ultimate therapy.

EXERCISES

As there is no specific content in this Chapter that you can now work on, I have given here a selection of Exercises that are excellent preparation to the work that you will later undertake as you learn the art of Tarot Therapy.

Take a look at each and every card in your pack and from this process, select the one that you like the most and the one that you dislike the most. Your selection procedure should be an intuitive one, so try to allow a response to occur within you as soon as you view the card and respond accordingly, without consciously thinking. If, during your selection, you put aside a number of cards that you like and dislike, consider afterwards what has made you react this way. Write notes on what you feel are the reasons for your choices and see what these may tell you about yourself.

On a different occasion, go through the entire pack and this time select the card that, simply by looking at it, you feel best depicts you. Follow the same process described above, making notes about your conclusions.

You can also try to select the cards that you feel best describe your partner, children, family and close friends. You can then show them your selection and see what their reaction is, but do be sure they are not likely to take offence!

Select between three and six cards at random, and without looking, from your pack, lay them out in the order you chose them. Examine the cards, without looking at any interpretation of them and allowing yourself to respond inwardly and intuitively to them as you look. Let your imagination open and from this process write a short story that moves from one card to the next. Do not try to be clever or an expert storyteller, but just have fun, letting your imagination and fantasy have free reign.

Put aside a period of one week and at the beginning of each day in that week, select a card at random. Examine the card and note any reaction you have at any level, knowing that it applies to you for that day in some way. Do not see the card as telling you what events will happen, rather that it applies to you as a person in some way, telling you something about your conduct and personal interaction at the time. Place the card on view in your home and examine it at the end of the day, seeing if your initial reactions proved founded or not. See how you feel about the card now and make notes as appropriate. At the end of the week look at the series of cards you selected and see if there are any patterns that you notice

CHAPTER 3 - THE CONCEPT OF THE TAROT

The Tarot is a vast body of work, a fact attested to by the number of works available on it and one I am in complete agreement with having begun this study on it and seen it expand effortlessly to three volumes! Its complete concept cannot be grasped by reading one single book alone or even a thorough study of one pack alone. We have seen its ability to shape shift, blending itself to the needs and interests of the day and this modern age is nothing new in this respect. Attempts to surmise the concept of the Tarot are therefore doomed before they have begun, but following the 'pointless optimist' spirit of the Fool, we must try our best, in order to familiarise ourselves with something of the true potential of what we now hold in our hands. Perhaps the best way to this is to explore what the Tarot is, before dissecting its structure and looking at how it works. We will also see what the strange word 'Tarot' actually is and means.

WHAT IS THE TAROT?

Attempts to define the Tarot are constantly thwarted as the Tarot has the ability to be all things to all people, reflecting in this its diversity and adaptability.. However, in an attempt to further explain just what the Tarot is exactly, I present below some definitions, culled from a variety of sources that you may take or leave as you wish:

- The Devils picturebook
- A Cosmos in miniature
- A means to connect the conscious with the sub conscious
- A psychic mirror
- A cycle of images defining the wheels of the Universe
- Spiritual life's journey
- Work on the nature of the Elements of the Universe, in energy form.

It can be seen from this that the use and ascription of the cards can be taken at many different levels, inclusive of both psychological and spiritual themes and relating at once to life on both an individual and Universal level. However, it is to the last definition that we shall turn for further explanation and help.

An atom used to be regarded as the smallest particle of matter known to us. With the splitting of the atom, humanity entered the nuclear world of energy and has come to recognise over 100 such chemical elements in existence. These have, since medieval times, been easily and naturally grouped into four main areas, corresponding, relating to and deriving from, the four Elements found in nature and all things, being Earth, Air, Fire and Water. It is these Elements, coupled with the fifth, as the product or quintessence of the four when combined, known as Spirit or Ether that constitutes the pack that is Tarot. First combined by Aristotle, the fifth Element of Ether comes from a Greek word meaning 'upper air', showing the higher, yet dependent nature of the Major Arcana to the Minor in the Tarot pack, as we shall discover.

The idea of these four Elements dates back at least to 430 B.C. and the Greek philosopher Empedocles. His elemental ideas were populated in mediaeval times with the exploration of the process of Alchemy, the secret of blending base metals into gold, an analogy for the search for unity of the human with the Divine. This alchemical process is also depicted in the Tarot for we can see within its pages, or cards, the individual in quest of reunification with the Divine that is its source. What better guide or source for therapy could there be, for those wishing to find a spiritual life in the realm of hard matter?

From this we can see that the nature of the Tarot has to do with the nature of life itself. By concerning itself with the five Elements that constitute that life, from a philosophical, psychological and spiritual standpoint, the Tarot is truly an explanation, in energy form, of life itself. This energy is the very stuff of life, the flow of power or energy that surrounds and permeates all things. The Tarot can be viewed as this life force in pictorial or symbolic form, at different stages and in different circumstances in our lives. By interpreting the cards at this same energy level, which requires a good deal of study and interaction, necessary to bring the cards alive for the interpreter, we are able to utilise a therapeutic method that can guide us to the best possible position we can hope to be in at any one time.

It is also significant interesting to note that the atmosphere of the Earth, upon which we all live, move and have our being by volume is composed of 78 % nitrogen, 21 % oxygen and 1% other gases, such as helium, argon and so on. The 78% reflects the Tarot as a whole, with the 21%, being the numbered Major Arcana cards that oxygenate, or give breath and therefore life to the inhabitants of the Earth, i.e. us. The remaining 1% we find in the card of the Fool, often seen as the key to the whole pack and with a unique role to play within it, signifying as he does the Seeker on the path to wholeness.

It is study, dedicated and thorough, combined with some 'inner' work such as meditation and journeying that allows us to access the power level of the cards, whereby the symbols release their store of energy, built up over the many years of use on and with them, from countless other practitioners and seekers. It is this practise that lifts the use of the cards above that of 'fortune-telling' and shows us the gulf between divination and therapy. We will discover more of this process when we examine the psychological nature of the Tarot and how it works.

For now it is enough to allow the knowledge that the Tarot speaks to us of life itself, with all its drama, heartbreak, pain and ecstasy. Such things must surely be sacred and our definition of what Tarot is should reflect this. As it is all things to all people, it is necessary to ascertain what it is to us, before we can make effective and therapeutic use of it. It may be worth bearing in mind however, that to define the Tarot is in some senses to limit it and the Tarot, like life, cannot be limited.

Since the Tarot reflects life (and life reflects the Tarot), it is necessary to ensure that our understanding of it and how it applies to us at any one time, is not a static thing, for such is also the nature of life. Change has been defined as the only evidence of life and since the Tarot is to act as our guide through that life, we must ensure that we are not limiting our understanding of what it is, to us. By constructing a personal definition of what the Tarot is now, we can monitor the understanding that this definition reflects, by checking periodically to see if we still agree with our definition, whether it now lacks something, does not specify our individual feelings and so on. Perhaps it is that we will find that our definition of what the Tarot is completely changes the more we use and so come to understand and appreciate the cards and their meaning for us. See Exercise 1 at the end of this Chapter.

Should a number of these definitions be compared it is likely that they will demonstrate the individuality of the Tarot and that it can come to mean many different things to different people. This ably shows the method of interpretation of the cards too, for this is as individual as our understanding of what a pack of Tarot is, of itself. It is to a unique and individual interpretation that this book will attempt to guide you. Very little space will be given to detailing what a card means. Rather, I will attempt to set out the material that constitutes each card, thereby allowing you to ascertain for yourself what the cards 'means', by analysing and working with the material presented, then checking it against your own understanding and experience. More will be said later on this matter, but for now the realisation that you can decide for yourself what any and all cards mean can serve as excellent motivation for the hard work that this process requires.

Chief in our studies must rank the awareness that we are dealing with life itself. The four Elements of such ancient power and strength constitute all that we are and all that is around us. The Tarot places these forces in a sequential order and structure that allow us to disassemble our selves and lives, examine the resultant pieces and then reconstruct the whole of that self and life, in a form more in keeping with that which we would aspire to. When we are aware that we are dealing with matters as important as this, it can only add to our view of the Tarot as a powerful, sacred tool, with the capability of acting as a mentor, guide, counsellor, medium, friend and even lover, such intimacy with the forces behind the Tarot are there able to be.

When you hold a pack of Tarot, you hold the ability to dissect, analyse and remould your or your clients' life. It is vital therefore that our approach to the Tarot and our clients is faultless and much will be said on this matter, chiefly to promote the professionalism of the Tarot consultant, something it must be said, sadly lacking in its current image and use. If we are to use the Tarot truly as a therapy, higher standards of practice, ethics, principles and methods must be met. This is the beginning of what this author (and I know from experience and conversations, many others) hopes will be a more positive and accurate image of the Tarot that the 'general public' will come to hold.

This process, a shift away from cruelly limiting the Tarot and pigeonholing it to that of a fortune telling device, used at the end of the pier or in the psychic fayre, will take generations to fully achieve, but as each one deepens their practice of the Tarot, or elevates it, to a dedicated therapeutic and developmental use, so will its image change and evolve. It is then that the Tarot can perhaps regain its rightful place, and be found in the practices of therapists of all kinds, from those involved in bodywork, psychologists, counsellors and spiritual practitioners of many varieties. Given that the Tarot is constructed from those forces that ARE the natural world, what more natural therapy could there be, to aid us in our understanding and development of body, heart, mind and soul?

On the subject of 'what the Tarot is' a great deal could and indeed has been written and the dedicated Tarot therapist would do well to avail themselves of some of the many works available on this aspect of the Tarot (See Bibliography).

Returning to our principle that 'the Tarot teaches us about life and life teaches us about the Tarot', we must also add to this that as we study the Tarot, we also study ourselves and it is the act of this process, i.e. studying the cards, that allows us to determine what we believe and understand the Tarot to be. The philosophical and spiritual search for wisdom and understanding has occupied many great souls across the centuries, but we can only truly know that wisdom by experiencing it for ourselves. It is not enough to read or hear their words, we must open ourselves to their experience; their feeling. The same is true of the Tarot.

The search for wisdom, the Holy Grail, Utopia, Never-Never Land or Tir na Nog (the Celtic 'Land of Youth') is the same journey as that of the Fool, the first card of the Major Arcana and in some ways, the Major Arcana itself. One of his main edicts is that he is the 'wisest Fool', the embodiment of wisdom. This is because he knows that he is a Fool and knows nothing, save what he experiences in each moment. This is truth, for there can be no other. To arrive at our own, real understanding of what the Tarot is, we must take the Fool by the hand, and plunge together with him over the cliff and into the landscape of the Major Arcana.

Here we enter that mysterious and fantastic world, known only to a select few of initiates. These people are initiates of the Tarot, those who have opened their souls to the power of each card and accepted it inwardly, allowing it to have whatever effect it may upon them. This process, as these brave and good people will tell you, is both a frightening and exhilarating one. Nobody is able to tell you what may happen, but the result will be that the Tarot will no longer be a mysterious pack of cards, or just a means of predicting the future. Rather they will be a very real presence in yourself and life, a spiritual ally and guide that enables you to act in a therapeutic and developmental way for those that come to you and seek your services, if you wish to offer them. You will have knowledge of yourself and the world and Universe that you live in. That royal road begins as soon as you make the inner decision that you wish to study the Tarot in this manner. This book will assume that you have responded positively to this and will I hope, enable you to experience the initiation into each card that you need.

This initiation is not some strange rite (unless you want it to be!), but a point at which you link into the card, you face the figure or symbol on it and are able to feel its meaning, its force and power and relate this firstly to yourself and your life, then that of others. In this way the cards come alive, the figures develop characters and personalities and can act to guide you in your therapeutic work. The active study of the cards, because the cards are active of themselves, results in interaction with them. This is the secret which you must unlock from all 78 cards of the deck. This is long and hard work, but its rewards, I am able to tell you, are well worth it. It would be possible, but self-indulgent, to describe here what these rewards have been for me, but it is what they will be for you that matters. In many ways, the sacrifice of long hours of study, meditation, note taking and just staring at the cards can seem pointless sometimes and again, if you have not the patience for this, Tarot therapy is not for you. If you persevere however, the potential rewards and benefits, for yourself and others, are limitless.

After a period of initial study, you will emerge at the end of the landscape of the Major Arcana, or rather ascended above it, having learnt the true nature of the Fool, that he is wise because he knows, understands and accepts his shortcomings and his lack of understanding of this! It is with such seeming contradictions that the Universe is littered. The truly wise one accepts these inexplicable truths and laughs. If you are able to do this, you have a very good understanding of what the Tarot is.

THE WORD 'TAROT'

The name of the cards called 'Tarot' is a very well known, if misunderstood one. Not so well known however, is the origin of the word itself and its meaning. Perhaps surprisingly, much can be learned of the nature of the Tarot by revealing this meaning. In doing so, perhaps it will be that some of the misnomers, limitations and inaccuracies that are widely held about the Tarot will be expunged too.

Historically, the word Tarot, in its popular and accepted spelling, is of French origin. However, this spelling is actually the French for the Italian Tarocco, from the game of the same name. These old Italian origins for the word lead many scholars and historians to claim Italy as the source of the cards themselves. This claim is, like many others concerning the cards, open to debate and we shall examine some of these when we look at the origin and history of the Tarot.

Interestingly, my Dictionary gives the above information, dating the word form the 16th Century, but gives us only a question mark for the origins of the word Tarocco. This echoes the very nature of the cards, in that as we have seen, one must effectively be initiated into the mystery of each card to understand it. Equally, each must consider the material and evidence available, inclusive of their own feeling and intuition, and decide for themselves where they believe the Tarot came from. One can justifiably ask why it matters where the Tarot originated, but we must remember that this book is being written by a self-confessed Tarot Addict, with the consequence that every nuance of the cards has much larger implications of significance and interest! Perhaps an anorak should be proudly worn at this point!

The word 'Tarocco' is actually the plural of 'Tarocci', but the earliest known name for the cards is as a game, called carte da trionfi', meaning 'cards with trumps'. This tells us little of the nature of the cards however, so it is to a combination of Hebrew and Latin influences, both large ones upon the Tarot, to which we can turn for further revelation.

The pronunciation of the word is of course, with the last T silent. This renders the effect and nature of this letter akin to that of The Fool, in that he occupies a place at the start and end of the word (or pack) simultaneously. Being numbered 0 (or not numbered) The Fool has no value as such, just like our poor disadvantaged letter T. This leaves it free to show us something of the cyclic nature of the Tarot, like the Egyptian Goddess Ta-urt and the Celtic Taranis, both linked with the origin of the Tarot, or at least the knowledge it contains, through being 'Mother of Revolutions' and 'Lord of the Wheel' respectively.

By leaving this letter aside, we can produce the following cryptic phrase:

ROTA TARO ORAT TORA ATOR

These five anagrams can be translated thus:

- **ROTA** - Latin for 'wheel'
- **TARO** - from two Egyptian words: Tar meaning Path and Ro meaning Royal, so the Royal Road or Royal Path of Life.
- **ORAT** - Latin for 'to speak' or speaks

- **TORA** - the Hebrew book of the sacred law, also spelt
    Torah
- **ATOR** - from the Egyptian Athor, the Goddess of
    Nature

Taking a paraphrased yet still close interpretation of this we can conclude that

THE WHEEL OF TAROT SPEAKS THE LAW OF NATURE

There is a distinct echo in this statement of our earlier edict that 'life teaches you about the Tarot and Tarot teaches you about life'. We saw how these two are intertwined and interdependent, each guiding the other by the very existence of their being.. If the Tarot has the ability to reflect the actions, feelings, thoughts and motivations of humanity, it takes as its tutor that which all living things are part of; what we call Nature.

It is a perhaps significant realisation that humanity has fallen away from the principles, teaching and dependency on nature, seeing itself now as separate and (mistakenly) in control. Perhaps this may go some way to explaining why the popular image of the Tarot is so far away from its true potential and capability. As we allow ourselves to (re)embrace the wonder of nature and learn respect for her forces again, so we may discover anew the true nature of this dazzling and wondrous set of cards.

STRUCTURE OF THE PACK

Due in the main to the adaptive nature of the Tarot and its ability to evolve alongside the spirit of humanity, the structure of the deck has also become something that varies. Since the advent of the technology capable of producing the exquisite effects and styles we see today in the cards, authors and designers have had 'carte blanche', literally, to adapt the Tarot to many different forms and inspirations. Consequently, the structure of the deck, the form they take and even the number and arrangement of the cards has become a variable thing. Given this state of affairs it is impossible to produce a guide to all such decks in one book. I will therefore concern myself with the most standard and accepted structure and form currently in use.

This is a 78 card deck, formed from two distinct yet interwoven packs. These are the aforementioned Major and Minor Arcana, the Major consisting of 22 cards and the Minor the remaining 56. The word 'Arcana' is derived in the main from the Latin 'Arcanum' meaning a secret or mystery. In its adjective form, arcane, the word comes to mean 'requiring secret knowledge to be understood, emphasising the need for initiation into the cards on both an individual and collective basis. Significantly, this is also one meaning of the word 'esoteric', showing us again the spiritual, sacred or higher nature of the Tarot.

These interpretations show us the inner nature of the cards, the sum total of the knowledge and information revealed when the seeker enters into them through study, application and meditation. Once this task has been achieved, that person is in a position to translate that knowledge to others, through the medium of a consultation, revealing the exoteric, or outer nature of the cards. In this way each who comes to the cards learns at least a little about the cards for themselves. Indeed it has been said with some justification that a Tarot consultation should be like a lesson in the cards.

We are first confronted by the mysterious and powerful symbols of the Major Arcana, a series of 22 cards that tell the story of the progression and unfoldment of the human spirit. Like a good Tarot consultation, these cards can be taken on different levels. Beginning with the Fool, he can be seen as the embodiment of the human spirit in physical form, the spark of life in flesh. What transpires over the following cards, in numbered sequence, is a series of images, figures and symbols, each depicting a lesson to be learned in the life of the Fool, as the spirit seeks it atonement and reunification with the source or Divine, whence it came. These lessons can be those we each must meet in the course of our life, or perhaps over the course of several lifetimes. This requires an acceptance of the principles of reincarnation, more of which will be explained in due course.

As each lesson is learned, each card encountered and its force and meaning absorbed into our being, so the Fool appears and questions 'Why'. This all important question and indeed the technique of questioning in order to learn, features strongly in another depiction of the search for wholeness and unity, that of the Quest for the Holy Grail. Here, those worthy are granted the vision of the Grail, when many strange things appear before them, not least the Grail itself. Then the question 'whom does the Grail serve' is asked, or taken another way, 'what is all this about, or more simply, 'why'? Should the aspirant realise the Grail serves them, that they must 'Know Thyself' before all else, they receive the healing of the Grail. Here the final card of the World in the Major Arcana is transcended and the soul joins again with the 'all that is' and receives complete and total liberation. Should the seeker fail in the asking of the question, the Fool appears once more and they return to living their lives until the required understanding is reached.

These are the lessons and teachings of the Major Arcana, the skill needed by the consultant being the ability to translate these lofty ideals to the everyday life of the client. The cards help enormously in this, as we will discover. We will uncover some of the inner meaning of each stage, lesson and card on this journey when we follow in the footsteps of the Fool and undertake the 'Seekers Quest'.

The Minor Arcana is split into four equal and again, distinct yet interwoven suits. These suits have given birth to the playing cards with which we are familiar. Though written references may point to playing cards being older, as some have claimed, the knowledge that is contained is certainly a good deal older than the modern form of playing cards, having their origins deep in the mists of myth. Indeed, such knowledge is beyond the limitations and restrictions that time and its associated linear thinking places.

The origin of the four suits lies all around us, in the natural world. We have seen how the Elements of Earth, Water, Air and Fire lend their form and force to all things, not least the suits of the Minor Arcana. Here, the name of each suit is taken by the symbol which is used as its physical representation, as follows:

EARTH	PENTACLES / COINS
WATER	CUPS / CHALICES
AIR	SWORDS / BLADES
FIRE	RODS / WANDS

It must be pointed out here that the variations of interpretation possible from the Tarot are such that even this simple list is open to debate and is hotly contested. The names of the suits may and do vary, without altering their meaning a great deal but the rub lies with the matter of which symbol and suit belongs to which Element. Earth and Water are aligned to Pentacles and Cups respectively in a consistent manner but when we enter the realms of Air and Fire, Swords and Wands, we find them to be interchangeable. In the above list I have chosen the way in which I have become used to interpreting them and have worked with on many levels over many years. I am subsequently familiar with the power that lies beyond each and feel comfortable with these ascriptions. What is required from the Tarot therapist is to explore what these Elements represent for themselves and make their choice accordingly.

One of Fire — FORCE

One of Earth — FORM

One of Wind — DAWN

One of Water — OPEN CHANNEL

The Elements of the Tarot (Tarot of the Spirit)

Whilst it is necessary to be clear and decisive in our choice we can do well to remember that our minds can change as we grow in awareness of what the Elements and the Tarot suits mean and represent. It cannot be stressed often or strongly enough that the art of interpreting the cards is an individual one. Each brings their unique gifts and outlook to their clients and so you must make your own mind up. The exercises at the end of this Chapter will help you to do this.

The four suits are each of 14 cards, following the pattern again familiar from playing cards. Thus we have a numbered sequence from 1 or Ace, through to Ten. These cards essentially combine the power and force of the Element to which they belong with the influence and energy of the number ascribed to it. Far from only showing events and circumstances in life, these cards contain information from such ancient and primeval sources as the Elements and numbers. Numbers may seem to have little to do with such supernatural subjects but as any good mathematician will tell you, the Universe can be defined and explained using numbers. Without their power and influence, necessary to give structure and order where there was chaos, we would lack a great deal in our society.

We must therefore be careful not to neglect or belittle the numbered cards, or the whole of the Minor Arcana, as some people are in the habit of doing. When we realise and accept that these cards too depict great and mighty forces and dominions, we can also realise their importance and relevance to ourselves and our lives and so are required to be taken notice of in our consultations. The skill, experience and ability of the Tarot therapist comes into play by again relating these concepts to the client on an individual and relevant basis.

It is reasonable to see each suit as a little like a mini Major Arcana in these numbered or 'pip' cards, since the task required is to move from the raw power and onset of the force of the particular Element depicted in each Ace, through its remaining 9 manifestations, within the life of the client and life itself. When, at card 10, we find the completion of the suit, akin to the World card from the Major Arcana, we again return to the Ace, perhaps of another suit, as we strive for a total liberation from the troubles and limits of the world and its demands. This is shown for us in the number 10 itself.

We shall enter into the inner workings and meaning of numbers and their associated power when we examine the Minor Arcana, but as introduction to the manner in which numbers apply themselves to our purposes, the number 10 will serve us well.

This number is comprised of two digits, a 1 and a 0 respectively, requiring that we apply the meaning of these to discover the resultant application of the 10. Thus, we have the beginning and the endless end. The 1 gives us the active and forward moving principle of life, the impulse to begin and the wild power of the life force within us and all things. This is followed by the endless circle of the 0, emptiness and potential from which to begin, again. In effect therefore, we have something, then nothing, like a vain gambler.

This reflects the nature of the journey through each suit of the Minor and the whole of the Major Arcana. When we begin, the Ace and the Fool, have in common that all they have is their untapped and untainted power or energy. By applying this to the reality they find about themselves, they gain the experience and knowledge that is required to guide them on through their future. By the conclusion of each stage of their journey, or the end of each suit, the best that they can hope to have realised is the truth that they know and have nothing. Paradoxically and typically of the nature of our Universe, all such knowledge is but naught compared with the need to realise our ultimately restricted human form and level. To progress to our next stage of evolution, or our next life if required, we must realise that we are like a blank canvas, a potential to display not only great beauty but truly fantastic achievements. When this inner truth is accepted and assimilated to our inner being, our core self, we are liberated from that which restricts, be it our individual beliefs and mental opinions based on what we have experienced, our emotional feeling and reaction to those experiences, the outward physical showing we make to the world or the higher spiritual impulse within us.

Now we are free to travel round the circle of the figure 0, back to our starting point, but a little higher on this spiralling circle. This is perhaps better explained by likening to the hardened heart that after such intense pressure from its outer crust, as protective and safe it may be, finally must break and give way, releasing the pressure from behind its dam to let loose a flood of tears. With the heart thus emptied, our view of the world and its state and our place within it is seen afresh. We can then sigh deeply, accept our humble position and errors and realise that we must step forward with ourselves just as we are. Now we are reborn into the 1 again, the next suit or the next card of the Major Arcana.

This leaves 16 cards remaining unexplained in the complete pack. These cards seem to give many Tarot practitioners problems and it can be easy to see why. The Court cards as they are known, feature four cards per suit, showing us a person or character on each. It is generally assumed that these represent the appearance and influence of a particular person in the clients' life in their consultation. However, it is necessary to see the Court cards as having the potential to mean much more, not necessarily in the person themselves, but in the type of force and power, or more accurately, the effect this has upon the client.

This is achievable when we consider the origin of the Court cards and the principles they illustrate. Here we again enter the Elemental realms of Nature. Considering that there are four Court cards per suit, it is easy to align an Element and its power to each card. The four cards of each suit of course go under different names depending on the theme and subject matter of each deck. As we will discover, the form and construction of present day packs is most commonly taken from medieval society for its foundation. Consequently the names most often given to the cards along with their usual Elemental ascription's are as follows:

PAGE	EARTH
KNIGHT	FIRE
QUEEN	WATER
KING	AIR

Again it must be mentioned that it is necessary for you to decide for yourself, as a budding Tarot therapist whether you agree with these pairings or not. Like the suits themselves, two of the above list seem interchangeable, the culprits this time being the Page and King. As we work through this pack there is ample opportunity for you to make your decision.

From this list we see that the form and force of the Elements again make their presence felt in the Tarot. Because of this and because we know that the Elements represent the life force from which all things come, in four different ways, we see that the Court cards have a much wider potential and application than only the appearance of a person in the reading.

This strength is made stronger and indeed doubled when we recall that the power of each suit comes from the same Elements. The two can then be combined in each Court card, so that, for example, the Page of Rods would be seen as Earth of Fire and the Queen of Cups, Water of Water. The results of this powerful combination will be seen in the examination of each card.

In the meantime, we will conclude our look at the structure of the Tarot pack by seeing the Court cards as forming a family, belonging to their respective suit. The Page is thus the Daughter, the Knight the Son, the Queen the Mother and

King the Father. This reflects the Celtic view of four such sacred figures in their tradition, the Creiddylad, Mabon, Modron and Dagda respectively. These figures we shall meet again exploring each card, so we will be content with our now widened view of the Court cards, to complete the structure of the Tarot pack.

In this way we are taking the 'traditional' and 'fortune-telling' meaning of the cards to a deeper level and this gives us a key difference in the use of the cards for Tarot Therapy.

Rather than applying the outer meaning of the card, by logically interpreting the scene we are shown to the client and their life, we allow the symbols on the cards to speak for themselves, letting the force and energy that it represents and carries with it affect and apply itself to the client. With the addition of sensitive discussion between the therapist and client a much deeper and holistic interpretation of a card and series of cards is achieved, restoring dignity to the power of the symbols so painstakingly and powerfully arranged on each card to reflect life and its sacred nature and process.

The necessity of the Tarot consultant to elevate themselves to the level of therapist becomes clear when we realise that in the energy of the Tarot cards, derived from the symbolic representation on them, is the very stuff and building blocks of life. This is done not only by a deep and personal knowledge and view of the cards, but by the practise and use of such methods as counselling skills, albeit within a spiritual context where possible, this being the only, true therapy and necessary here since the Tarot includes the spiritual as part and parcel of the everyday life, a practical spirituality if you will.

By applying the symbols and energy of the cards directly to the client and their life, we can restore something of their originally intended meaning. Just as this is done for each card in a consultation each time it appears, this microcosm is also reflected in the restoration of the general view of the Tarot as a whole at the same time, healing the damage done to the macrocosm of the complete deck by years of use and abuse as that which predicts the future and little else. With the focused, ethical and purposeful use of the Tarot as a therapy we can help to recapture something of the sacredness so sadly and prominently lacking in many people and in society as a whole, by bringing about the inner and outer healing that is the highest and full result of the Tarot Therapy session.

HOW IT WORKS

By examining the nature and structure of the Tarot we have come to see how it is formed and utilises the ancient power of Nature and the universal life force energy that all things come from and essentially, are. What is yet to be revealed is how these apparently abstract forces can relate to ourselves and the intricate workings of our lives, when they are laid out before us, usually by somebody who does not know us well or may never have even met us. How can it be that 78 pieces of plastic are capable of telling us about ourselves and our lives and more importantly can be utilised in a therapeutic manner that allows us to take responsibility for our own actions and beings and so grow and develop to achieve our fullest potential, such is the aim of the Tarot therapist here? This is perhaps one of the most vexing of all questions regarding the Tarot.

For our answer we will first turn to the psychological interpretation of the seemingly random deal of the cards. Here we often meet with derision and scorn, for it can be claimed that 'it's all in the mind' and we see what we want to see when consulting the cards. When looked at a little closer, we discover that this is indeed the case and is as it should be, due to the nature and contents of the human mind.

It is known and accepted that the 'average person' (a horrible concept!) uses only approximately one third of their brain and its power. The remaining portion is that with which we are concerned and indeed what it is necessary to tap into when using the Tarot for therapy. This dormant part of the mind must be awakened and a bridge made between the two. This can be taken quite literally for the human brain is made up of two halves, or hemispheres, each with their own function. The left hemisphere is the realm of the conscious mind, the everyday functioning, logical and rational part of the brain that you are using to read these words and that you use in the course of your everyday life and activities. This is necessary to use when relating your interpretation of the cards to a client in a consultation and to discuss the issues arising as a result with them.

What must be added to this however, are the messages and information arising from the right hemisphere of the brain. This is the un, or sub, conscious parts of the brain, wherein instinctive and intuitive responses to external stimuli are formed. For the Tarot therapist it is therefore necessary to enter into the dark and mysterious realms of their own subconscious so as to be able to act as a wise guide and counsellor when the clients is laid bare before them during a consultation. The Tarot is fully and wonderfully capable of producing and revealing this information, that the client would not otherwise have access to, for themselves. This it does by utilising the most profound and direct language known to humanity - that of symbols. This language is also that of the subconscious mind and so the Tarot comes to be seen as the perfect therapeutic vehicle, not only for the mind but body, heart and spirit too, tapping as it does into each of these worlds and aspects of the human being and the wider world and Universe about it.

At this point a study of symbolism will repay dividends later, when we come to experiencing and feeling the process of the symbols at work, by interpreting the cards. The study and use of symbols is based on the principle that the

Universe functions and is, a unified whole, in which all things are related. It is for this reason that ancient symbols are meaningful and potent today and have relevance to the modern life and person. Symbols are seen as expressing the patterns of the psyche, with the sequence of the cycle of life and the interaction between the two. As such, they demonstrate the 'binding force' of the Universe, which in modern parlance is known as energy or 'life-force'. In this light, symbols are seen as being able to heal the gap or chasm between the conscious and unconscious minds. Symbols have been aptly defined as a 'precise and crystallised means of expression'.

Further to this, symbols can be seen at a more transpersonal level, since they depict the methods and means of the created or physical, everyday world, with the supernatural or higher realms. In essence they unite humanity with spirit. The philosopher and writer Erich Fromm defined three classes of symbols:

1. **The Universal** - a symbol which comes from the 'intrinsic relation' between the symbol and what it represents, i.e. the literal. This type of symbol has a clear and definite meaning wherever and whenever it is viewed.
2. **The Conventional** - a symbol stripped of any basis, such as those used in industry and mathematics, i.e. the abstract. This is a blend of a standard meaning for the symbol and the personal, individual response to it.
3. **The Accidental** - coming from transitory conditions, with associations made through casual contact, i.e. the intuitive. These symbols allow for a completely individual, momentary interpretation to be made by the viewer.

In the context of the Tarot we can see that any one card is actually a composite, or blending of the three types of symbol. For the Tarot therapist, it is necessary to be able to perceive the type of symbol you are looking at on the card and respond accordingly. Further down the line, it becomes important to realise and be aware whilst interpreting the cards, that a symbol can be more than one or all three of the types of symbol defined above. The Tarot therapist must develop the ability, by repeated study, meditation on the cards and practise of interpretation to discern how the symbol they are perceiving is communicating, first with themselves then on to the client. By this method the three types of symbols can be seen as stages, of unfoldment and revelation of their meaning, for the client in that particular consultation.

This brings to light the difference between a sign or emblem and a symbol. A sign is created purposely, usually (to illustrate) a specific purpose. Such is the vase with company logos in modern times, though it is debatable at which point they become symbols, since there use is so ubiquitous as to lodge themselves in the psyche of humanity across the globe, this of course being the intention of both the designer and the company that sells it. A symbol however, just 'happens'. Rather like new words that appear in common usage, due to some new understanding or technology, symbols have the ability to manifest from the ethers, as the realm of our imagination and projected thoughts. They are the outworking of this inner reality, encapsulated in an accessible form for all 'with eyes to see'. It is through this connection to the force that shapes and dictates our lives and selves that they enable the redirection of energy to be employed and facilitated by their understanding and employment. Changes brought about at this level are the only real solid and sustainable ones. In the hands of the Tarot therapist, the symbols depicted on the cards become powerful gateways to the understanding of the inner motivations and workings of all that we are.

Consequently though we may have learnt and memorised the meaning of any one symbol, we may only use this as the essence of our interpretation of the card as a whole. Whilst many symbols on a card may have a standard, accepted interpretation, in combination with the other symbols on the card and subsequently other cards in the consultation, it is necessary for the Tarot therapist to allow an intuitive response to the symbol to occur at that time and be able to relate this to the client. From this we can see that the process of interpreting a card for each client individually is a progression from the Universal use of the symbol, through the conventional to the accidental.

The choice of the term 'accidental' is an interesting one, illustrating the paradox of the workings of intuition, a ubiquitous term that is rarely explained on investigated. In the context of Tarot symbolism and therapy, the intuition needs to be utilised a great deal. The symbolic function is regarded as occurring 'at the precise moment when a state of tension is set up between opposites which the consciousness cannot resolve by itself'. By bypassing the rational mind, which has already responded to the symbol it perceives at the Universal level, the power of the symbol kicks in and the conventional response to the symbol is arrived at, bringing us to the conclusion and revelation of the accidental, or intuitive response and interpretation.

This intuitive response cannot however be remembered and used again, churned out in subsequent consultations. A definition of intuition will illustrate this point: 'immediate mental apprehension without reasoning; immediate insight'. Our intuitive {literally 'inner tuition'} faculty is alive, and responds as such to the stimuli given it, in this case, Tarot cards. This is why I have repeatedly instructed students to learn what they can of the symbols, then forget it, since this knowledge needs to be brought to this intuitive, transpersonal level, something that is beyond the Universal and belongs to the moment. This reflects something of the magic of a Tarot consultation.

Intuition bridges that gap previously mentioned, by bringing information from the shade and retreat of the unconscious and into the light of the conscious. It is then a matter of the

Tarot therapist utilising their skill and ability, drawn from what is within them rather than something that can be acquired, in relating the information flowing to their brain and heart to the client. This needs to be done sensitively and supportively and in terms which the client can relate to. The way in which this is done will be explored later.

It must also be realised that a Tarot card is a collection of individual symbols. This gives us two levels at which we can respond to the Tarot card, which should be seen as a chance to deepen and make more relevant and meaningful our interpretation, rather than a complication that must be endured! Initially, individual symbols need to be examined and an appropriate response made to each that strikes us as relevant at that particular moment. This does not mean that every symbol on every card must be explained in every consultation. This is clearly not practical or realistic. Rather the intuitive skill of the therapist must be used to discern what is necessary to be explained to the client. Of course it may be that the client may make mention of something they have noticed and this process should be encouraged.

Once the necessary symbols have been examined and revealed, it is then necessary to look at the Tarot card as a whole. Now the true power of the card and its symbols can be loosed. It is here that we truly arrive at the complete 'accidental' meaning of the card. Each symbol on a Tarot card will relate in some way to the others on it, adhering to the Universal theme on which the card is based. It is because these themes are concerned with the passage of life and our place within it that the Tarot presents for us what is known as 'ageless wisdom', deriving as they do from the source of that knowledge: nature and its forces, which in turn relate to the wider Universe of which we are a part. Understanding the role we play in that Universe and fulfilling the potential of that role should be the highest goal of the Tarot therapist for their clients. It is their job to enable and empower the client to discover this for themselves and after the consultation to be armed sufficiently with knowledge and understanding to act on.

This process is known as the 'symbolic line', the 'common rhythm' of a series of symbols, such as that on a Tarot card. This follows the thinking in symbolism that nothing is meaningless, or that everything is significant. Equally symbolism sees nothing as independent and everything as related, not least the symbols themselves. In this way, the microcosm or one individual can be seen as a related part of the macrocosm of all symbols, or put another way, the microcosm of one card in a consultation can be seen as a related part of all cards on view, the macrocosm.

The translation of abstract information from the cards to methods of acting is likened to the 'true basis' of symbolism. A symbol can be seen as the 'correspondence linking together all orders of reality, binding one to the other'. Taking symbols as having the ability to 'transmute systems of vibration', we see how effective they are in relation to the Tarot when we see that all things consist of vibrations or energies, moving at different speeds. It is this that gives their different qualities. In Nature, these give rise to the four Elements, each having their own distinct vibrational pattern and speed that results in a corresponding response within the human being, thereby controlling and regulating the functioning of certain systems in our selves.

This adequately describes a Tarot card too, since each is a symbol of itself. At a greater or more Universal level, the whole of Nature, of which humanity is a functioning and intrinsic part, can be seen as a symbol. When we recall that the structure of the Tarot is derived from the structure of Nature we begin to realise the potential for the Tarot to be used as a therapy, by using the same power or force, depicted as symbols, for its working.

Carl Jung, the Swiss psychologist who embraced a spiritual element to the Universe and the human being coined the term 'archetype' for such symbols. These symbols, which must include many of the symbols on the cards and the cards themselves, are those which possess the greatest efficiency in communicating their meaning and relevance for us as individuals at the time of our consultation and so have the highest potential for 'psychic evolution'.

This reflects the way in which symbols can be interpreted, on two distinct yet related levels, being the objective and the subjective. The objective is seen as the understanding of the symbol and the subjective the application of that understanding to given examples and situations, in this case, the clients. It is stressed that the individual prejudices, the clients' likes and dislikes concerning the symbols, must also be taken into account. Psychologists have argued that the use of symbolism is distorted when an interpretation is applied, since any one symbol exists as itself, pure and untainted by any human reasoning. The intuitive, or 'accidental' response to the symbol however, bypasses the conscious mind which such people are so often bound up in.

Jung saw archetypes as 'ready-made systems of both images and emotions'. It is for this reason that both the mind and heart must be used when interpreting the cards. The workings of symbolism are commonly seen as being a mental functioning but for our purposes our emotional response to the symbol must also be noted. Intuition can adequately be defined as a blend of the inner response to both the minds understanding and the hearts feeling. By including an emotional or feeling level to our consultations we also serve to relate to the client at a level which draws them in to the process and includes and values them as a holistic person, made of body, mind and spirit. To be truly therapeutic the Tarot consultation must address the needs of each of these aspects of the client.

Jung however, viewed humanity as being 'pitifully unaware' of these forces in our world. It is this, in the psychological view that gives rise to conflict in humanity, resulting in our present world of poverty, disease, greed and violence. This global crisis is perhaps indicative of the individual endemic fear we can have at facing what we may have chosen to have forgotten and so pushed to our unconscious or subconscious mind. By keeping and effectively imprisoning such information and experiences we are preventing ourselves from becoming whole, blocking the process of individuation in Jungian terminology. The Tarot, in the hands of the sensitive and skilled therapist, has the ability to bridge that gap and return the client to a state from which they can progress to an ultimate wholeness and completion.

These 'deeper' parts of our mind also house all the matter that the conscious mind cannot or does not, wish to retain. They can, in this sense be likened to the 'bottom drawer' of our minds, the rarely unexplored contents lying undisturbed within until a catalyst is experienced that throws light onto them.

That catalyst is the Tarot. This process also shows us further the therapeutic nature of the Tarot. It is accepted in psychological terms that for the human to become whole and complete they must face what limits, restricts and fears them; they must face and accept and thereby transmute the power of what they suppress or repress. These things are the contents of the right hemisphere of the brain and so the process of individuation, which we can liken to the Seeker's Quest, or journey of the Fool, is depicted in the cards of the Tarot. By utilising the power of symbols the Tarot is able, in the hands of a therapist, to shed the required light into even the darkest corners of the client and gently and safely, coax and nurture the fears, nightmares and memories that have taken refuge within that darkness.

For those filled with trepidation or what is often more coldly seen as denial at the thought of facing their fears, let us remind ourselves of the inescapable maxim that 'there is nothing to fear but fear itself'. Of course it is only by facing our fears that we are able to discover the real truth of this statement and so the journey of the Fool becomes one for the stout and brave of heart, who can at least take comfort from knowing that they possess the best and wisest of companions on that journey, the Tarot itself.

The power of symbols has been demonstrated to extraordinary effect throughout history and continues to be used so today. Symbols can be seen prominently as far back as ancient Egypt and beyond. Hieroglyphics are one of the most profound and expertly used languages of symbols, the power and effect of which many other tribal cultures were also aware of. Armies marched under their banners, symbols proudly fluttering on the flag and carried resolutely on the shield. More recently the world-wide spread of some companies and corporations have overcome the language barriers of the world by using symbols and in this lies the real clue as to their power.

Global companies need to find cheap yet effective ways of advertising their goods, so as to maximise profit, at whatever other cost they seem to incur, for which read exploitation of workers' rights, environmental destruction and so on. The advertising world has clearly realised the potential and power of the symbol and so incorporate an image or logo into their advertising and everything associated with the company. Every time a person sees this image, an immediate and instinctive association is made with what else is seen and that companies name and product. This is why modern adverts feature scenes of happiness, desire and affluence, so as to convince us that the product shown will result in such things for us if we have it. The reality is far from the case of course, and the advertisers are well aware of this, yet untroubled by it.

This is because the power of the symbol does not discriminate between what is good and positive and what is damaging and detrimental. Indeed, it is unable to do so for the symbols it encounters are received by the right hemisphere of the brain, the irrational, feeling half. As soon as the symbol is seen a response occurs and it is this response, triggering synaptic messages to the deeper brain that advertisers seek to effect. It is this that has seen many extreme forms taking place, such as encoded, tiny words appearing in television adverts, as well as the blatant exploitation of the truth 'sex sells'. Before you scream 'conspiracy; however, watch some television advertising and see how many use sparkling effects, flashes of light and words or images flashed on the screen very quickly. This same process has been used recently in the unlikely arena of the rock music concert with the band U2 using the same techniques to get across their own, rather more empowering message, on their 'ZOO TV' tour.

Here we enter the world known as subliminal but fortunately for us, the symbols appearing on Tarot cards are, for the present at least, static. One wonders however what advances in the use of the Tarot a 3D, moving and speaking, interactive Tarot computer programme might achieve. Fantasy role playing may never be the same again!

The power of the symbol thus lies in its ability to form that aforementioned bridge between the two halves of the brain. The symbol, being a global language can be interpreted more at a feeling and intuitive level than a thinking one. This comes after the initial response when we are able to consider our reaction upon looking at a card and draw conclusions as best we are able. The role of the Tarot therapist then becomes first one of interpretation of the symbol, on behalf of the client which, most importantly, is taken in conjunction with the clients own reaction. It is for this reason that a Tarot consultation should never be a one way process, but an exchange between client and therapist.

This is also why I have always exhorted students of the Tarot to learn the cards thoroughly and mentally absorb what each is able to about each card and then forget it! This is so that the information, learned in the conscious mind is able to sink into the deeper levels and so a response to the external stimulus of the card itself can be trusted as an accurate one, unbiased or distorted by the therapist themselves. The power of both symbols and the Tarot is thus revealed.

The language of symbols has been called 'the art of thinking in images' and so the Tarot can be seen as the most eloquent of such languages. Any one Tarot card, is or at least should be if correctly constructed, a precisely and deliberately arranged series of symbols creating one unified concept. The power of one individual symbol is amplified by its use alongside other images and symbols that all relate to the same theme, that of the message and meaning of the card itself.

We can consider the individual symbols to be the physical representation of those very life forces and energies from which all physical reality comes from and is formed. The human mind has energy with great potential and power and the Tarot has, through its ability to go to the very core of our own energy in these deeper levels of the mind, the ability to translate that raw and unfocussed energy into a form that lightens rather than darkens, expands rather than restricts and heals rather than destroys the human condition. This it does through the instinctive and unstoppable language and power of symbols.

When we realise that all things are formed of energy, be they human, animal, mineral or vegetable, thought, word, deed or feeling that result in action, we must also accept that true therapy or healing must also occur at this same invisible yet real level to be the most effective and complete it can be. It is for this reason that many Eastern systems of medicine, such as Chinese and the Indian Ayurvedic, examine the life force of the patient in its varying circumstances and situations rather than their outer physical symptoms. Energy in the human system and being takes many different forms that can again be linked to the four Elements we have already discovered. Because the human being itself consists of these same elemental forces, and the structure of the

Tarot is also formed from these same powers, the cards are truly unique in their ability to address our needs at all levels.

When we consider the potency of these symbols and combine it with the matter of the Tarot - the meaning and nature of life, fuelled by the knowledge that the Tarot speaks the law of nature, we come to fully understand and realise the perfect position the Tarot is in to act as a therapy able to address any need, be it physical, emotional, mental or spiritual.

EXERCISES

Write your own description or definition of what the Tarot is, in no more than 3 sentences.

Re-read the section regarding the ascription of Minor Arcana suits to Elements. By looking at your own cards, especially noticing their general colouring and how they feel to you as well as what you see on the card, decide which Element you feel best belongs to which suit at this stage. You are of course free to change these as you progress.

.
Repeat the above, this time with the Court cards as your subject. Remember that each Court card already has one Element ascribed to it, from its suit. Add to this the Element of the Page, Knight, Queen or King and see if you feel the combination of Elements and what you know of what this represents 'fits' the card. Decide which Court cards belong to which Element in this way.

Consider any times or situations in your life that you can think of where you have used your intuition in some way. Think back to how your perception was at this time and how your intuition may have arisen to direct you. Make notes about this and consider its relevance to your use of intuition with the Tarot.

Choose three cards from your pack, either at random or by conscious choice. Examine the individual symbols you see on this card and note down any responses to these in the same way as above. Having done this, repeat the exercise, this time examining the card as a whole, rather than as individual symbols. Note down your mental and emotional (i.e. intuitive) responses as you do so. Do be aware that your responses are accurate for the time you are looking at them, not necessarily as well as in the future. Do they tell you anything about your current state of self and life? Repeat this process gradually as you progress with your cards until you have done this at least once for every card, perhaps by picking one card per day, or three per week, over the coming months.

TAROT DEDICATION CEREMONY

This Ceremony is intended to provide a vehicle for you to come to regard your Tarot cards as a sacred object, since that is their nature and use. What is given below are brief suggestions and guidelines only. Your own particular Ceremony will be all the more potent and meaningful if you add your own words and actions, as you feel fit. Read the guidelines before attempting your Ceremony. Make notes afterwards regarding what you felt and experienced.

Prepare first by clearing a sufficient space around you and ensuring that you will not be interrupted. Light a candle and play some suitable music, if you like it. You may like to take a cleansing bath to enhance the mood and the occasion, perhaps using some purifying essential oil in the bath, or sprinkling sea salt into the water, which has a cleansing effect on the aura..

Begin by creating a protected and safe space in which to perform your Ceremony. Do this first by walking around your room or area in a circle, sunwise (clockwise), slowly tracing your steps and imagining that a field of energy is created as you go. Come back to your starting point and then walk around the circle one more. This time pause at each of the four directions, welcoming each Element as you go. Begin in the North, asking for the power of Earth to be present, in your own words as you feel moved. Continue to the East, for the Element of Air, South for the Element Fire and West for Water. Having done this you might like to address and acknowledge any higher power you identify with, be it a deity, God or Goddess etc.

Then be seated, close your eyes and relax. If you meditate enter into your stillness. Feel yourself connecting with your own inner self and feel the sense of balance and peace there. Now take your Tarot cards and hold them for a time. Let yourself and your inner senses feel any response that comes to you as you do so. Light some incense and allow the smoke to waft up before you. Fan your cards through the smoke, allowing the properties of the incense to clean and clear them of any previously held vibrational patterns. Perhaps say a request or prayer as you do so, asking for them to be cleansed and sanctified for your use.

Now read a previously prepared statement of dedication to your Tarot. This needs to be in your own words to be effective and should contain a statement of the use you will make of your cards, your purpose in having them and particularly how you will utilise them for positive change and growth, in yourself and others. You may address this dedication to any higher power that you acknowledge, but also to yourself. Consider what you must do to honour your agreement and fulfil the promises you should make at this time. The unseen powers that exist take us at our word in such times so be sure that you mean what you say. Read this aloud, perhaps from a carefully prepared written statement, that you should keep carefully for as long as you use your cards. Follow your conscience at all times in this.

Now choose at random three cards from the pack, face down as you choose them. These cards will tell you about the effects and meaning of the dedication you have just made and may give you information regarding your use of the Tarot. They may be relevant to you at this time but principally will represent how you interact with and can utilise the cards. Study the cards, perhaps meditate on them and allow any feelings and thoughts to come to you. Make notes as you feel suitable.

Make a prayer or statement to the Spirit of the Tarot, thanking it for its guidance and communication. Add any other words or actions that you feel appropriate following your previous experiences. Now put your cards away. You may also like to purify your silk and box in incense smoke before you do so.

Now close your circle, by walking round in the reverse order to before, thanking the power of each Element in turn with words you feel are appropriate. Do not forget to thank any higher power that you work with too. Extinguish any candles you may have lit and pause before leaving to take a few deep breaths. 'Ground' yourself back in the everyday world by pressing your feet and/or hands on to the floor a little. Ensure you do not feel light headed afterwards. If you do, take a drink and snack to ensure you have returned your consciousness fully.

CHAPTER 4 - THE SEEKERS QUEST

The point of our lives, and there surely must be one, can partly be to learn what we can in the short time we are here, and grow and develop as best we are able. This is by no means the whole point, but does give us purpose. A brief glance at human history shows that what is missing from this equation is the ability to apply what we learn to each other and so learn to live in tolerance and harmony. For this to occur, a critical number of individuals must learn to live in harmony with themselves. Only then can we hope and expect to not kill, maim and do harm in any way to each other.

This is a very tall order, as history again confirms for us, yet it is not impossible. An ancient and significant spiritual truth and principle is that of the microcosm and macrocosm, expressed as 'As Above, So Below. Applied in the current context, this principle tells us that what occurs at an individual level is reflected at a collective one also. This can be applied in the reverse too. This echoes the view that we each have a 'spark of God' or Divine aspect within us, often termed the spirit. Within this, it can be viewed, is a miniature Universe. The workings and very construction of our DNA also confirm the principle.

If as suggested above, the purpose of our lives is a progressive one it is clear from history that we need a guide to help us. Enter the Tarot! For a guide to be effective on all points on this Quest, it must by definition, illustrate the clear stages of that journey at both an inner and outer level. An exploration of both Major and Minor Arcana shows this to be true in the case of the Tarot. Whatever its true source and origin, the Tarot shows us vividly the progressive nature of life and how we can achieve a measure of both individual and collective harmony and wholeness. This we term the Seekers Quest. This is commonly called the 'Journey of the Fool' also commonly being applied only to the Major Arcana cards. To act as a true guide and therapy in ourselves and lives the whole Tarot deck must be seen as part of the quest, which we shall explore in this context.

The Seekers Quest is the path The Fool takes as he moves through the other 21 cards of the Major Arcana. It is by the consistent questioning of what or who he meets at each card that the Fool learns the lesson of each card and so progresses to the next. Over the course of one life time or the accumulated memories and wisdom of many lives, The Fool evolves to be a complete and whole human being, as the living embodiment of the spirit from which all life comes. He then takes and applies what he has learnt to the outer, everyday realm illustrated by the Minor Arcana.

The Major Arcana should always be seen in this context, particularly in the work of the Tarot therapist, since it is this path to wholeness that is the fulfilment of this use of the Tarot. In working with the cards of the Major Arcana, the Tarot therapist has a need to be consciously aware of this level of the cards as that to which the client needs to aspire and inherently understand. The interpretations of the Seekers Quest can perhaps best be viewed as the higher meaning of the cards, when they are viewed as complete in this way.

This is a cyclical way, one that moves freely and fully to its next stage as a direct consequence and result of the Seeker taking the energy of the card within, its power or force that brings about the transformation required. This transformation can occur at any level, be it physical, emotional, mental or spiritual. This will be revealed by the details of the Minor Arcana cards chosen by the client in a consultation. Included in the following Chapter are details of the way in which the Arcanas are linked, to serve as an introduction to the whole pack, seen in the light of therapy. For these purposes, the Minor Arcana serves as the place or realm in which the Seeker works out or manifests what he learns at the deeper level of the Major Arcana lessons.

By opening oneself, often via meditation or exercises such as the ones used throughout this book, performed by the client themselves under the guidance and supervision of the Tarot therapist, the transpersonal level of the card is reached and its changes are allowed the space to bring about their effect. This, as mentioned above, is a transformation. The transpersonal level of the card is precisely that - beyond the individual. The understanding of this level may never be put into words (though I will shortly try!) but this is unimportant. What does matter is that the client is able to respond appropriately in the relevant level of themselves and their lives.

Being beyond the individual level does not imply that you must be an expert in the Tarot in any way. Rather, with the happy innocence of the client in the ways of the Tarot, to whatever degree, the power and depth of the symbols dealt with, are able to unleash their full transformative potential. It is then up to the client to respond as they feel fit. Changes of this kind cannot be forced, however strongly you, as the clients Tarot therapist feel, for change must be made willingly and freely for it to have a lasting and positive effect. When the client is ready for this, they may do it. In consultations, the explanations are given, discussed with the client and exercises suggested or carried out. It is then necessary to release the client to work the changes through, offering your further support and guidance when necessary. The burdens of accepting clients own problems can easily fall squarely on the shoulders of the Tarot Therapist if they are not careful and if so, they will soon crumble and fall as the weight of successive clients bears down on them. It is for this reason that I have included elsewhere some pointers towards the construction of your consultations and mention of counselling techniques.

This unfolding process of the Fool is known as individuation by psychologists, the term being coined again by Jung, the spiritual friend of psychology. This is seen as an analytical method of exploration of the self, resulting in the understanding and integration of the parts that make up this whole. Seen in this light, the Major Arcana is the ultimate pictorial depiction of the means and stages of the individuation, when seen from a sacred or spiritual viewpoint. When the Minor Arcana is then added as the method of working out what has been learned in the everyday life, it easy to see how the Tarot can act as a therapy.

As a pictorial depiction, of symbols rather than words, the power of each card is allowed free expression and given the ability to do its work. Change is at the heart of our lives and indeed, is the only constant process we have. It must therefore be 'faced and embraced', accepted willingly and positively, however uncomfortable or painful the outward results may be of such transformation. The fortune teller may have previously looked only at the outer change taking place, from a standing of the cards simply explaining what the forces of fate or destiny have in store for the client. The Tarot therapist however, must be able to take this to a deeper level within the client and explain the until now mysterious forces and energies of the cards before them. It is this which allows the client to maximise the considerable potential, both of the cards and themselves.

Psychologically, these symbols that contain such miraculous ability are seen as archetypes. A possible definition of an archetype can be 'an abstract form that represents an inner truth'. Because they speak of 'truth' or maxims and principles that disseminate the accumulated knowledge of humanity to its present stage of evolution, the archetypal symbols of the Tarot possess within themselves, the means to be the therapy we need. Since such truths apply to one and all peoples, they are also able to bring the client to the transpersonal level required for the knowledge of the truth to be implemented in the self and life of the client.

Further to this, because an archetype is an abstract image and as such unlimited by the current mental level of understanding reached by humanity as a whole, it is alive and able to evolve alongside its human counterpart. It is this that enables the Tarot to reveal more of itself as the human race does the same. Truth is still the truth as we know it at any given point in time. What we recognise as this truth may change and a new interpretation or understanding of an archetype may emerge to express and allow for this change. This is the case with the Tarot. This is also the reason why the Tarot therapist must also be on their own path of truth in their own selves and lives. It is not necessary for them to be a complete and whole human being to use the Tarot as a therapy, for there are precious few people like this alive physically. When they do occur, they generally do not hang around for very long, since there is little on the physical earth to teach them. Rather they evolve or ascend to a higher level of existence which we must eventually all come to know. What is required from the Tarot therapist however, is the motivation to reach these heights, one day, and a willingness to change and evolve in their present life time towards this goal. They are then open to understanding of the cards at the depth required to facilitate the changes spoken of earlier in others and to have enough mental comprehension of what they see and are dealing with to explain them in acceptable terms to the client.

Indeed it has often been stated that those who use such tools, teach them or otherwise act as healers or therapists do so because at the deepest level, it is they who need the therapy. This is why I have always alerted my students, as I do now, that studying the Tarot is a study primarily of the self. As the therapist is open and flexible enough to accept what is revealed to them in their study of the Tarot, so they are enabled to pass on these understandings and revelations to their client. Without this, a Tarot consultation can become merely an exercise in word games, or be open to misunderstanding and the exploitation of any vulnerability the client may have or show. Such practises are not in the spirit of the Tarot or of healing and indeed the evolutionary and progressive principle of the Universe and so must be roundly condemned.

When conveyed to the client, the mental understanding of the archetype as it relates to the client in that particular time and place in their lives, occurs and they are empowered in a way that only they can truly know. Under the guidance of the Tarot therapist they are directed to allowing this change its full force and range and so the Tarot brings the Seeker to wholeness, or at the very least contributes significantly to this process.

This path to wholeness has been depicted in areas other than the Tarot of course. Fairy tales and stories, whether for children or not provide a fertile ground for allegory and many have utilised their talents to produce great works. The film 'The Wizard of Oz' is in reality a perfect depiction of the path of individuation, as Dorothy continues on her quest, following the yellow brick road to the wizard who will give her what she wants, a return to 'home'. Along the way she meets those who are each lacking something of themselves, which all discover of course at the end and so live happily ever after, as they should.

The Seekers Quest is also known as the Masonic Harmonies in Freemasonry, the Great Work of the Alchemists and can be seen as a programme of initiation, into and through each card.

On a more mythological level the story of the Quest for the Holy Grail, carried out by the Knights of King Arthur, also represents the same Quest the Fool pursues through the Major Arcana. Here the Grail is that which is able to give to each according to their need and so return or restore them to a state of purity and completion. Each who comes to the Grail must be worthy however and imperfection shows itself at the critical moment. Lancelot is blinded by the light of the Grail for his part in the eternal triangle between himself, Guinevere and Arthur. We can take heed of this in the context of the Tarot by realising that the lessons of each card must be taken to the transformative level, implemented to ourselves fully and then allowed the freedom and space to express themselves in our practical lives.

In surveying the Seekers Quest we are therefore exploring the very essence of the Major Arcana cards. This chapter thereby serves as an excellent introduction to these 22 cards allowing for the beginning of the individual journey the aspiring Tarot therapist must take. It must be made clear that the order of the cards detailing this journey has varied through history and continues to do so, in keeping with the evolutionary spirit of the Tarot. The order given here is the most accepted in these times, the main point of contention currently being the placing of cards 8 and 11, Strength and Justice, which are often transposed.

There follows a short piece on each card, both to welcome you to each one and to attempt to explain the evolutionary and cyclical, progressive nature of their sequence.

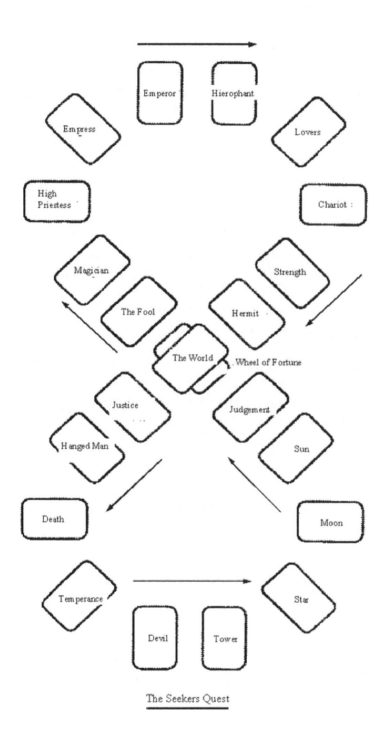

The Seekers Quest

THE FOOL

The Fool has both no and every place in the Major Arcana and indeed the complete Tarot. He has no number, or is numbered 0 and this reflects the position he has in the Major Arcana, being everywhere. He is thus the beginning and the end, as well as every point in between. He is the Seeker, embodied for us as the itinerant traveller, the ragged boy who is perfect in his innocence. In the Quest he plays the part of Seeker perfectly, for he knows no other way. We refer to the Fool as 'he' but he is really hermaphrodite, or of both sexes. In this we see his true nature; that of the human spirit personified. This is the eternal part of us that belongs to the wider Universe, the spark of God if you prefer. At the outset of his quest he knows nothing and is free of all fear, emotional conditioning and mental understanding. He must travel on his journey, questioning everything he encounters and accepting everything. By this process he is guided to encounter the symbols of the 21 cards on his journey, just as we encounter challenges and decisions through our life. By this process each successive card comes to him and he must respond as he sees fit, just as must we in life. The Fool is the symbol of life, of existence, akin to the new born baby and exemplifying the curious spirit we can see in the new born. As he thinks, so he is. He is a physical form of pure life-force energy, just as each of us truly is. He represents the egoless state of purity from which we all come and must, at length, return. We call him the Seeker.

THE MAGICIAN

The Magician is conscious of his own existence and it is this awareness that separates him from the Fool. The Magician is the result of the blossoming of awareness in the Fool. He has realised he is alive and must now come to terms with and accept this and the reality of who and what he is. Like the growing child, he explores all he sees and finds and seeks to master it. By the identification and then exertion of his newly realised will he must become fully aware of his physical, emotional, mental and spiritual faculties, as exemplified by his magical working tools. The ego, the 'weapon of consciousness', has emerged and must be integrated into his existence and being. He must in all senses, learn to live with himself, with his physical drives, emotional feelings, mental judgement and spiritual consciousness. The Magician must learn the lessons of his outer self and existence before he can progress. This is the externalisation of what is within.

THE HIGH PRIESTESS

Just as the Magician is the outer, masculine side of the human being, so the High Priestess is the inner, feminine half. Each of us, whether physically male or female, must learn to balance and blend these two 'complementary opposite' halves, a principle we shall meet time and again in the Tarot. Having explored and learnt to accept all the Seeker encounters without himself, now he must turn within and explore what he encounters there. The inner mysteries of the human condition must be acknowledged and accepted. This is note a state of resolution, for this is the process of the journey itself, but a recognition that this state exists. This is the receptive side of the human personality and in the first of four Jungian 'ego-powers', the personification of intuition. This must be balanced with the active, aggressive will of the Magician as a passive, subtle force. When this is achieved, the lesson is learnt and progress can be made on the quest. This is the balance of the inner and outer.

THE EMPRESS

Staying with the feminine, the Seeker now discovers the creative potential within himself, the urge to care for, nurture and protect those he encounters as he discovers the essential unity and brother/sister hood of all peoples. This is the ego's response to the feelings it identifies, as expressed in the symbol of the crescent moon, which was atop the head of the High Priestess but is now beneath the foot of the Empress. This is the beginning of the understanding of why all things have been created, principally the self, manifesting in the actualisation of the mental consciousness, through feeling and emotion. This is the eternal mothering potential within us all, the need within to express that which we feel in our hearts. The Fool must learn now to balance his inner feelings with outer action, being neither so full of feelings nor devoid of them that reality is distorted. He must learn to express his feelings and work with his emotions, as neither a destructive or constructive tool, but simply as a force, or energy. When this is utilised efficiently the lesson has been learnt.

THE EMPEROR

Here, as we might expect, is the father principle to the mother Empress; Father Sky to Mother Earth. As the Empress discovers the container, the Emperor fills it. The ego now learns to assimilate sensation to its experience, as does the Fool or us. The Emperor is the controller of all under his power and so the Fool must learn to control and implement that which he has learnt so far, in the physical realm of his life. Through effort and application, the Fool becomes the fully realised Emperor, having learnt the way of the material world around him. Progress is made when this awareness is aligned with the natural world around him and he applies what he knows within it, thus becoming Emperor of all things.

THE HIEROPHANT

When he has been out and become the symbolic Emperor of the world, the Fool must now sit back and assess what he has learnt. When we have reached the stage in ourselves and lives when we see that the material life can offer us nothing in the way of inner peace and development of who we are, we must look elsewhere. Now the Hierophant appears and introduces the possibility to us of an existence beyond that which we know. Offered here under the guise of the teaching of the established church, we must look for the nuggets of wisdom in the doctrinal teaching the Hierophant gives us. The ego-power of thought flowers and we must assess what we know in its new light. This can give rise to religious belief and feelings as opposed to true spirituality. The Fool's attention is still in the physical world so he now seeks a belief for himself, something that he can cling to in times of distress or trouble. This creates a safe boundary within which to continue his quest. The teaching of the Hierophant can be seen as those of morality and conscience, offering a bridge to the higher awareness and self.

THE LOVERS

The Fool reaches a turning point on his quest where he faces a decision that we all must make at some stage. The Lovers exemplifies the principle of choice and here the Fool must decide whether to stay with what has become safe and familiar or venture onward into the unknown. In the context of a consultation the only wrong choice is no choice at all, but for the purposes of the Seekers Quest, the Fool must at some point choose to move forward, for that is the purpose of his existence.. Until he does this, he stays, as if never moving out of the honeymoon period of a marriage and never facing the reality of his life and self. The call of independence and self-responsibility can no longer be ignored. The Fool must learn to recognise the basics of Divine love in this form. He must also learn how to relate to others and both give to and receive from them. This can be seen as a choice between a rational, masculine approach to his life or a feeling, feminine one. Given the freedom, the Fool must decide.

THE CHARIOT

Once his decision is made, the Fool moves forward, as if propelled by some unseen force that carries him ever onward. Now he must experience the full power of his being, as a human being. If he can learn to control the careering path of his chariot, he keeps going. If he loses control, gives way to the pull of his senses, symbolised by the horses, he is in danger of succumbing to sensory pleasures and stagnating. Then the horses will eventually throw him and he must recuperate and move forward once more. A clear direction and dedication to the Quest are required now to keep on the dreaded 'straight and narrow' path to wholeness and liberation. Single-mindedness and discipline are the qualities the Fool must learn at this stage, which promise great rewards when carried out selflessly. This is the path of the true disciple. On a more mundane level, the Fool must also find his place in society, adapt to this and accept it. He must learn to take himself seriously in the light of his acquired knowledge and experience, but not too seriously. Control and application of the energies of one's being is the key to progression now, using method and purpose to move straight forward, in both the material and spiritual realms.

STRENGTH

Once his future direction and focus is found, the Fool moves on with his chariot to encounter the figure of Strength. His self-control must now extend to face and learn to integrate his darker side, his previously untapped shadow. This is exemplified by the 'lady and the lion', the one pacifying the other by force of valour, not physical strength. A balance must be found between the masculine and feminine aspects of the Seekers character and self. He must learn that repression is not an option, rather an integration of his two 'complementary opposite' halves that must be achieved by co-operation, negotiation and usually some compromise. Once achieved, the natural strength and power of his ability and self are able to emerge, giving him the fortitude and wisdom to continue. The basis of his existence must now be in love and truth.

THE HERMIT

Once the balance required of the Strength card is achieved, the Seeker is led up the mountain path the meet the Hermit. Now his balanced and powerful personality leads him on a mental quest as he seeks to uncover for himself the knowledge of who and what he is. The Hermit is that part of himself which must face his truth alone. This may mean a change of direction as a result of what he discovers. A turn inward is required as the Seeker meets with isolation and the inner levels of his being for the first time. His forward path must now be illustrated from within, guided by an inspired wisdom. Meditation, silence and study will be his teachers now as he attends to the work of his soul, motivated by service to humanity.

THE WHEEL OF FORTUNE

Now the Fool can emerge into the outer world once more, with the knowledge he has acquired from his studies. Transformed as he is, he now sees and feels the greater forces directing his life which he is here challenged to accept and integrate. This means that the forces and strange images of his subconscious mind rise to greet him, as well as the power of fate and destiny. He must learn to 'go with the flow', not of surface, material situations and circumstances but of the underlying energies and unseen forces that propel him forward. He must utilise his Hermit's wisdom and knowledge and tap into the flow of these forces within and without his being and follow accordingly. This can herald pleasure and pain and each must be responded to appropriately, without reaction or objection. The Fool must also reorient himself to find his place in the world as the result and outworking of these inner forces. This is the preparation for the greater spiritual life ahead.

JUSTICE

This is the centre point or axis of the Seekers Quest. Justice is the middle card of the Major Arcana journey and all revolves around her. At the very centre of his being now, the Seeker faces a direct encounter with the truth of his existence. In the mirror image of himself which Justice shows him, he must be still and unmoved by what he finds. This requires an acceptance of his complete being that he must release to a higher Judgement than that of his own self. If he is found wanting in any way, the sword of Justice falls and he begins again. If he can accept what he is given by this powerful figure he may be permitted to pass and move to the higher stage of his journey. In short, his conscience must be completely clear for progress to be possible and he must balance both his life and self.

THE HANGED MAN

Given access to Otherwordly realms now, The Fool is first introduced to the Hanged Man. Here the challenge is an acceptance of his position, as one now able to know of things other than that which he is aware of with his outer senses. Faith is a key issue now, when his inner senses prompt his consciousness to open to a trust in the greater power he now identifies, if not explains. The higher purpose to his existence in this life must be explored and opened to, in trust that all will be well. The knowledge of the inevitability of his own Death comes to him and he must accept this without question, assured by his faith and a deeper sense that he will continue to evolve and is immortal. This requires him to be free of the constraints of his conscious mind, letting go of all that he knows as certain, for all is now a matter of faith and trust. He must be devoted to his cause and devoid or self-motivation or interest, thereby offering his whole being and life as a sacrifice for a higher purpose. It is this that gives him the required spiritual at-one-ment.

DEATH

The reward for the Fool, in letting go all that he knows and clings to is a meeting with the figure of Death, the skeleton beneath the cloak. This means the complete freedom and liberation from his old way of being and living. All roots must be weeded out for him to succeed and successfully answer the question that Death poses him. Any trace of lower or baser human desires will be severed most painfully by Death and so this must be embraced, not in a physical sense of course, but symbolically. Fully aware that his human life and body is but one aspect alone of his full and truthful being, he must detach himself fully from what is around him and dedicate his being to the higher quest in a complete way. His spirit is thus set free, to operate through the vehicle of his physical body and the Seekers life will never be the same again. Illusion is stripped away to reveal the bare bones of existence. This transfiguration signifies the process of maturation in the cycle of the spirits existence.

TEMPERANCE

Given over to the spiritual way, the Seeker meets the blessed and welcome Angel of Peace in the form of Temperance. This is a great reward and a wonderful card. Now the Fool becomes the seed and inspiration of new life. He feels a complete passivity and satisfaction at his new existence and is able to have a foot in both worlds. Grounded and connected the Seeker is now perfectly placed to act as mediator between the two, living a sacred life of practical spirituality. His consciousness is now fully placed in the higher echelons of his existence and he cannot turn back for he has gone too far. Both his conscious and subconscious minds are in full communication and so he acts as his own guide and advisor in this respect. In this delicate balance he must find peace before he can move on. The full conscious knowledge of his immortality is unleashed and he is once again the free and youthful spirit he was at the outset, liberated by giving himself body and soul to the

Divine. He is aware of himself as a being of energy and power, unlimited by the physical casing around it. This is the unification of the spirit and soul energies when the human personality becomes infused with those of the divine.

THE DEVIL

The Seekers reward for his new found spirituality is to meet the Devil! Here the Devil reveals any last vestiges of his old humanity and burns them in the flames of his power. The Seeker must be willing to relinquish all that he has kept secret, knows has held him back or otherwise sets stock by. All his inner urges and desires must be transformed to manifest a higher motive. He will now find that everything at a human level is shown to have its higher equivalent and he must learn and understand that all is energy. The Devil teaches this by way of example of the Seekers own energy. Often misunderstood and misplaced, the Devil is that which binds us, so telling us of our need for and the means by which we can be set free. This is achieved by embracing the darkness and thereby merging it with this light of the divine, giving healing.

THE TOWER

The effect of the lightning that strikes the protective Tower the Seeker has built around himself is to force him into the limelight. The rush of adrenaline that follows must be gathered and all the wit and will the Fool has must be summoned to weather the storm. Any unnatural energy or action within the Fool is destroyed, as the full glare of the light of his own consciousness combined with that of the Divine, is first revealed, even if only for a moment. He must accept the state of the world and his life, leave the debris behind and move on, facing onward and upward for that is all he now knows. He can have no belief, trust, faith, ambition or other awareness that is not illuminated by the lightning and cast into oblivion. Instead he must simply be.

Thus the ego is cast aside and the basis for life becomes the pure spiritual forces.

THE STAR

In the darkness that follows the Star rises and the Fool is given gentle hope and a direction to follow, to take him home again. The Star, though still distant, is a sign that the end of his quest is now in sight. He must fix his sights unfailingly on this, open himself to the energy of stellar guidance and the hope of what will be. Inwardly he can feel this stellar power, know that he is 'star stuff' and so begins a knowledge of the Divine within himself, that he lost and forgot when he became the Magician, so long ago. This must become conscious knowledge as the transformation here takes effect and he lives a life that enables the Divine to have its place within him. The ideal of his being and existence must be followed and eventually reached. This is the rekindling of divine light within the Seeker as he reconnects with the higher forces.

THE MOON

Closer than the stars, the Moon appears now, full and round in the night sky. Its light casts shadow and illusion around and over the Fool and he is opened to the full force of this mysterious power. His instincts and intuition must guide him alone now and he must put aside all but these things if he is to survive this 'dark night of the soul' It is to his soul that he must connect and allow the freedom to guide him. He must be receptive to the subtle yet powerful pull of the moon and what it will dredge up from the shadows it creates. Logic and reason must be abandoned and he must follow the way of the Divine as he prepares through the night to be unleashed to its full force and power. The Moon is the light of the Sun reflected and his preparations must be complete come the dawn.

THE SUN

With that dawn comes the rising of the Sun, the most direct encounter yet with the goal of his quest and the face of the Divine. The Sun is still separate from him, yet he can feel its heat. If he is not to be burned up in the intensity of his encounter with and realisation of Divinity he must be completely open and honest and employ a spirit of reconciliation with what he realises he always was but never knew. A prerequisite is that he must be in harmony with all beings and nature around him, again which he realises he is a part of. The sacredness of all is made known to him and this too must become a part of his being. This is a time of truth for the Seeker and of great happiness. The Light of the Sun, as the energy of the Divine is the source of all he is now. It is time for him to bask in that illumination and align himself with the Divine.

JUDGEMENT

The trumpet is blown and heralds the beginning of The Fool's ascension process to full unity with the Divine. The tombs of his old earthly life and sphere of existence are left behind as he faces the angel before him in full and complete liberation and rapture. His consciousness is completed now, all the bonds and limitations of the physical life are removed and understanding is granted, of that which he is, was and shall be. His full potential is finally realised and achieved. The Seeker enters the timeless realm of existence where the past, present and future merge to become one in the being that he is now. This is the call to rebirth in human form.

THE WORLD

In ecstasy the Fool becomes the dancer, dancing in tune with the rhythm of life. He moves freely, instinctively and with Divine expression. This card is seen as the outer expression and result of the previous one and the Fool sees and feels himself as a part of the Universe, a free and fully Divine being. He is one with all things and is united with the source again. Here he enters a time of gestation before a new cycle of earthly existence. He recalls that which he forgot and is restored to his original state of joy. The microcosm of his being is united with the macrocosm of the Universe. The Seeker is home once more and is fulfilled.

THE FOOL

In keeping with the cyclical nature of all things the result is that the Fool is reborn and becomes as he once was, with the addition of full and conscious recall of all that he has encountered and learnt. He is enlightened and free. If there is need he must descend again, incarnate to physical form and undertake the next stage of his ultimate quest. This however is the province of beings greater than us, in whom we must show complete confidence and trust in their task. The Fool happy in his position, is for now untroubled by this.

The above briefest of examinations of the Major Arcana cards serve to introduce us to the characters we meet on our own journeys. It is these very journeys that the aspiring Tarot Therapist must tread in some way if they are to utilise the valuable quality of empathy in their consultations. It is worthwhile to note here that the client is of course on their own Seekers Quest. The difference between the quest of the Therapist and the client, is that the Therapist has access to the store of knowledge the Tarot gives them, thereby affording them the opportunity to make their quest a conscious one. This conscious ability does not make the quest easier however, if anything it is likely to make it more difficult! The quest is largely an inner one but will always have its reflection on the outer. This gives us the simple and general comparison of the Major Arcana being the inner realm of our beings and the Minor Arcana being the outer level.

Whatever the difficulties faced by the Therapist, it is always worth remembering that the hardships, challenges, blood, sweat and tears of the quest are valuable signs for those following on bravely in our wake. These are of course our clients who rely on the faltering, incorrect steps we make, partly on their behalf, so as to be able to guide them to where the ground is firm. Once on 'terra firma' we are able to lay foundations and orient ourselves through the physical, manifest world around us. It is to this equally strange and wonderful realm we now enter.

EXERCISES

As stated above, to be truly learned of the lessons of the Tarot, it is necessary for the aspiring Tarot Therapist to undertake their own Seekers Quest. This does not mean that you must reach a state of enlightenment before you are fit or qualified to use the Tarot in this way, but that it is necessary for you to be on the path towards that final, heady goal. One way in which you can begin your journey and an excellent means of introducing yourself to this level of the cards is to work through the Major Arcana card by card. As you go, allow yourself to respond inwardly to the cards, from a place that is neither emotional nor mental, but a combination of both - that of the intuitive. This process will allow the beginnings of an individual interaction with the cards to take place, which can be deepened and confirmed, when the cards are examined individually in subsequent chapters and exercises. Make notes of your responses as these may in time, turn out to be the very deepest interpretations of the cards you can arrive at, such is their nature and power.

Based on that same intuitive response, allow yourself to examine the Major Arcana and select the card that you feel best represents you at this stage in your life. Remember that this card needs to be as close as possible to the complete picture of your whole being, for this is the level at which they work and to which they communicate. Write down why this is so and any other thoughts or feelings you have in relation to this card. When you have finished working through the exercises in this book, go back and examine what you have written here and see if it still applies and if not, why not; what has changed?

Select the person that you feel knows you best and describe and explain to them your choice of Major Arcana card. Ask them their opinion and if they agree and the reasons why. Show them the card and ask them to offer any thoughts or opinions they have in the light of this knowledge. How do you feel about what they have said?

Looking at the notes you have made on the Major Arcana cards, examine them along with the cards and see if any of the cards typify, describe or illustrate any specific periods, times or circumstances in your life. Knowing what you do now about the cards, how might this awareness have helped you at that time?

In your own words and taking as much 'artistic license' as you feel is required, write your own story of 'The Journey of The Fool' or 'The Seekers Quest'.

The following exercise is included here by way of introducing you to the esoteric, or inner aspect of the Major Arcana, as you relate to it at the deepest level. Some prior experience of meditation is useful, but not essential. There is a tape available of this and other Tarot meditations, to help you. Please see the details given in the book for these.

Begin by becoming comfortable and letting yourself relax. Allow your body to settle and gently but firmly place your focus and concentration on where you are and be fully present in the moment. Allow the outside world to drift away and let all your worldly concerns, troubles, aches and pains drift away from you. Let go and relax. Let your breathing settle into its own natural rhythm.

As you become deeply relaxed, maintain the focus of your mind on what you are doing. This will have the effect of putting your body effectively to sleep, but keep your mind awake and alert, yet functioning at a deeper level of consciousness than is usual. It is from this level, or the right side of your brain, that you will respond in this exercise. Let go and let the process carry you along. Your instinctive and intuitive, immediate responses and reactions are what will give you true responses and occurrences, so simply let them happen. Try not to understand them consciously (until after you have finished) but immerse yourself in their happening while doing the exercise.

Now let yourself become aware of the life force and energy within your body and your being. Your 'being' is the whole you, your physical body and its energy counterparts, that make up your aura. Let your imagination, your higher, creative mind guide you. Feel the life force responding to your thoughts and concentration, as it is bound to do by the spiritual law of 'energy follows thought'. Focus your thoughts on your feet and the base of your spine. Imagine energy, in whatever form comes naturally to you, flowing down to this area and then spreading out below your body. Focus on 'grounding' yourself, rooting in to the Earth like a tree. Ley yourself relax and become heavy. Feel the warmth of the soil around you, the rock beneath you, supporting, guiding and comforting you. Imagine the goodness and the nutrients in the soil seeping into you and beginning to flow up into your being. Let the energy of the earth move into you and give you its strength and support. Imagine this flowing up into you through your feet and your spine. Let this earth power flow up until it reaches your heart, where it rests.

Now focus on the energy flowing up from your heart and leaving your body, this time through the crown of your head. Feel it flow out into the air around you. Sense it moving up, still following your thoughts, into the clouds and the sky and the light above you. It continues to move upwards, above the sky now and into space. Imagine this energy flow moving out

113

among the stars and settling on the farthest star that you can see. This is the source of light and spiritual guidance for you and connects you to your own highest awareness. As soon as this connection is made, feel the energy flowing back down into you, from above. See it move down through space, then the sky and the clouds, through the air around you, then the crown of your head. You have become lighter and finer and now this energy balances with the earth energy as it reaches your heart. Feel this place of power, peace and balance at the centre of your being.

Now, using the power of your creative imagination, see yourself standing outside what you know is a Temple. You can see the door before you, which is closed at present. Nobody else is there. Walk around the building you see. This may be any kind of building. Notice its shape, colour and its state of repair - does it look new or old, well kept or ramshackle. Let yourself notice the details of the building as fully as you are able.

When you have walked around the building, return to where you stood in front of the door. This time you hear a sound and you see a figure standing in front of the doors. This is the Guardian and the building is the Temple of the Major Arcana. Observe the Guardian closely and see how you feel about their presence. Approach them. They greet you and ask your purpose. Explain, in your own words, what you feel this is and why you are here. Sense their response, in whatever way it comes. The Guardian may allow you to enter, and if so will open the doors for you and usher you in. You may sense in some way that they are not allowing you to enter at this time, or make no response. If this is the case, you must accept this and return from the meditation to try again at another time.

If they allow you to enter, go inside. You will see before you a staircase, but little else. It is dimly lit, just enough to see the steps ahead of you. Begin to climb these. You may count the stairs as you go. If you do, you will find that there are 78 in all. When you reach the top, you emerge into a large hall, lit by burning torches fixed to the wall at intervals. At the far end of the hall is an altar, on which are placed several objects. Approach the altar and see if you can discern what these are, but do not touch any of them.

Now turn and look back at the hall you are in. When you look around you, you will see that on the walls are large, 'life-size' depictions of the Major Arcana cards, in sequence. It is difficult to make out the details clearly as the light flickers and dances about you, but you can just see that the figures and scenes are the same as on your own cards. Walk slowly around the hall now, observing each card in turn and noting any strong reactions you may have.

When you are ready, find your way back to the steps and begin to descend them. When you reach the bottom, the Guardian is waiting for you. They may have some message, or a gift for you, in some form. Thank them, whatever if anything, they do or say at this time and walk away from the Temple, without looking back. You hear the door close, but you know you can return when you wish.

Now let the image fade away and bring yourself back from your meditation. Do this slowly and gently by focussing on your body and where you are sitting or lying. Increase the level of your breathing back to its usual, everyday depth. Become aware again of your surroundings and move your fingers and toes. Be sure you have returned fully and completely and when you are ready, open your eyes.

Make notes of your experiences as soon as possible. These should be a concise account of your journey to the Temple. This meditation forms a vital link to the inner study you will make of the cards, so care and attention should be taken here. You should perform this meditation a number of times so that it becomes clear and you feel comfortable whilst in the Temple. It is from this place that you will later undertake journeys into each card, so it is necessary to establish a good foundation in the Temple now before you can achieve this. Make notes each time that you journey to the Temple and observe any changes that occur and progress you are aware of making, trying to be objective as to the reasons for these.

CHAPTER 5 - THE MAP OF THE QUEST

In the past some Tarot authors and practitioners have utilised the Major Arcana alone in their work. It is a popular practice to define the Major Arcana as more important than the Minor, because what the cards represent have more power. In a consultation it is common to hear the 'reader' (a disagreeable term) single out the Major cards chosen as being the ones to take note of, often at the expense of the Minor cards. This practise denies the client much of what they may glean from their consultation and detracts from the power for good it may have.

Whilst it is not denied that the Major Arcana cards are important, it is argued that all cards are equally important. The view of the Tarot Therapist is that the Major Arcana cards and their associated interpretations speak to and reach a deeper level of the client. This transpersonal level, as seen above, is vital to reach through a consultation if effective and positive, lasting change is to occur, to assist the client in their development and progression.

Once reached, through the Major cards that have been selected in a consultation, the lessons, tendencies, blockages and so on indicated, must be drawn out and placed in the context of how they are affecting the client and what they need to do about them. This is the place of the Minor Arcana cards. The effects of what individuals are working on and the testing ground for these lessons is the everyday world. Much spiritual teaching tells us that there is a direct reflection between the inner and outer levels, a principle further explored in Volume 2 of this work. The Tarot is no exception and so the practice of Tarot Therapy must embrace this working.

This presents no problem as once again we find that the design and structure of the deck easily adapts itself to this need. The Major Arcana is therefore not more significant that the Minor, only different. The Major cards show us the inner journey the client is making at the time of the consultation, the Minor the outer. Each balances and is vital to the other. The one cannot exist without the other. This principle represents a significant difference in attitude and approach to Tarot consultations and the cards themselves that is part of the re-appraisal required before the cards can begin their move back to the sacred regard in which they demand to be held. It should of course, always be obvious that it is not the cards themselves that are sacred, but what they contain and represent, which is life itself.

In order to illustrate the equality of Major and Minor Arcanas further we will explore (in part) the links between them and show how they need to be seen together, for correct application during a consultation. This has the added benefit of allowing us to give a further introduction and explanation of the nature of the Minor Arcana.

This requires first that we examine the last card of the Major Arcana, The World. As can be seen from the illustration, the traditional image of the card contains a figure inside a garland, dancing. This figure, as with all figures in the Major cards, is the Fool, or Seeker, at the conclusion of their quest. In The World, they are seen dancing the dance of life, since they are now 'at one' with it. This results in the natural inclination to move in tune with the rhythm of life, whatever this may be for that individual.

21

The World

21

©R. gloud 1989

There are stars gleaming behind the Seeker. These can be seen as the other cards of the Major Arcana, to which the Seeker has travelled on their journey. The significance of the garland is of the victory the culmination of the journey brings. Beyond the garland in the four corners of the card are traditionally a man, lion, bull and eagle. These have much symbolism attached to them, which will be explained in Volume 2. To illustrate our purpose here it is necessary only to know that these figures represent the four Elements of Earth, Air, Fire and Water. These have been intelligently shown in their natural state in the card pictured. As we know, this is the realm of the Minor Arcana, each suit being the dissection of its particular Element.

Everything in our everyday lives can be seen as belonging to, or constructed of, one or more of these four basic states of being. Though the science of chemistry has given us many more Elements, they each derive from these four general and powerful ones. The World card shows that the Seeker has learnt the lessons required of them, or in the case of an individual consultation, the particular lesson they need to learn at that time. This can only be achieved when an understanding and application of the principles taught is applied at all four levels, represented by the Elements of the Minor Arcana suits.

This applies at two levels, individual and collective. The individual is as illustrated above, in the context of a client receiving the therapy they need at the time they receive their consultation. The collective level is illustrated in the journey of the Seekers Quest. As the Fool learns the lesson of each card he becomes a little more whole and complete. When he assimilates all 22 lessons of the Major cards he must then learn to apply them in his everyday life and demonstrate that he can lead the sacred life required of him, in whatever manner is appropriate for the individual time and place he is in. This spirit of time and place is shown in the World card and its outworking explained in detail in the Minor Arcana.

Spiritual teaching and the development of the self is useless and pointless if it does not have direct and practical application through our actions and in the way we live our lives. A good test of the teaching being offered to you, from whatever source, is to consider how it can be applied to your daily life. If it cannot something may be missing. Further to this, we need to apply what we lean at all four levels of our self and so address the needs on the physical, emotional, mental and spiritual selves. The Tarot is shown to be the perfect guide once again, as its structure is based on this principle.

These four selves are aligned to the Elements and are seen as constituting the whole human being. Each person is the sum of these four Elements: Earth, Air, Fire and Water, resulting in the fifth one of Spirit. We have examined the correspondence of this previously but it is repeated here to illustrate the links between the Arcanas. At the beginning of this Chapter we looked at the principle of the Microcosm and macrocosm. Now we can see how the Minor Arcana is the Microcosm to the Macrocosm of the Major Arcana, each subject to, yet dependent on the other. We can no more divide the Arcanas than we can divide a person.

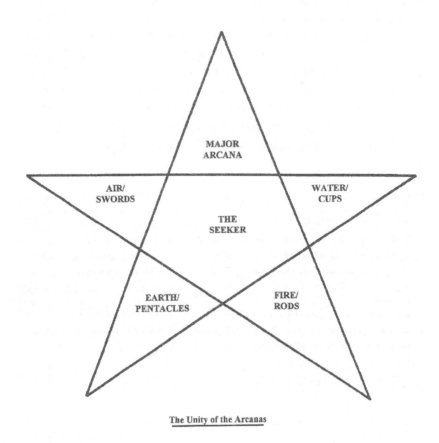

MAJOR
ARCANA

AIR/
SWORDS

WATER/
CUPS

THE
SEEKER

EARTH/
PENTACLES

FIRE/
RODS

The Unity of the Arcanas

It is also possible to place the whole of the Tarot around the 'wheel of the year', a process that easily illustrates the unity and integration of the Arcanas. For the present it is necessary only to explain the seasonal ascriptions to the Minor Arcana suits, showing immediately how the human being is intertwined with the natural world around it. The seasons and suits are usually linked as follows:

SUIT	ELEMENT	SEASON
PENTACLES	EARTH	WINTER
SWORDS	AIR	SPRING
RODS	FIRE	SUMMER
CUPS	WATER	AUMUMN

Like many aspects of the Tarot, not least what the cards actually mean, these correspondences are open to debate. The Tarot Therapist should therefore be clear as to which Element, or suit, they feel belongs to which season. This is achieved by study of the cards and experience in their use, combined with interaction with the natural world, which will always act as a faultless teacher. The seasonal linking to the four suits is often taken as a means of placing timing on events indicated by the cards in a consultation. In Tarot Therapy a deeper linking is enabled, by examining the inner nature of the human being as it relates to the eight-spoked festival wheel now widely used in the Aquarian Age and Pagan communities.

The Major Arcana cards are also linked intrinsically to this wheel, a feat achieved by the creators of the previously mentioned Greenwood Tarot, for which they are to be heartily congratulated. Their multi-level approach to the Major Arcana tells us much about the true nature of the cards, serving as pointers in the direction of their inner, therapeutic nature.

The Minor Arcana suits represent the gradual and cyclic flow of the seasonal energy that constitutes the annual round of nature, repeating in a spiralling and evolving pattern. Built into this round are eight marker points for change in the nature and quality of energy we receive from the natural world. These are times of critical events in the passage of the Sun and outer planets, as they relate to the Earth, these being the vehicles by which we receive the energy from which derive our being and of which we are ourselves made.

As the Minor Arcana cards are the gradual or outer change, so the Major Arcana are the specific or inner changes we undergo. This subject is explored fully in Chapter 8 of this book and expounded further in Volumes 2 and 3.

In the therapeutic context, this means that the combination of Major and Minor Arcana needs must be addressed. The Minor cards appearing in a consultation illustrate the needs of the individual at the physical, emotional, mental and spiritual levels, whilst the Major cards will show their deeper origin and source, in so doing illustrating the requirement for the whole persons needs to be addressed.

In the working of the four Elements, it is that of Earth which is taken as the foundation, the heaviest platform upon which we build. This equates to our outer actions in life, that which we do from day to day. As such, Earth is the starting point of the outer journey, the point of birth of a new project. The Ace of Pentacles card, or One of Earth as it can be known, illustrates this and shows us how the Minor Arcana follows on from the Major, taking what has been learnt within to the outer realm of existence.

The traditional image of this card depicts a clear gateway at the end of a path, leading through a garden, as seen by the Robin Wood card depicted on the left here. The garden can be seen as the garden of the Major Arcana, leading out through the archway to an as yet unexplored landscape, that of the hills and mountains of daily life, the landscape of the Minor Arcana.

In the Rider Waite card pictured on the right, from the deck that is taken as the standard for cards of the 20th Century (but not the 21st, it must be said!) the archway is clearly shown to be the garland from the card of The World. The Seeker is seen to need to go through the arch/garland and out into the world of the Elements, applying what he has learnt and now knows from his previous journey through the inner, starry landscape of the Major Arcana cards. Here comes the test, to see if he can address his needs on the four Elemental levels. That the landscape ahead is one of hills and mountains indicates that there are peaks and troughs he will experience, as do we all, and that the lessons are hard and the going tough. The requirement of a guide to help him is still paramount and so the role of the Tarot Therapist is clear at this stage. This is to assist the client to fulfil their needs on the four levels of their being, as indicated by the four suits.

In order to introduce the Minor Arcana in its therapeutic setting we will explore something of these needs now, by examining the four suits. There is no significance to the order these are presented in, but the suit titles are added to with their respective Element deliberately, as these express the basic nature of the suit and should ideally be seen as the suit. It will be noted that the Tarot of the Spirit, utilised throughout these three volumes does this in the names of it cards. For a complete analysis of these needs, I would refer you to my book 'Practical Spirituality'

PENTACLES/EARTH

This suit deals with our needs at the physical level of our being. This is shown through the suit as the need to live in the world of form, rather than force. There are many who profess to follow a spiritual path that fail to apply their beliefs in the mundane world around them. Rather they try to focus on the development of the higher faculties, believing these to be the only spiritual ones. A true and complete spirituality integrates the whole of life, from birth to death and beyond and at all levels. We are the same sacred person when we are doing our washing-up, cleaning the car or sitting in meditation. The suit of Pentacles shows us how.

Through its inception with the Ace, the Pentacles suit traces the nature of form as it manifests physically. An equation for this can be the growth and development of the physical body. Consequently, Pentacles shows us the need for physical health and balance. Chief among this is the need for us to realise that we are a sacred spirit within a body. When we begin to have this regard for what we are, our view of our physical needs shifts. Too often in the pressure to achieve in the modern, material world, we neglect the need of the body to rest and regroup its strength. The body must be honoured and treated with respect. It is an incredible machine, capable of amazing feats. However, it needs healthful, unpolluted food, clean water, rest and exercise to maintain its strength. The suit of Pentacles illustrates all this and more.

Our need here is to establish ourselves in our bodies and grow alongside it. As the awareness of our body grows we must make the effort to establish and maintain its health and balance. This can then be utilised in our work, allowing us to provide for our own and our loved ones material needs. The strength that comes from health acts as a shield in times of imbalance or dis-ease and we realise the true value of what we have. As time progresses we work hard to keep providing and perfect what we do. When at length, the time comes for rest and retirement from our outer work, we are able to utilise the material gain we have in the security we feel and see around us, enabling us also to guide those that follow us, our children and our loved ones.

All this and a great deal more besides is depicted in the suit of Pentacles. Its wisdom and value may seem somewhat detached from the spiritual life and therapy we are working on here, but do not underestimate its place in the scheme of things. A full exploration of the Minor Arcana will be undertaken in Volume 3 of this work, which will reveal its true value and need. Until then, it is sufficient to recognise the equal part all four of the Elements play in the constitution of our being and all things, allowing this to give us acceptance of its significance.

SWORDS/AIR

The suit of Swords and Element of Air relates to the needs of our mind and shows us what is required at the mental level of our being. Our minds will, if we are not careful, adopt a central position in ourselves and lives and assume control of our whole being. This creates an imbalance in the person that results in our doing only what we think is applicable to us and only if the deeper levels of our mental processes grant approval. We cannot then, do something just because we feel like it or because we want to. The mind will bring up all kinds of irrational fears, based on its previous experiences. Working exclusively at this mental level creates a world of illusion that we believe to be true. Anything that does fit this view we have created of the world is dismissed as bunk.

If we recognise these tendencies in our mental processes we can become objective, tempering what our minds tell us with what we see is physical fact and what we feel is in our hearts. This allows for a deeper truth to emerge, that of an instinctive or intuitive one. It has been my experience that the intuitive can be defined as a combination of the heart and the mind. This combination takes us to a deeper level than either is capable of by themselves and which lies within us a constant and natural source of guidance and wisdom. The suit of Swords is ideally created to act as an outer form of this guide, showing us the developing stages of the mind.

The mind contains more than one level, yet few of us bother or are brave enough to delve down and explore the deeper levels. The subconscious and unconscious contain all kinds of horrors that lurk in the darkness, quietly working away to remove our potential and keep us trapped in their grip. The Seekers Quest has shown us that we need to explore these strange images at some point and the suit of Swords shows us how.

128

Our minds can give us a great deal of work if we allow them free reign and unchecked power. If we stop the flow of thoughts for even the briefest time we gain a glimpse of how things could be if we checked the contents of our minds. The need for relaxation of the body has been made clear and the same is the case with our minds. This does not necessarily mean that we must become expert at the art of meditation, but a calm and 'meditative' state of mind is most certainly of benefit as we seek to tame the wolf that lurks within. This is best done by opening to the darkness and letting the contents empower us by accepting what we find and working with it. Nothing then can harm us.

Just as we need clean food and water for our bodies, so do we need clear air for our minds. The lungs control many functions in the body and it is amazing how mentally refreshing it can be to talk a walk to a windy place and just stand there, letting the wind blow the cobwebs of our mind away. We need do nothing else, nature's power being easily sufficient.

The workings of the mind are strange indeed and the suit of Swords suffers from much misplaced malice because of this. All too often Swords are seen as the negative suit of the Tarot, those cards that point out 'bad' things happening in the clients' life. This view is unrelated to the purposes of therapy, but such is the strength of our minds that conflict can often result if we do not heed our needs at this level. When viewed therapeutically, Swords actually show us how to do this. Perhaps this negative view of the suit tells us more about the minds of those who have expressed it!

Beginning with a thought or our first conscious awareness as a baby, we must learn the power of choice and decision, seeking the balance that comes with this. If left unchecked we see the pain and anguish that can follow. This requires a peace of mind to be established that can only come from the deeply relaxed in body and mind. The power of meditation should not be underestimated, nor should the influence of outside suggestion. This can cause as much distortion, or be equally helpful, depending on our previously established strength and presence of mind. This poise allows for harmonious ideas and co-operation to flow, but we must warn ourselves against the corruption of greed at this stage, avoiding thinking only for ourselves. This leads to a place of imprisonment and isolation that take a good deal of objective work and cold, hard truth to escape from. Pain and doubt plague us through this process and the contents of the deeper mind come up to haunt us. If we allow ourselves the sweet release from fear that we need, understanding and truth result that stand us in great stead for our progression.

RODS/FIRE

The suit of Rods and Element of Fire show us the needs of our spirit, as symbolised by the fire within our beings. This can burn and consume us if not tended to carefully and lovingly. If this is achieved, a powerful force that offers protection, warmth, guidance and comfort can endure all the pain and stress that life may throw at us. Our spirits, perhaps not as accessible and 'conscious' as the needs of our body, mind and heart are still one quarter of our being and must be held in due regard lest we fall prey to a life that is cut off at and from its source. It can become easy to spot the person in whom there is no belief or regard for the sanctity of life, for a cynicism and coldness takes over that betrays there view. Whilst completely free to have such a view of course, the end result becomes plain to see in the futility with which such a life can only be led. We need to heed the message of the suit of Rods and carry our spirits lightly within our beings.

Fire is a source of heat and heat is an energy, just as is the spirit within. We need then to learn the ways and workings of this energy if we are to be balanced in body, mind, heart and spirit. Energy is a term much used in the current spiritual trend, but little understood. Its true nature is akin to that of our spirit, as that which exists in all things and indeed, is all things. Recognition of this is of paramount importance in dealing with the needs of our spirit.

Our spirits need expression as well, in the same way as the other urges and drives of the human being. This may manifest as a need to pray, meditate, perform ritual, sing, dance and so on, in accordance with the beliefs on the individual. With the advent of such items as the Universal Declaration of Human Rights, which acknowledges the right of each person to conduct their 'religion', we are beginning to see the world wide recognition of the needs of the spirit. This means a great deal for the future of humanity and represents a major step forward in our evolution. When we can see and accept the spiritual alongside the material, we can begin to work at achieving the inner and outer balance required for sacred living, at both the individual and collective level.

A spirit of tolerance is of great value for the needs of the spirit to be addressed. All too often we have found ourselves at 'holy war' (surely a contradiction in terms) because of differing beliefs. The true spirit instead finds celebration in the similarities and the differences of individual beliefs and cultures across the world, recognising as it does the great diversity in the same spirit that the human being houses. The suit of Rods points out these similarities and differences in turns, as we each learn to address the needs of our spirit.

This process begins with the acknowledgement of the spirit within the child, even with the ritual of the naming ceremony to present the child to whatever deity is recognised. Tuition is needed in the ways of the spirit, keeping a balance approached looking inward, then outward. The long-term view and development of the spirit must be allowed for in our actions, which results in the attraction of those whom we need to mirror ourselves and create the stability we both require. External forces may seek to knock us off balance or steer us nearer our goal, dependent on how we approach obstacles. Victory is granted through persistence, strength of belief and conviction. This will become a true shield and mighty weapon in times of weakness and despair. This creates a rush of awareness of the spiritual self that pushes us forward to achieve our goals. Later in life we can rest a little and reflect on what have striven to achieve. We must always be vigilant that the ways of the spirit do not cloud our judgement, keeping the balance that is required in all things. With this balance we can bring about the meeting of the needs of the spirit shown in the suit of Rods.

CUPS/WATER

The needs of the heart, as expressed through the suit of Cups and Element of Water are perhaps more immediate than the previous ones. Emotional pain is all too familiar to the majority of us, but we rarely seek to explore the source of that pain. This can be others or circumstances, but if we look deep enough, we can usually see that it is ourselves who are the centre of the cause. The needs of the heart must then be addressed with an openness and honesty that requires much courage and strength. It is for reasons such as this that a balance of addressing our needs at all four levels is required.

Like water, our feelings must be kept flowing lest they become static, stagnant then poisoned, becoming devoid of potency and meaning in the process. Without water we die quickly and without the strongest of emotions, love, we suffer the same fate. We can only experience love when we are open to its force and softness. For the human heart to truly feel love, it must be soft. This does not mean that we are weak, in fact quite the opposite, for it takes a great deal more strength to cry than it does to harden the heart. The needs of the heart are many and varied, but chief among them is the need to love and be loved.

Contentment, being the peace felt in the heart at what we have in our lives, beyond that of mere possessions, is another important facet in addressing the needs of the heart. This peace and satisfaction can only be felt when we give ourselves what is our hearts desire. This does not mean that we rush out and buy what we have always wanted regardless of cost, but that we need to look deep within to the centre of our emotions and consider what we find there. It is only by accepting what we find in the depths of our soul that we discover that which we each lack. This can be something different for each of us, but the suit of Cups can be an excellent guide in this process.

The process begins with our first feelings, and the purity of the feelings we experience and the immediacy of our expression of them. Next comes a recognition that others have these feelings too and we begin to be conscious of love for the first time. This results in great joy and liberation and release from some of the fear than can plague and limit us if we allow it to. The fear of what may happen can prevent us from the wonder of childlike love and trust that is so beautiful and poetic. Our dreams and fantasies can be a help in encouraging us but we must ensure they do not become dominant in our hearts and psyche. As we struggle against the strength of our feeling we must sometimes swim against the tide of our feelings and stick to what we know is right, despite what we want to do. We must also take care not to allow ourselves too much emotional freedom, taking an arrogant attitude or become bogged down in depth of feeling that we become too serious. When we achieve the balance indicated at the end of the suit of Cups we experience the unconditional love felt in the functional family that is quite Divine in its expression.

It is very clear from even these brief and basic descriptions of the Minor Arcana cards that their application in Tarot Therapy is a distance apart from the traditional meanings given them. Readers with experience of the Tarot may have noted that the last paragraph under each suit here follows the cards through from Ace to Ten. These short tales show us how the numbered cards of the suits can form their own mini Seekers Quest, each addressing the needs at their level of the client. When utilised in this manner, the Minor Arcana is seen as an equal part of the Tarot, requiring the Major cards for their substance and each half of the pack being useless without the other.

The intricacies of the progression of energies through the numbered cards of the Minor Arcana are explored in Volume 3 of this work , but there follows an introduction to this principle, as it applies to the work of the Tarot Therapist, so as to familiarise ourselves with the workings of numerology, as they applied here. The most effective, logical and direct way to achieve this is to examine each number in turn. During this process we shall also introduce the geometric shape associated with each number, also reproduced below. These serve as a pictorial and symbolic expression of the numbers and will also repay meditation for those so inclined.

The science of Numerology is far more than the ascription of selected interpretations and meanings to each Number. In truth it is a method of explaining the structure and workings of the Universe in mathematical terms, a subject still widely utilised in modern physics. This deeper and more powerful way of looking at numbers forms an easy and harmonious marriage with the workings of Tarot Therapy. This method also forms a correspondence with this more archetypal use of numerology applying over and above the traditionally accepted 'fortune-telling' meanings, just as we see the interpretations of the cards themselves.

This approach to Numerology brings all numbers back to their single digit, by combining them until a number between 1 and 9 is reached, giving it its vital or primal power. These 9 digits (together with the additional 0, just like The Fool in the Major Arcana) form the skeleton around which the body of the Universe, and the Tarot, is constructed. Following this analogy, if the Minor Arcana cards are the bones of the body, the major organs (heart, lungs, kidneys etc.) will of course be the Major Arcana cards, leaving the Court cards to be the outer personality, features and expression of what is within.

The number One is looked upon, not surprisingly, as the birth or initiatory point, the urge to create and the active principle from which all things come. It is pure energy and requires something to connect itself to for its continued existence. It must 'go forth and multiply' if it is to fulfil its mission and reason for existence. It brings identity and awareness and can be likened to the human will, the knowledge that 'I Am'. The Ace, as it is called in the Tarot, brings force into form; brings energy to manifestation, if it is acted upon in the correct manner (by the client). One makes the unreal, real. It can be symbolised as a circle, viewed as the continuous unbroken line, the infinity of existence and all life. It is perhaps best viewed as the raw power of its particular suit, or the root or source of its Element.

The Two is the principle that divides the One and is therefore seen as the number of balance, harmony and duality. This is achieved by forming an opposition, in effect the 'equal and opposite reaction' to what is envisioned and created at the One; the 'parallel universe' to the Ace. Two is seen as the number for reason and understanding, since this is the agent of reaction to the raw strength of the One, force being met with skill, brawn being met with brains. It is shown graphically as the line extending into infinite space in two directions.

When these two opposite yet complementary principles find their balance they result in the third principle: the number Three; just as the Sun shines upon the Earth and causes growth. As the number for expansion, it is linked to the planet Jupiter, as the only planet in our Solar System that gives off more energy than it receives. This tells us much about the nature of the Three. Three is the tangible result of the flowering of the balance of ideas. This is where the idea of the one is brought into tangible reality. The shape of the Three is the triangle, seen as the highest active, energy force shape and often used in healing for this reason.

Once created, balanced and manifested the energy must be stabilised in physical reality, which is the province and responsibility of the Four. This is the number representing foundation, stability and security. Like the square of its shape, the four shows us the boundaries which we must not cross as yet, lest we lose the power we have created and contained within. When we are ready we can move forward into the five, but for now we must recognise our limits and seek to consolidate what we know. We must not run before we can walk. Four moves the triangle to the square, solid and dependable. Now is the time to realise what has been produced.

This stability can become a trap, if we settle for the easy life, resting on our laurels. The nature of energy however is an active one and it cannot be contained. Nature abhors a vacuum and so the fifth principle comes to challenge and provoke us to move on and build on what is known. This can be welcomed or reacted against, but must ultimately be accepted and embraced if we are to succeed. Five can be unexpected and uncontrollable, yet is necessary. It is an active, expressive number, only destructive if we see it that way. A little like the time of adolescence, five is a number for change. It shape is the pentagram, the five pointed star, an ancient symbol of oft misunderstood significance and power.

When the power inherent in the pentagram is harnessed, we reach the Six. Here energy is harmonised on the outer levels of life. Significant progression results, from the product of the blending of the power of the energies we have realised thus far. A state of co-operation and satisfaction is reached. The best description of the Six is in the word 'synergy', a beautiful word whose dictionary definition is "the potential ability to be more successful or productive as a result of a merger'. This is a wonderful interpretation of the function, purpose and use of the Six. Its beauty is also reflected in its geometric display of the six pointed star, consisting of the upward and downward pointing triangles. This reveals a deeper layer to the Six, consisting as it does of two three's.

The active principle of the Three is multiplied by the balance of the Two, producing the more holistic harmony we now have. This is summarised in the maxim. As Above, So Below; As Within, So Without'.

The Seven is seen as the mystic number, the number of Earth and Creation, for reasons which are (partly) revealed following this numerological examination. The Seven is the energy of awareness, the knowledge of what we have created so far, the perception that comes from the objective view. There is the need to begin something anew in order to avoid becoming stale. This may involve a risk but the sense of knowing or of intuition that the Seven brings will guide us faithfully if we are still and listen. The multiples of See are well documented, including the planets, days, chakras, colours and so on. These are shown graphically as a seven pointed star, around which creation hangs like a web.

The higher energy and knowing of the Seven must be controlled and established. This is the province of the Eight. It is clear to the astute reader that the Six, Seven and Eight in particular are a repetition of the Two, Three and Four respectively, at a higher or more evolved level. The Eight is therefore the foundation of the Four having been built upon, as a result of its multiplication with the balance of Two. This gives us the wisdom of experience and a regeneration of our power, resulting in knowledge with power. The shape of the Eight is the octagon, or eight-pointed star.

When the power and knowledge of the Eight are focussed positively, the Nine is reached, as the highest number, of perfection and achievement. Completion and fulfilment are the realm of the Nine. This is seen as the highest number we can have, more so than the Ten as we shall see and since it is the last single digit number. Nine is the recognition and acceptance of ones real value and attainment of the goal. Nine shows us the true path to optimum quality of life and contentment. Nine is the Spirit or Divine in clear and direct, unhindered communication with the Earth plane, or individual human, as its physical aspect. Its shape is the nine-pointed star, formed from three interlocking triangles, the significance of which is clear. The Nine is looked upon as being the active energy of the Three multiplied by itself, giving us the highest energy we can have. This results in understanding that is before or beyond words.

Lastly we have the Ten. This is not specifically one o the numbers in our workings of the energy of the creation of the Universe, as we see them here, but is included here since we have ten cards to each suit of the Minor Arcana. Ten can be seen as the reverberation of the Nine, echoing out across the planes, as this perfection I realised, then released, as surely it must be. Energy, as we have seen, cannot be static and all things must die, to be reborn. This is function of the Ten. It is seen as the One and the Zero. The One is the power of energy, just as explained above. This is combined with the principle of life, the Zero, resulting in the release of life, the blending and merging with the all, when the perfection of the Nine is realised. Ten is basically therefore something and no-thing. It is from this no-thing, that the next something, or one-thing can be produced. The Zero is the infinite energy, the pool of the Universe of energy without from to which we all return, ready to be born anew, into our next incarnation.

This leaves the Court Cards available for explanation. Following the title of this chapter as the map of the Seekers Quest, w can view the Court cards as guides showing us the way to take as we follow the map. We have seen previously that the Court cards are in reality combinations of multiples of the Elements of the suit to which they belong and from which their archetype is taken.

Here we can remind ourselves that the four Elements can be seen as the outer expression of the workings of energy as the physical level of its evolution and expression. The Court cards are the personality types that result from this expression. They are not (necessarily) a particular type of person, but a stage of our understanding of ourselves as we come to process the energy that we receive at different stages of our life. This is explained further in the section that follows and I would refer readers to the charts of the Rays which shows the Elements that belong to them, including a reminder here that the four 'lower' Elements combine to the fifth 'higher' Element of Ether or Spirit.

The workings of energy as they are expressed though the numbers are then combined with the power and realm of the Element to give the interpretation of the individual numbered cards of the Minor Arcana and seen in their expression as the Court cards. This process is deceptively simple and is given its application to the client when it is combined with the intuition of the Tarot Therapist at the time of the consultation. Intuition is here looked upon as that of pure reason, the natural product and outworking of the Therapist aligning themselves with their own Soul prior to the consultation commencing. The necessary practice and method of the consultation is covered in a later Chapter, but the therapeutic nature of the Minor Arcana is now revealed to us.

THE TAROT AND THE SEVEN RAYS

In Volumes 2 and 3 the concept of the Major and Minor Arcanas will be explored in detail. For now to further our studies of the Tarot as a therapy, the links that can be made between the structure of the pack and the Seven Rays are introduced. This is a complex subject and one that fully deserves the deeper exploration given it in Volume 2.

In order to introduce the subject, we must first familiarise ourselves with the division of the Major Arcana into a threefold pattern, linking the Minor Arcana to it by the usual suit divisions. This split is known as the Three Septenaries and will again be explained in detail when we do the same with the Major Arcana, as the subject constitutes the whole of Volume 2. The basis of this teaching is to align the holistic structure of the human being to the realms of the Three

Septenaries. The first horizontal line in this layout then becomes the Realm of Body, the middle line the Realm of Mind and the top line the Realm of Spirit. This gives us the following:

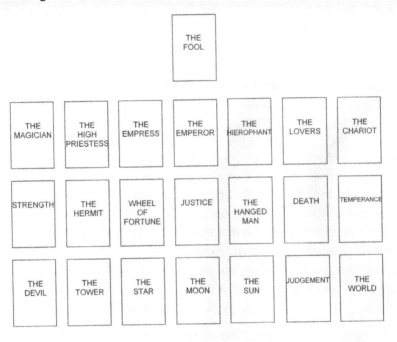

THREE SEPTENARIES

The three fold division of the Major Arcana shows us exactly why the Tarot as a whole reflects the esoteric nature of existence and so is the embodiment of Universal Truth and so the perfect and complete therapy. The explanation of this grand statement is to be found in the teachings of the 'Ageless Wisdom' of the Theosophists (H.P. Blavatsky, Alice Bailey, C.W. Leadbetter, A.E. Powell et al). These invaluable teachings tell us, alongside a great deal of information of much importance and relevance, of the Seven Rays.

The Seven Rays are, most basically, energy outpourings from higher levels, from which all things take their form and substance. These are equated with the Biblical Seven Spirits before the Throne. The Rays are seen as being equal in nature, no-one being better or worse than the other. In this they follow the working of energy itself, being neutral. The qualities assigned to them reflect the characteristic type of that particular energy. The qualities are "like the colouring that the prism takes when subjected to the rays of the sun". The individual rays are seen as being an energy type vibrating at a specific set of frequencies. Though they are numbered, this does not reflect any order of preference. The importance and significance of the Rays cannot be overestimated, both in the part they take in explaining the structure of our Universe and the place they take as a consequence in the understanding of the therapeutic nature of the Tarot.

It is with the qualities of the Rays that we are here concerned. Three of the Rays are looked on as being 'Major Rays', as those that have greater force than the remaining four. These three Rays can be seen as the dominating forces in the manufacture of our Universe. These Rays can therefore be equated to the three 'realms' of the divisions of the Major Arcana in the Three Septenaries layout. The Major Arcana is divided as follows for this division.

REALM	RAY	QUALITY	ELEMENT	CARDS
BODY	1ST	WILL / POWER	ETHER / SPIRIT	1 – 7
MIND	2ND	LOVE / WISDOM	ETHER /SPIRIT`	8 – 14`
SPIRIT	3RD	ACTIVITY / LIGHT	ETHER / SPIRIT	15 - 21

Blending the Rays and Realms of the Major Arcana in this way serves to illustrate further the true esoteric and therefore therapeutic nature of these 21 cards. Since each of us is on a path of evolution, conscious or not, the only true therapy must address this inner walk, guiding our faltering footsteps as we commonly stumble and stagger as best we can along it. It is to be remembered that the abundant use I have made of the word esoteric is in the sense of it meaning 'inner' or 'within', from its Greek root. It is only when we look within that we find the truth of who and what we are and what motivates us to do what we do and be who we are. Therapy

141

must therefore employ methods to reach within and, gently and lovingly, draw out that which we need to know to help us. The Tarot is, once again, perfectly designed to achieve this, in the hands of the sensitive therapist.

The briefest of commentaries will suffice here, by way of explanation, since it is for the aspiring therapist to study and make of these divisions what they will. It is to be noted that The Fool is set apart in this concept, since it is he who embodies the human form of the Rays, being their physical end and manifestation. He represents each of us, as the Seeker, making our way through the subsequent levels the Major Arcana represents in turn. He can fulfil his role of Divine Joker with abandon, popping up at opportune moments to question and provoke us to doubt. It is these very questions and doubts that are the catalyst we require to propel us forward on our quest. Without his vital input we would remain the lazy victims of comfort we can easily become in this world of convenience and automation.

The first realm of Body and Ray of Will shows us that the seven cards of this level are concerned with the application of what the individual has at hand. The Ray is seen as that of Spiritual Energy. The discovery of this begins with the Magician, in his masculine nature, complemented by the feminine High Priestess, then supplemented by the Empress and Emperor, as the inner and outer manifestations of the physical nature and will of the person. The Hierophant serves as a guide for his will and physical energy, while the Lovers indicate the choices of freewill that must be made. The Chariot is the mastery of this freewill and manifestation of the energy, directed and focussed upon the individuals chosen goal.

The second realm of Mind and Ray of Love-Wisdom show us the result of this direction. The Ray is one of Magnetic Force. This must first be tempered with the wisdom of love, through the fortitude that Strength gives us. This results in a higher wisdom from the study of the Hermit and an acceptance of that which is our fate, as the result of the lessons we have agreed to learn in each lifetime, shown in the Wheel of Fortune. Justice takes us to the centre of that which we are and know at this time, where our mind is laid bare before us. This requires a reorientation to the love that pervades all things at their highest level. This brings about a Death experience, by way of revelation in the Seeker, resulting in the peace that comes, in the Temperance card; a peace of mind that 'passes all understanding'.

The third realm of Spirit and Ray of Active/Creative intelligence takes us to awareness of the true nature of ourselves, as physical aspects of the Divine. This Ray is one of Radiant Glory. his activates the higher faculties of both body and mind that have gone before, giving a truly spiritual person, fully alive and in possession of all that they are. This process begins with the Devil, when we must first realise all that we are not and shed that which limits us. Freed from this Tower of Maya (illusion), we are guided onwards and upwards by the Star, first as a faint and distant awareness, then as we begin to trust and integrate our process of intuition (inner-tuition), closer with the Moon. The blazing reality and truth of the Sun warms and fuels our spirits fervour and we can reach our highest aspirations, responding to the call of our spirit with our activated intelligence. This gives us the full possession of the being that we are, the active, creative person, following the holistic ideal of body, mind and spirit, symbolised here by the World.

These first three Rays of the Seven that exist are seen as primary, and greater than the first four, just as the Major Arcana is seen in relation to the Minor. This does not diminish their significance however, as we have seen. The remaining four, or sub rays equate perfectly with the four suits of the Minor Arcana, as follows:

RAY	QUALITY	ELEMENT	SUIT
4TH	HARMONY THROUGH CONFLICT	AIR	SWORDS
5TH	CONCRETE KNOWLEDGE	FIRE	RODS
6TH	DEVOTION	WATER	CUPS
7TH	ORGANISATION / RHYTHM	EARTH	PENTACLES

As stated above, further explanation of the alignments will appear in Volume 3 of this work, in its proper place and context of the structure of the Minor Arcana. There is a vast wealth of information available concerning the Seven Rays, some of which will be digested in Volume 2, as it pertains to the therapeutic nature of the Tarot. It is important to realise now that these Rays encompass all that is in the Universe and indeed the Universe itself. When utilised in healing and the determination of the cause of disease in the individual, coupled with their alignment with the Tarot, it is easy to establish a quantum leap in understanding how and why the Tarot can be used for therapy in this way.

It should be stressed that meditation on these subjects alone will repay themselves and begin a work in the aspirant that will benefit clients accordingly. The names of the Rays describe the nature of both the Ray and the suit to the extent that this alone tells us with what we are dealing with in the client when cards of this suit appear. Suffice to say now however, that the alignment of the Tarot with the Seven rays can represent a leap forward in the appreciation of its context as a sacred therapy, whilst giving the dual benefit of helping us to understand the workings and nature of the Universe in which we live. So it is that the Tarot itself does the same as the Rays. For the present let us accept this information as a carrot dangled tantalisingly before us, to take when we are ready.

A great deal is required of the Tarot Therapist in the perfection of their art, which will be explored shortly. Here are the tools of the trade, a wonderful and versatile mix of images, symbols and colours that in their myriad

144

permutations of selection in consultations have the ability to answer every need that occurs in those who have the privilege of enquiring of them. The Tarot Consultation becomes something a great deal more important than the brief and surface half-hour chat in a noisy and crowded hotel room fayre. The therapeutic process takes the consultation out of this scenario and into the comfort and peace of the consulting room. It is through these hallowed portals that we now step.

EXERCISES

Select three cards from the Minor Arcana. Place these alongside each other and see what they may tell you about your current needs, based on the information given in this Chapter. Try this same process for somebody close to you, ensuring they are aware that you are training and learning and not to take anything you agree upon too seriously yet. See what you can agree upon together from the selection of cards they have.

Looking at the information given so far in the book concerning the Elements and the nature of the suits, write a description, in your own words of what each represents, in yourself and your life so far. Focus on your own needs at each of these levels and explore these. Allow yourself to be honest in this work and as objective as you can be. When you have written notes for your needs on all four levels see what common traits and underlying influences you may be able to identify. You may decide to select some Major Arcana cards to further identify and work with these deeper causes. Refer to the notes and your own instinctive and intuitive reactions to them to help you. Trust what comes to you and try not to question it, even if what you receive surprises you. Remember we can be our own worst enemies in this kind of work.

Read through the notes for each of the numbers and write down your own understanding of the energy of each number, including Zero and Ten. Try to do this in your own words. The notes you produce from these exercises will form the basis of your interpretations of the cards at a later date.

This is a good time to examine your motivations in working with the Tarot. Answer the following:

What use of the Tarot do you wish to make and why?

What do you think the Tarot can teach you about yourself?

What do you think of the prospect of discovering unpleasant things about yourself through your study of the cards?

What are you prepared to sacrifice to be a Tarot Therapist?

In many senses it does not matter what your answers are. It is more important that you have a clear answer and that your conscience is quite happy and at ease with it. It is also good to review your answers to these questions as you progress, checking your conscience to see if they still apply, have changed or you feel differently at any time. The study of the Tarot is a study of the self and this will undoubtedly give rise to some dramatic and powerful change at some point.

CHAPTER 6 - THE SPIRIT OF THE TAROT

It is of paramount importance to realise that in the workings of Tarot Therapy an attitude must prevail, of service. This service is first one from the Therapist to the client, but is one that is sourced from a higher level of awareness. Here we pay due and proper homage to the Spirit of the Tarot, in whatever form we consider this to take.

That there is a Spirit governing the workings of the wisdom in these cards is undoubted. We talk here of the energy behind the cards, the life force that gave birth to the form they now take. We remind ourselves at this point that it is the knowledge and ageless wisdom that is represented by the cards, not the cards themselves that are important. In so doing, we find the purity and sanctity of the Tarot. This may be seen as a congruence of energy, drawn together over the millennia of the existence and accumulation of the knowledge of humankind. This energy is constantly changing and evolving, yet always retains its true and perfect nature in its essence, as it is born not from human, but divine origins.

For the aspiring Therapist the question is not one of the facts of existence, but of the form they wish to imagine it takes. This does not necessarily mean that some spirit in a divine yet human form is governing the workings of the Tarot at a higher level, though this traditional image may be appropriate for some. Indeed it is good and productive to envisage a form of deity that oversees the workings of Tarot Therapy, to ensure that the ageless wisdom is not only preserved as it should be, but perhaps more importantly is used in the manner for which it is intended.

All things are open to abuse, in particular it seems, that which is given freely, as is the case with the ageless wisdom of the Tarot. The history of humanity is replete with mistakes and the atrocities that occur when we lose sight of our divine nature and interconnectedness. The damage that is wrought when we seek to guide our own affairs is far reaching and must be balanced out by the workings of karma over a good many of our years. When we delve into the mysteries of life, through means such as the Tarot, it is vital that we allow ourselves to be guided in our work for others. It is equally vital that the Therapist know of the source of their guidance and is able to feel the connection they have to this source as a real one. For this reason a meditation to establish this connection is included in the exercises for this Chapter.

However, it is futile to suggest or hope that every Tarot Therapist will perform such a meditation prior to a consultation, or utilise some other method of establishing a connection with the Spirit of the Tarot, or their own guides or guardian angel. The necessity of correct preparation for a consultation is covered later for this can be the key to a successful and lasting, positive change brought about through it. For this reason we must seek to establish a more tangible form of guidance for Therapists to follow and adhere to.

It is stressed that what is presented is not done by way of laying down rules and regulations, the transgression from which results in punishment, by way of extradition or humiliation. Rather, the necessity for establishing good practice and the highest standards becomes clear when we consider the abuse of power open to the Therapist, in any position in society and at any level of practice. As stated before, the mistakes of the past have shown us the need for insurance, in the minds of those trying hard to stick to the strictest principles that we must establish at the outset. It is only by the continued application of such principles that we can hope, in time, to reverse the low, astral glamour of the Tarot that currently holds sway.

The necessity for professional practice and conduct through Tarot Therapists the world over must also be as uniform as possible. The scenario of what passes for acceptable behaviour in a consultation setting being different from one town to another must be avoided. It is this that may give rise to the disparity and consequent weakening of the Spirit of the Tarot.

We cannot simply lay down a set of rules that dictate what we can and cannot do in a consultation, any more than we can say that any one card means this that or the other. The nature of the spirit with which we are dealing is just not like that. Rather, the form that our guidance must take must be open and accepting of some differing practices, just as the interpretation of cards will differ between Therapists. It must be seen and accepted that it is these very differences that illustrate the strength in diversity that has allowed the Tarot to adapt itself to the changing and evolving needs of humanity over the centuries of its existence.

The different interpretations of cards is an often challenging subject amongst Tarot consultants and one that offers a potential trap to its students. The workings of intuition, or pure reason, provide the best answer, when we realise that true intuition occurs from a connection to our own and individual source of wisdom or knowledge. This source, whether we call it the soul, God, guide and so on, is formed when we make the connection spoken of earlier, prior to using the cards. Our creative imagination is brought into play as the eyes look upon the symbols of the cards, forming the seemingly random associations they make. These links are formed from the combination of the cards laid out before us for that particular consultant, as they apply to that particular client. Beyond the basic, accepted, core meaning to each card, the intuition is allowed free reign to speak as it may in the consultation and it is this process that allows the Spirit of the Tarot speech through the Therapist.

It is the job of the Therapist to 'translate' this information into a form readily understood by the client and in speech that is applicable to their self and life at that time. The nature of such working may at first glance seem distanced from the professional, clinical therapies we have become used to, but it as well to mention here that we are dealing now with the medicine and therapy of the future. This is one that allows and accepts the workings of energy.

This energy is one that flows and affects all it touches. It is coloured a little differently in every living being and its nature must be accounted for in the therapies we choose to utilise as the medicine of the future. Energy medicine is a true and good definition of Tarot Therapy. As we learn more of the way of energy and its workings, it will be seen that the flexibility it brings with it is an integral part of the professional standards that we must seek to import and apply in this context. Intuition in truth is as scientific as the laboratory experiment.

It is this intuition and the individual nature of the Therapist that gives rise to the differing interpretations of the same cards. The strength and beauty of the Tarot consultation lies in the observance by the Therapist of the way in which cards make combinations, rather than the linear and therefore limited view afforded by interpreting first one card then another. A Tarot consultation is a wondrous thing, a process of uncovering deeper and still deeper levels and layers of the card interpretations, the clients' heart and mind and their needs at each level of their being. As the cards are constructed from the very form of all these levels, they are perfectly able to consider and deal with all the needs they come across in those brave enough to open themselves to it. Such bravery deserves to be rewarded with the highest standards of practice from the Therapist they choose or are guided to.

At a solely human level, Tarot Therapists must be seen to be accountable if they are to gain recognition for their services. They must be accountable to themselves, in the form of their own conscience, often viewed as the voice of the spirit within. They must also be accountable to their clients, to each other and to the wider public. This entails the settings of the highest standards and practice and the establishment of uniformity amongst those adhering to them. The most effective way to do this is to propose and suggest here a Code of Conduct, Ethics and Practice.

These are not rules, as said previously, but suggestions, thrown willingly into the waiting hearts and minds of those who read these words. Cast into this pit, it is hoped that at some stage what emerges will be useful and practical and help to establish the good practices required.

It is recognised now however, that the establishment of some recognised body to administer these codes is vital if the Tarot is to take again the respect it so richly deserves. To this end, I offer the following suggestions as a blueprint for a 'Professional Association of Tarot Therapists'. That this book is published at all is a good indication to me that the time is ready for such an organisation to come into existence. The nature of our tangible reality is such that it must first exist as energy. The energy from which our reality is formed is largely constructed from astral (emotional) and mental matter. That is, what we think and feel is what we experience. This is true both individually and collectively.

For these words to be manifesting themselves, as they truly are, in the knowledge that they will be published in this form, is a clear indication of the readiness for the acceptance of the Tarot as a therapy and that the necessary preparation on the inner planes has been done, to begin to bring this about on the outer planes of this Earth. As the energy of all this congeals and takes heavier form and shape it is my feeling and deepest wish that it will evolve into some kind of Professional Association. This must surely be a basic requirement before we can truly say that the Tarot has taken its rightful place once more alongside the other sacred, natural therapies available to us, to facilitate our growth and development that enable us to fulfil our potential.

The convergence of the energy particles that result from the thoughts and feelings of those who first realised what we now know as the ageless wisdom began this same process, so long ago. Here in the watery mists of Atlantis, or perhaps before this in some other, lesser known time and place, the Spirit of the Tarot was first formed. In seeking to preserve the body of knowledge and wisdom they had amassed through the long successful and flourishing years of their land, the priesthood of Atlantis took the energy from the inner planes and gave it form. Thus encoded, this energy was able to manifest according to the understanding of those who viewed it at any one time. In this way the Tarot was able to present itself in the form best suited to the understanding of that time in history. It is still doing this and so the Spirit of the Tarot is alive and well. In presenting the Codes that follow, it is hoped this will breathe new life into this Spirit and let it live on, healthily and abundantly, into the Aquarian Age.

This will in turn be achieved by the truly focussed hearts and minds of the Tarot Therapists who utilise the cards in the manner suggested, with due regard and acceptance of its timeless and scared nature. As this process unfolds, the Tarot will feed from this positive energy and bring itself back to its hallowed position, no longer clouded in mystery and mysticism. Rather it will stand clearly and brightly. In the consulting rooms of those who fully understand, appreciate and can correctly focus the power that it represents and that lays within it.

CODE OF CONDUCT, ETHICS AND PRACTICE

It is recognised that no code can resolve all ethical and practice related issues. This Code of Conduct, Ethics and Practice does however, seek to provide a framework for addressing such issues.

The purpose of this Code is:

- to establish and maintain standards for Tarot Therapists

- to inform and protect members of the public seeking the service of Tarot Therapists

- The Aim of this Code is:

- to establish and maintain optimum levels of practice amongst Tarot Therapists

- to establish a common frame of reference within which to manage their responsibility to clients, colleagues and the wider community.

Tarot Therapists should endeavour to use their skills and abilities to the clients best advantage. Tarot Therapists must take all reasonable and necessary steps to work competently and to the best of their ability.

The welfare of the client has the highest priority. Tarot Therapists should take all reasonable steps to ensure the clients safety during consultations, both physically and emotionally. Tarot Therapists should also attend to the need for their own safety.

Tarot Therapists should work without prejudice and due recognition of the value and dignity of every human being.

Tarot Therapists must respect clients' values, personal resources and capacity for self-determination.

Tarot Therapists should take all reasonable steps to take account of the clients' social and cultural context. Tarot Therapists must undertake a commitment to sexual and cultural equality. Tarot Therapists must have respect for the client irrespective of race, colour, creed, sex, sexual orientation and belief.

Tarot Therapists should not raise the issue of their own religious beliefs, unless specifically requested to do so by the client. There should be no attempt made at 'conversion' or other persuasive implication made by the Tarot Therapist to establish a similar belief in the client.

Tarot Therapists should not be judgmental and should recognise the clients' right to refuse treatment or ignore advice. It is recognised that it is the clients' prerogative to make their own choices with regard to their health, lifestyle and finances.

The terms and conditions of a consultation should be explained and agreed in advance between the therapist and client. This should include cost. Any subsequent revision should be agreed before any changes commence.

Tarot Therapists must take the same attitude and degree of care whether the work is paid, voluntary or on an exchange basis.

Tarot Therapists must not accept tokens such as favours, gifts or hospitality from clients when this might be construed as seeking to obtain favourable treatment.

Tarot Therapists shall not make false claim to their training or make comparison with other therapists.

Any unnecessary conflict of interest should be avoided and any other relevant conflicts of interest should be made clear to the client.

Tarot Therapists should not offer consultations when their functioning is impaired due to personal or emotional difficulties, illness, disability, alcohol, drugs or any other reason.

Tarot Therapists reserve the right to refuse a consultation to any client clearly under the influence of alcohol or other substances or perceived to be mentally incapacitated, at risk or dangerous.

It is an indication of the competence of Tarot Therapists when they recognise their inability to satisfactorily meet the needs of a client for any reason. Tarot Therapists may choose in this situation to make appropriate referral to other professionals.

Tarot Therapists must not exploit clients financially, emotionally, physically, socially or sexually. It is recognised that sexual activity with clients is unethical and unprofessional.

Tarot Therapists must not give medical diagnosis unless a Registered Medical Practitioner. Tarot Therapists must not offer any kind of diagnosis they are not trained and qualified to offer.

If a client is found to be suffering from any disorder or disease of a medical nature for which they have not consulted a Registered Medical Practitioner, Tarot Therapists must advise them to do so. This should be recorded for the Tarot Therapists   protection.

Tarot Therapists must not use titles or descriptions to give the impression of medical or other qualifications unless they possess them.

Tarot Therapists must honour and accept the role of other health professionals and not interfere with their treatment and advice.

Tarot Therapists shall be personally responsible for actively maintaining and developing their personal professional competence and shall base delivery of their work on accurate and current information in the interests of best quality practice. All Tarot Therapists have an individual responsibility to maintain their level of professional competence.

The maintenance and development of professional standards is a requirement of continual practice. Tarot Therapists must ensure they undertake continued learning.

Under no circumstances must any Tarot Therapist who witnesses malpractice by any other Tarot Therapist remain silent about it.

If the client is under 16 years of age, permission of a parent/guardian must be obtained before giving a Consultation.

Consultations room must be clean, adequately lit, properly ventilated and in a good state of general repair.

If the consultation room is not directly accessible from the street, all entrance ways and stairways should be kept adequately clean and well lit.

Tarot Therapists should take all reasonable steps to ensure the accessibility of their consultation room to those with a disability. Should a consultation room be located so as to be inaccessible, Tarot Therapists should consider alternative options, such as travelling to the client to give the consultation. Limitations to access should be clearly stated on all Tarot Therapists advertising (i.e. 'one step access' etc.). Wording for advertisements and promotional literature should be designed so as to be visible wherever possible by those with visual impairments. It is recommended that a computer font size 12 be the minimum used in Tarot Therapists literature and advertising where possible.

Any advertising should comply with the British Code of Advertising Practice and meet the requirements of the Advertising Standards Agency. Adverts should be dignified and should not claim a cure or mention any disease in this context.

A Tarot Therapist must not attempt by any means to entice a client to leave another Tarot Therapist to become their client.

In the event of a referral of a client by another Tarot Therapist, no form of commission or split fee may be paid or accepted.

Criticism of other Tarot Therapists should not be implied either in writing or verbally, before clients or the general public.

Tarot Therapists should at all times act in a courteous and honourable manner, with integrity, sensitivity and tact. Tarot Therapists attitude must be competent and sympathetic, hopeful and positive, so as to encourage the same in the client.

Tarot Therapy is not given unless requested by the client.

Tarot Therapists shall if possible ensure that their practice is fully covered by a substantial professional indemnity insurance, insuring them against professional malpractice/public liability.

Prior to the introduction of a recognised and accepted governing or professional body, Tarot Therapists should instigate an individual Complaints Procedure which they should abide by. In the event of the formation and membership of such an organisation, Tarot Therapists should agree to abide by the complaints procedure wherever possible.

CONFIDENTIALITY

It is recognised that any limitation to the degree of confidentiality can diminish the effectiveness of a consultation.

Tarot Therapists must ensure that the welfare and anonymity of the client is protected.

Tarot Therapists must provide privacy for consultations. Consultations must not be observed by any other person without the clients consent.

Tarot Therapists must ensure the privacy of any third party involved in any aspect of a consultation, apart from the clients' perspective. No disclosure should be made to any third party without the clients consent unless required by process of the law, whether that law be by statute, statutory instrument or order of Court.

If consultations are taped, clients should be made aware of and agree to this prior to any recording being made. Clients should be made aware of the number of any copies made.

All personal information about clients must remain confidential. This includes name, address, biographical details and details of the clients' life. Tarot Therapists must not pass on lists of names and addresses to others for any promotional purposes.

It is recognised that exceptional circumstances might arise which give the Tarot Therapist good grounds for believing that the client will cause physical harm, or have harm caused to them. If possible, client permission to break confidentiality should be sought or after consultation with a supervisor.

Confidentiality continues after client death.

Tarot Therapists must ensure they are compliant with the Data Protection Act.

RECORD KEEPING

It is advisable to keep records of consultations. Clients must be aware of the existence of such records and have full access to them on request. All records must be held securely and confidentially.

Record keeping is advised so as to make the client history available should the client move to another Tarot Therapist and request their records. Records should be kept in such a manner as to be fully understandable by another Tarot Therapist in the event of referral. Tarot Therapists may choose to note the Tarot cards used in a consultation in clients records.

Notes from an Initial Consultation/Medical History must be signed by the client as being a true and accurate record of their present condition.

SUPERVISION

Tarot Therapists must take appropriate steps to monitor and work within the limits of their competence.

Tarot Therapists should receive appropriate and ongoing supervision and support wherever possible.

It is proposed it be an ethical breach of the code to practice without supervision wherever possible.

The purpose of supervision is to ensure the efficacy of the therapist/client relationship.

The volume of supervision should be in proportion to the volume of work undertaken and the experience of the Tarot Therapist.

Supervision can be given by one or more of the following models:

One-to-One, Group, Peer Group, Co-supervision.

A suggested ratio for supervision for every 20 hours of client work is:
1 hour one-to-one, 2 hours co-supervision, 1 hour for each group member.

It is suggested that an increase in these times be implemented for new Tarot Therapists and that extra supervision time be arranged when required. During supervision the identity of clients should be protected wherever possible.

ESOTERIC ETHICS

Tarot Therapists should not make claim to accurate future predictions, but stress the nature of possible futures, dependent in part on the clients' emotions and thoughts.

Tarot Therapists must consider if it is in the clients best interests to know the nature of any information they perceive regarding their future. Tarot Therapists must not predict death.

Reason and common sense should always be applied to any 'impression' Tarot Therapists may receive to say or do certain things during a consultation.

Intention is all important.

We are responsible for our thoughts and actions. Harmful thoughts and actions return to us.

We are all part of a greater pattern or plan.

Three basic senses are required for acceptable Tarot Therapy: Common Sense, a sense of proportion and humour.

This last section of 'Esoteric Ethics' are those that apply more specifically to the work of Tarot Therapists alone, the previous being largely applicable to Therapists of any kind. As mentioned before the Code, the implementation of the standard suggested by it require the formation of some kind of recognised, professional governing body with elected committee members willing to undertake the hard, selfless work required of such roles. Until that time, one can only hope that the morality and honour of aspiring Tarot Therapists leads them to abide by the suggestions outlined by what is given here.

Because at present there is no one recognised standard for Tarot Therapists to aspire to and follow, I have given the widest possible reign to the area of coverage of the Code, if nothing more than in an attempt to illustrate the nature of such work and the situations Tarot Therapists may deal with and the responsibilities undertaken by them. It is my view that this can only benefit the Tarot and help to rectify the damage done to the image of the cards.

As this process gathers pace and energy, so it is that the Spirit of the Tarot will be wakened anew, stretching its weary and aching limbs from their current foetal position, in time adopting a stance once more proud and dignified. As the Spirit issues forth its healing and regenerative power to the clients of Tarot Therapists so it is enabled to heal itself and the cards can once more be seen to be shining a sacred light.

EXERCISES

The above Code can only be a theoretical one until such time as some kind of governing body be implemented to the world of Tarot. This does not mean that its principles and guidelines cannot be adopted in the hearts and minds of all those willing to seek the sacred recognition due the Tarot and who are aware of its therapeutic and healing potential. To this end, read the Code thoroughly and consider if your current or aspired for practice aligns with the guidelines of the Code. You may need to consider if you are in agreement with what is presented here and if there are areas not covered by the Code. In effect what is required is that you draw up your own personal Code of Ethics, Conduct and Practice and morally commit to abide by this. You should endeavour to make your Code available to all who wish to see it on request, as there should be no doubt or guilt within you that shames or prevents you from doing this. In considering your Code, it is good to consider the reasons for any disagreement you may have with any of the points or areas of the Code as this may reveal certain subjects that need attention in your own self or practice methods. Honesty is the best guiding policy here and listening carefully to the voice of your own conscience.

The other Exercise appropriate at this stage is a further meditation. This builds on the meditation given in the Exercises for Chapter 4, where you were taken on a trip to the Temple of the Major Arcana. This journey returns you to that place, wherein you encounter the Spirit of the Tarot. It is therefore necessary to be familiar and comfortable with the previous meditation, so that this one is effective and meaningful when undertaken. Again, the voice of your conscience and intuition is the most effective guide for you to know when this is so. When you feel ready, undertake the following journey.

Enter into meditation in the way that should now have become familiar and easy for you, following your practice of the previous meditation. When you have deeply relaxed yourself and so entered the altered state of consciousness required for these purposes, allow yourself to become centred, arriving at an awareness of the place of peace and rest that truly passes all understanding. From here you can begin your journey on the inner planes, to meet the Spirit of the Tarot.

Find yourself once more before the Temple of the Major Arcana. See its shape and outline forming clearly before you and take a little time to adjust to the sensation of being here once more. You may choose to walk around the building again if you wish. As you approach the entrance the Guardian will be there and will greet you, telling you that you are expected. You may choose to greet the Guardian yourself or they may have some message or instruction for you as you enter the Temple.

When all has occurred outside, enter. Climb the stairs, counting them if you wish, until you have climbed all 78. Adjust your senses as you enter this deeper part of the journey and allow yourself time to settle and be at ease when you reach the Temple itself. Take some time to walk around this inner sanctum of the Temple, observing the cards on the walls. You may feel drawn to pause before any of them as you walk around, but be careful not to be drawn into them too far, no matter how strong the pull may be.

When you have walked through the Temple to your satisfaction, find your way back to the altar. Stand before this and examine what you find there. You will see that a candle or other small light is lit and it occurs to you that somebody must have entered the Temple before you. Hearing no one, take a seat beside the altar and become comfortable. Now the purpose of this visit is reminded to you - you are here to meet the Spirit of the Tarot. Perhaps with a little apprehension but certainly some excitement and expectation, you close your eyes and silently make request or prayer to the Spirit to come to you and be in the Temple with you.

After a short time you will hear someone approach. This stage of the journey is an individual one that no guidance can be given for. Simply take as long as you need in your meditation for events to unfold as they wish. No harm can come to you and you are perfectly safe. The Spirit of the Tarot may choose almost any form to appear to you in and this may not remain the same throughout your workings with the Tarot. You will be able to communicate to them, but they may choose not to communicate with you! This you should accept. Your conduct should be faultless whilst in their presence as this is an ancient and powerful being, yet has suffered much over the years. You will find that they still retain a benign presence and intent however, but they will know your intentions in your work with the Tarot, better than you do, so it is advisable for your conscience to be clear before meeting them!

Take as long as you need for this stage of the meditation and when you are ready, prepare to make your return. It may take several journeys before the Spirit will appear to you in a physical form (or you perceive them that way). You may notice only a slight change in the colours around you for a time or an alteration in the atmosphere. Persist with your visits and do not be disheartened. True contact of this kind with inner plane beings often takes many attempts before being successful.

When all seems done, as will become apparent in your meditation, give your thanks to the Spirit of the Tarot. Remember that you may ask them any questions or ask for help that you feel in need of in your studies with the Tarot so be sure you have said all you wish to before you bid them farewell. You can return when you wish and once a good and clear contact has been made they will become an invaluable guide and confidante for your work.

Come back to the altar and see the light once more. Become aware of the surroundings of the Temple and when you are ready find your way back to the stairs. Descend these and make your way outside. Ensure that the door to the Temple is closed, by yourself or the Guardian. They may have some other message or gift for you, which you should accept with thanks. Walk a little way away from the Temple and then the let image fade away, making your slow and full return to the everyday, physical world, following the process that has become familiar and comfortable to you. Do not forget to make brief notes of your experiences, as should have become standard practice for you now.

Contact with the Spirit of the Tarot is a key initiatory stage of your studies with Tarot Therapy and one whose importance should not be underestimated. Repeat this journey when you feel you need to. Always be humble and polite before the Spirit, however you perceive them or they appear to you. Honesty should also be by your side at every visit and in all your conducts with the Tarot. Given these conditions, the benefits of the contact afforded by this meditation are invaluable, giving clarity, guidance, reassurance, perhaps challenge but certainty and comfort to the aspiring Tarot Therapist. It is also quite poetically beautiful and inspiring, as such contacts often are.

CHAPTER 7 - THE ACTIVE THERAPIST

The new light the Code of Ethics, Conduct and Practice throws upon the familiar Tarot consultation is a transformative one. Strict observance of the Code results in a drastically different approach to the provision of a Consultation, but as we have seen, this is entirely what is required if the restoration of the Tarot to its sacred origins is to be achieved.

Even the slightest observation of the Code will give the aspiring Tarot Therapist much to strive for by way of the application of their therapy. The situations and circumstances that Tarot consultations are currently given in are many and varied. The popular and detestable image is of the fortune-telling booth at the end of the pier. With the advent of the widespread popularity and commercialisation of 'New Age' ideas, the Tarot 'reader' found themselves employed by the local emporium, housed more often than not in the back room, basement, or as I have observed on some occasions, in the window of the sudden mushrooming of these shops and centres. From here, various entrepreneurial promoters, some lacking in the ideals they were promoting through their activities, organised 'Psychic Fairs', promising all kinds of encounters, all it seems, with 'the country's top clairvoyants'.

As someone who has travelled this bejewelled and sadly sought after road through the 1980's, it is tempting to catalogue the indiscretions, absence of spirituality and motivation for profit that seemed to accompany the great majority of events and individuals I encountered during this period. However, this serves little purpose, other than selfish ones. Looking back, there are many stories to tell, each one serving to illustrate the conditioning of the society we have created and human nature within it. What this time did teach me was to act in my own way, that the only way of life is your own, to steal a quote from these times.

Though it appeared necessary at the time to 'do the rounds' of this scenario in order to establish a reputation I experienced a growing sense of disquiet and unease that I could not work adequately in the environments in which I was placed. Many times, the inherent nosiness that exists in the unsatisfied human spirit, as a manifestation of its quest for peace and fulfilment, meant that a consultation was observed at very close quarters by those in search of the 'best' reader in the room. Coupled with the choking stench of tobacco fumes and alcohol (the readers as well as clients!), I could no longer feel that the spirit of what I was involved in was being honoured.

At length I took the decision that the appropriate place for my work was in the private consultation room. This necessitated a good deal of adjustment in my working practice, to create the environment I needed. This also meant that I would reach a good deal less people, but I felt this was necessary if I was to follow the promptings I felt and move forward in my work. The unseen workings of the higher forces that guide such matters have ensured however, that my needs have always been met. Here I must give due regard and honour to the patient and accommodating spirit of my wife. It has also become clear to me that the quality of the work done is more important than the quantity. This process is one of continuing unfoldment and progression, in keeping with the aspirations I still hold as the therapist I try to be.

What has been learnt from these years of work, in terms of the nature and delivery of consultation from the therapeutic perspective, I attempt to pass on here. This is done by way of offering and suggestion, rather than rules and regulations, as with the Code of the preceding chapter. What you adopt as your own practice and custom is of course entirely your affair and I feel should be done so in a spirit of openness and willingness to be wrong. It is only by trying things and discovering what works and more importantly what doesn't, that excellence of practice and standard can be achieved. It is to the highest standard that we should all strive for and aspire to as Tarot Therapists, if for no other reason than our love and regard for the Tarot itself demands this respect.

As someone who has tried many things, retained some and rejected others, in the search for the most effective and appropriate consultation, there are many areas which simply do not come to mind until they happen in practice. So it is that I can offer the following suggestions and guidance from what experience I have. Some are obvious and have been initially mentioned previously, while others are more obscure and surprising. Here we can place such subjects in their proper and full context.

BOOKING CONSULTATIONS

For an effective and smooth, clear procedure to your Tarot Therapy operation a booking procedure is essential. Obviously in your promotional literature you must give means of contact your clients may use to book you. This will usually be your telephone number and the initial call that results is an important time, during which impressions are formed by your client that can have a large effect on the success or otherwise of a consultation.

You may need to answer questions prospective clients have which you must demonstrate the patience and understanding to answer fully before any decision is made as to whether they have a consultation or not. You should never push any client to book if they are unsure. Indeed, it is far better to advise them to wait until they are sure if you consider them not to be so. Doubt will equal confusion and unclear goals when the consultation occurs, reducing its effect and your reputation accordingly.

You need to be clear about the details you must impart to the client by 'phone. This will include taking their name and possibly address, as well as a contact 'phone number in case you are ill. It may be necessary to assure them of your discretion in the event of your having to call them, in case nobody else knows they are visiting you. Refer to yourself as a friend or making a personal call if asking for them by name over the 'phone.

You may need to give directions to your home or place of work and sending a clearly marked map to them is a good idea. It is good to outline the length your consultation is likely to take and whether you set a clear finishing time or let your consultations be open ended. This is also the time to inform the client and agree with them any charge you are making. You will therefore need to be clear about your charging policy and whether you are going to operate a reduced charges system for those on low incomes for any reason. If doing this, I recommend asking the client to provide written proof of benefits and so on, as I have known clients take advantage of a good nature.

The subject of charging for consultations often causes distress and difficulty. There can be no clear guidelines to give as only your own conscience can determine what, if anything you feel you are worth. I would strongly suggest however that you make some charge to clients, particularly if you have taken and passed some recognised course of study for your work. Charging is in esoteric reality an exchange of energy and you should set your fee at a level which you feel best represents an equality in this awareness. This may vary according to the length of time you give in a consultation and the area you are in. It may be you need to charge clients more if you pay rent for a workspace. You could also consider the initial consultation being more expensive, dropping the price for subsequent consultations as part of ongoing therapy, a practice common in many complementary and orthodox therapies.

When beginning your career as a Tarot Therapist, or whilst you are training, you may decide to offer consultations for just a small fee. This can add incentive to you to develop yourself and gain appropriate qualifications where necessary and if you decide to adopt this practice, do ensure your clients are aware that you are in training.

I have always tried to operate on a system that does not preclude any person from obtaining a consultation when in clear need. I have found that the provision of a free consultation occasionally is always returned, usually to excess of what I have given away, by some unexpected income or other expression or goodwill. It seems that the gods always respond generously to a similar spirit. What matters perhaps most on the subject of charging for your work is that you are clear about your policy and stick to this, always being willing to explain your reasoning to clients, should they ask.

I would also suggest that on taking the booking a deposit is requested. This is for several reasons. Firstly it helps prevent the annoying but inevitable occurrence of the client simply not turning up. You will have expended some time and energy to prepare yourself for a consultation to be left waiting until you are sure the client is not going to arrive. If they have paid a deposit, clients are more likely to make the effort and less likely to let any fears or worries that might dissuade them from attending getting the better of them. It is a rare client brave enough to inform you they have changed their mind and wish to cancel, such is modern human nature.

That the client bothers to send a deposit to you also indicates they are serious about their consultation and are more likely to take notice of its results and effect. I also believe that this system is in the best interests of professionalism and demonstrates an awareness of your own worth as a therapist, whose time is of value. I have found that very few clients object to a deposit, those that do usually expecting something quite different from the work I do and therefore more appropriately referred elsewhere.

Should you not receive a deposit when promised, you are then able to 'phone the client and ascertain if they intend coming to see you or not, thereby avoiding a waste of time and energy and offering the allotted space to another client. This practice also encourages the professionalism necessary for Tarot Therapy.

In conclusion on this subject, the system of energy exchange can be extended to the most pleasurable and worthwhile practice of swapping your consultations for treatment with other therapists, Tarot or otherwise. As a practising therapist, supervision is required as indicated in the Code and therapy to help maintain yourself is always beneficial while working for others. There is something very sweet and pleasant about work done by this method and there are usually many therapists willing to trade work.

Returning to the booking of your consultations, be clear about the date and time for each one booked. It is a good idea to determine the number of clients you can see in any one day (three being an absolute maximum for me) or perhaps week and what times you can reasonably be available for, without over committing yourself or causing inconvenience to your household. It is easy to always say yes, but the good therapist will be aware of the need to say no on occasions and retain the ability to do so, clearly and politely. Clients will not take offence and if they are genuine about their consultation will rather wait in order to receive you at your best, which you also have a duty to give to every client.

If you have one client following another it is good to set a cut off time for late arrival, to avoid creating a backlog, or being still engaged when your next client arrives. Allow yourself plenty of time between clients, not just to avoid overlapping and catering for overrunning slightly, but also for giving yourself a chance to rest and recuperate your energy. The need for this period will soon become very apparent should you not include it.

A professional and friendly telephone manner can be important, both in honour of your Code and also in putting the client at their ease. Using the clients name is both courteous and professional, demonstrating that you are listening to them and recognise them as an individual, as opposed to just another client. Thank them for calling you, whatever the outcome of the call, but do not be condescending or patronising at any point, whatever your view of any questions they may ask and what you think this shows about them. Your clients' morals and conduct are not a subject for your judgement, only areas they may look to you for assistance with. Your personal opinions are irrelevant and should remain so throughout the consultation and beyond. Always be clear about not giving your own view, but that of the therapeutic stance. Clients may press you for your opinion ("but what do you think I should do"), but this must be refused. It is best to reflect this kind of questioning back to the client and if they persist explain gently but firmly that you are not in a position to offer this. If they push further, just refuse.

This brings me to the matter of providing consultations for friends, as will inevitably occur and the difficult area of when clients become friends, as many do over a period of time. In accordance with professional conduct it should always be made clear that the consultation is just that and is not discussed outside of this environment. It should be understood that what you say during it is done so as a therapist, not a friend and that further activity should take place in the proper setting, not in the casual conversation. Your policy about charging should be equally clear for friends as well.

The matter of seeing clients socially or just in the street also arises here as this can create embarrassment or awkwardness and have potentially serious consequences if you are unlucky. It is the best policy to allow the client all possible polite chance to acknowledge you first, as they may be in the company of someone unaware of their visit to you and wish this to remain the case. Do not mention the consultation unless they do so, but still do not discuss its content, even if they seem to want to. A basic conversation can be polite, but anything further is best diverted to the next consultation. Be prepared to be passed off as an acquaintance or vague friend without taking offence in these circumstances. As indicated at the start of this Chapter, there is more to being a Tarot Therapist than meets the eye!

Once your booking is made, you must prepare yourself for the consultation, which also contains many unexpected pitfalls and details that deserve your attention.

PREPARATION FOR CONSULTATIONS

Correct preparation for a Consultation, both in practical terms and that of the therapist, is of vital importance to its successful and effective outcome. The responsibility the therapist has towards the client and that they should feel within them, dictates the necessary preparation be undertaken. The highest regard must be present in the Therapist for what they do and how they do it and it is this that must guide them in the preparation they make, each and every time they consult the Tarot with a client.

The question of duty and responsibility can be addressed at this stage. These are often areas that are underestimated in the value placed upon them for the best possible consultation. The Code of Conduct, Ethics and Practice outlines in practical terms the role and responsibility the therapist must have in their work, but there can be items only implied by the formal language utilised in such things. These are more of an emotional nature, including such things as the sensitivity of the therapist to the needs of the client, the need for empathy without belittling them, tact, diplomacy and honesty, all without sounding or implying negative possibilities. The therapist must cultivate the attitude of detached involvement, being able to impart to the client that they are alongside and supportive of them, yet objective enough to provide a balanced view.

Such qualities can truly only be achieved by practice and experience, both of Tarot Therapist work and life. The acquisition of the tenderness to feel the clients pain can only come about by feeling something of a similar, identifiable pain in one's own self and life and the objectivity needed can only arise from the discipline of professional conduct over a period of time spent in this or similar work. This is just one example from the sampled list given above, but serves to illustrate our point here. The career of the Tarot (or any) Therapist is not for the uncommitted or indecisive. It is a work that requires great sacrifices but also brings equal rewards, though usually not financial.

It is for this reason that the question of training for such work must be mentioned. As at present there is no one recognised body to promote and administer the Code of Conduct, Ethics and Practice, so there is no body to do likewise with the training of aspirant Tarot Therapists. It is hoped and envisaged that this will soon change however, for the standards we must seek to arrive at and implement in all true Therapists require such a group of dedicated souls.

Training of this kind must inevitably lead to an examination of the individual's ability so as to ensure the necessary standard has been reached. What form this examination may take is beyond the province of any one person, but should be the synthesis of a committee of opinions. This committee should ideally be formed from a cross section of opinions and backgrounds so as to instigate the widest possible use of possibilities in the examination outline.

An examination should therefore be aimed at an assessment of the Therapists understanding of the cards and the way in which they relate together in a consultation. More will be said on this vital aspect of Tarot Therapy in the following Chapter. The Therapist should be able to demonstrate an understanding of the energy from which the cards are formed and their working in everyday life and in people. There must obviously be a clear knowledge of the basic interpretations and structure of the cards and the Therapist should also demonstrate an ability to relate these to the client in a manner that supports and assists them in dealing progressively with what is revealed. The form this takes is outlined in the Code.

The utilisation of Counselling skills must also form a portion of a Tarot Therapy consultation and it is to be recommended that the basics of this approach to therapy be undertaken as part of ones training to become a Tarot Therapist. It should be made clear however, that the Tarot Therapist is not a counsellor, but utilises some of the methods and abilities of the counsellor as part of their work. This perhaps subtle sounding difference is worthy of distinction in that the Tarot cards enable the therapist direct access to all levels of the client simultaneously, including the spiritual, that is denied the counsellor. A greater emphasis is placed on working together with the client, unfolding the multi-layered interpretations and applications of the cards as they appear at the time of the consultation. The benefits of counselling techniques become clear as one uncovers the application of the cards in practice and begins to appreciate the potential they have in the setting of the therapeutic consultation.

The intricacies of counselling methods and techniques are the subject of a great many books and could easily form many more as the links between them and Tarot Therapy are explored. Until such time as the inauguration of a 'Professional Association of Tarot Therapists', it again falls to the conscience and dedication of each one that comes to the Tarot to work with it in a therapeutic way to instil within themselves the levels of professionalism and competence such as reflect the training necessary to utilise the sacred knowledge of the cards.

The edict in the Code for ascertaining if information obtained through a consultation is in the clients best interests to know has further implications that need to be addressed here, for how is the Therapist to determine such things on the clients behalf and by what right do they assume such a position. Hopefully the right of determination is given from undertaking approved training and by obtaining a recognised qualification, then gaining experience in their field.

This is deemed so because of the nature of Tarot Therapy work. The correct use and application of the Tarot results in the Therapist acquiring information about the client that they may not otherwise have access to themselves. As we have discovered previously, such information originates in the unconscious of the client, wherein lie many repressed or suppressed matters yet to be resolved. As Therapists, we must consider why the client may have chosen not to face or deal with the contents of the subject we are exploring in the consultation. This can often be the result of pain or suffering on their part, deemed too great to face and accept at the time of its occurrence and so 'relegated' to the deeper, quieter levels of the mind. Here the pain can lay forgotten, until awakened by actions such as ours.

Yet within this scenario must be brought to attention the fact of the clients' ownership of this level of their being. You may feel that because the information or pain is the clients own they have a right to know what it is. The very fact that the client has come to the Tarot and that such cards as have appeared to lead the consultation to reveal the painful contents of what they have previously faced or dealt with, can be an indication that the time is now right for this to occur. It has often been my experience that the very reason the client has come to me at all is because something is troubling them but they do know what lies at the root of it and so how to tackle it.

These are classic symptoms of unconscious activity, bubbling up like a volcano about and needing to erupt. As the therapist, it is our job to do our best to steer the lava flow in as progressive a direction as possible, though this may cause some pain in its release. For the client to evolve the lava must flow, just as all energy must be expressed. If it does not, it seeks some other form of outlet, often resulting in physical disease, since this is the most dense and so last means of expression of life force energy. The realms of the Tarot Therapist are those of a faster and lighter level of energy flow, that of the astral (emotional) and mental. It is to these levels that the information in the Tarot largely addresses itself and at which transformational change can be brought about by the understanding granted by the explanation and interpretation of the cards.

It is at this point that first the intuition and second the sensitivity of the therapist must be brought into force. Intuition, being the direct and higher perception of the mind, is the best guide for the therapist to use in the determination firstly of the accuracy and secondly of the relevance of what they perceive for the client in a consultation. When intuition is seen as coming from a higher source, whether this is deemed to be the clients or therapists guide, God, Goddess or other deity, it can be recognised that its use steers the therapist to truthfulness in their understandings of the cards selected.

It is then a matter of whether it be in the clients' best interest to know what has been revealed. It is difficult to categorically say that one should or should not tell the client everything that is perceived, as this must be a decision based on what is thought best at the time and the above guideline is perhaps the best that can be given. We can perhaps add to this the necessity and essentiality of gentleness, sensitivity and tact in the way the Therapist approaches the subject. This is a subject that must be inherent in the Therapist at some point. It can be enlarged, heightened and honed by experience but must first exist within the persona of the Therapist. For this to occur there must be a love of two things: the Tarot and people.

For one to be a practising Therapist there must be a love of the tools of one trade, whether this be the construction of the body in the case of physical doctors and therapists, the workings of the mind for psychologists and the like and for healers and Tarot Therapists a love of the whole human being, inclusive of body, mind and spirit. The Therapist must be able to recognise the potential vulnerability of each client that comes to them and react to this with compassion, empathy and objectivity, all while reading the Tarot! It is for this reason that the Code includes the suggestion of the Therapist being in therapy themselves and that they seek to continually improve themselves, their being and their work: all these things are interdependent and interrelated. It is only by discovering and 'facing and embracing' the unconscious memories and suppressions as sources of pain and fear in themselves that the Tarot Therapist will be able to empathise with the client and so be of any use in assisting them to deal with theirs. Though this may be a difficult task for some and constitute a tall order bringing blood, sweat and tears in its wake, the reward of the beauty visible as the hardened shell of a client melts away with the recognition, understanding and acceptance of a subject you uncover together, possibly after years of guarded hate or anger, in a consultation, is something of pure spirit. This promise should serve as motivation alone for the aspiring Therapist, such is the closeness to Divinity possible through the grace we see and feel at such times.

Contact with a higher power is an oft recurring theme in Tarot Therapy work, as the majority of clients acknowledge one or another. This does not mean that the minority are wrong of course and this must be respected. Equally however, as Therapist your own views, beliefs and opinions must be clear and any practice you wish to adhere to as part of your work must be equally clear and carried out in such a manner as to be completely unobtrusive to the client, to the point of their being unaware of them.

As part of your preparation, it is necessary to consider if and then why, how and when you wish to pray or speak to any deity or your own higher self or intuition. I have mentioned the importance of intuition earlier in this Chapter and so include the following as recommendation for ensuring your connection to it is clear and that its messages can flow without hindrance to your client. These things can also be applied to what guiding forces you choose to acknowledge and work with. Whatever you choose to do, it is vital that you are clear about it. Reserving the freedom to change and adapt your views and beliefs as you change in life, what must be avoided is an indecisive weakness that results only in hesitation and doubt, which serves no purpose.

In preparing yourself for a consultation you may like to grant yourself some time for quiet or meditation, so as to 'centre' and balance yourself and ensure detachment from your own concerns. The Code points out the wisdom in recognising when you are unable to do this, but small everyday concerns can easily be side-lined by a few minutes stillness and focus on the task in hand. These should all be completed with plenty of time for you to prepare yourself and your room. I always ensure that everything is completed 15 minutes before the client is booked. Should they arrive before this I sit them down, perhaps offering a drink and politely explain that they are early and I will be with them shortly. This is very unusual as clients do often arrive before their time, being both eager and nervous, but will sit outside in their car, or loiter at the end of the street before approaching the door.

Central to my preparation is the time spent in meditation. During this I 'pray' or ask for protection as I open myself to the impressions from - wherever - both for myself and my client. Being trained to work with such 'things' I ask for the presence of both my own guides and those of the client. Secure in the knowledge that since I have asked it is the case, I then forget all about guides and concentrate on what I am doing. The relationship seems to work best when we are both left to do what we are meant to be doing. I will usually wait and see if I receive any impressions in my meditation that are relevant to the client. If you feel you may forget these, as is possible since they come in a subtle form, it is a good idea to write them down. You may find however that they are not relevant to the consultation or the client and so choose to ignore them. One recommendation to make here is that it is best to avoid proclamations that begin along the lines of 'my guide says' as this may offend the client if they do not accept the existence of such beings or cause them to ridicule or disbelieve what you are saying throughout the consultation. Far better and more effective to mention the impression received during a preparatory meditation, then leave the client free to choose or reject the information as they wish

The content or method of your preparatory meditation is of course for you to decide and will doubtless change as you progress. I have found that entering into meditation is now enough in itself to ensure that I am detached form my own little concerns and that I operate from a balanced perspective and also that I am positively aligned to the client. This last is necessary to ensure that one does not inherit the conditions of the client. Meditation in this manner is not a compulsory thing, for you may find that simple prayer or statement recited will do the trick. What is compulsory is constant monitoring of yourself to ensure the objectives are achieved before each and every consultation. Occasional change in your preparatory methods is helpful as it helps to avoid the slothfulness that habit can bring.

Setting the Scene

In summary, a meditation prior to a consultation should:

- still, centre and balance the Therapist
- free the Therapist from their own concerns
- align the Therapist to their own intuition, higher self/power/guide/deity
- provide opportunity for the reception of information from this level
- leave the Therapist ready for the consultation

The meditation is actually the last thing carried our prior to the beginning of the consultation. Prior to this comes the preparation of my consultation room, the setting of which can indicate many things about the therapist and their work. Attention should therefore be given to this aspect of Tarot Therapy, to ensure it says what you would wish it to and so that it reflects the standards you aspire to. Like physical disease of the body, the surroundings we choose to put ourselves in can say much about ourselves and for this reason care and attention to detail in setting the scene for your Tarot Therapy work is helpful to its overall effectiveness and image.

You will need to pay attention to the heating and lighting in your consultation room, to ensure that these are as they should be prior to the client's arrival. Heating should have reached the required level, not be still getting warm or cooling down. If your room is likely to be hot, consider adequate ventilation. Equally, do not overheat the room as this will have the effect of making both client and therapist drowsy and a yawning therapist is guaranteed to put your client off! Check that neither you nor the client will be sitting in a draught as this will not only cause coldness but is highly unpleasant and creates muscle tension.

In the original design of your room, try to be aware of the likely changes it will undergo as the year turns and the seasons affect it. It is as well to mention the safety aspect here too, being conscious of what is near your source of heating and any trailing leads or wires, which should be securely fastened so as not to be an obstruction. You may need to have a fan available if the client finds it too hot or a portable heater if the client complains of cold. People are different and the comfort of your client should come first. They need to feel comfortable and relaxed if they are to find the session as beneficial as possible and from a business point of view, want to return!

Depending on the time of day of the consultation, and how long it is likely to last, the light may change during it. You may feel it is wise to have lights in place and turned on before starting the consultation as a sudden change can have a drastic effect on the atmosphere you have worked hard to create. Atmosphere can be an important aspect of a consultation as it can allow the client a chance to be aware of the deeper level of the consultation more easily. Your clients initial reaction on entering the room is vital and should ideally be one along the lines of 'oh, what a lovely room'. They may be quite nervous and unsure of what is going to happen so a pleasant and welcoming environment can do much to put them at their ease. If they make some comment like this, it can also be a good indication of some inner sensitivity about them, which it is useful to know!

The level of lighting can be a significant factor in creating an atmosphere. Obviously it is vital that you are both able to see the cards clearly, but you may find that too bright a light creates a harshness you do not want. Experiment with different lighting effects, positioning lamps and different colours and wattage of bulb until you have the effect you desire. Have somebody play the role of client for you and check shadows do not fall on the cards and seek a number of opinions, as your idea is not the only one that matters. You will not please everyone, so first please yourself, but check that you are not the only person with this reaction!

In arranging your lighting ensure that both you and your clients faces are visible to each of you as this is necessary for trust to occur, which is important in a therapeutic consultation. Dim lighting can play tricks with our view and you should be able to see your clients' eyes and expression clearly.

If you decide to use candles, as many people like to do, the safety aspect is all important. There is nothing quite so distracting a having to extinguish a fire in the middle of a consultation and this does not lend itself to a relaxed, healing environment! Consider where and on what candle wax may drip and if the candle will mark a burn on your prized antique table. Experience has shown me that it is better to spend a little more on a better quality candle that a cheap one that will drip wax everywhere or whose wick will collapse shortly after lighting it. Place the candle away from any likelihood of it being knocked by you or the client. Lastly here, check to see that your candle flame does not flicker in a draught, as this can create an annoying effect over your field of vision.

Another aspect of creating the appropriate atmosphere is smell. If your consulting room is in your home the ordinary household smells will need to be eradicated by some means before you client arrives. This applies primarily to cooking smells, but consider pets and any activities that have taken place recently that leave any lingering odours. Opening a window may not be enough and mid-winter is not a viable solution.

Incense provides one option, but is not liked by everyone. Though they may like the smell, clients may not like the smoke and some are strongly irritated by it, causing coughing, sneezing and streaming eyes. Advice here is to buy a good quality incense and experiment with it first. Also ensure that it has finished burning before the client is present, which usually avoids any irritation. Again, check where you place the incense and its holder and ensure the ash does not collect on a valued or polished surface or may be knocked. Stick incense is much more manageable than the granular form for these purposes. Often a whole stick is too much in one go, but they can be easily broken off and will still burn happily when re-ignited.

An additional and powerful adjunct to a relaxed and welcoming atmosphere is the use of music, but this needs to be done sensitively. Music playing low when the client enters the room can be lovely and is an excellent method of blocking out or taking the edge off any surrounding noise from the house or area around your room. If in your home, others members of the household will need to be aware of your activity and respect this, avoiding their own loud music, television etc.

Obviously your choice of music is relevant. The music should be of a relaxing nature and there are a myriad number of compositions available these days, but the quality varies considerably. You will need to consider whether you are going to play the music throughout the consultation, but this can be a distraction. The benefit here is in detracting from any awkward silence that may occur if of course, you find silence awkward. Experiment beforehand to discover the correct volume of music that allows for normal conversation to be carried out, without the need for raised voices. Music should be playing so as not to be conscious of it, but so that it creates a pleasant and relaxing backdrop, adding to the overall mood and ambience of your room.

If you are recording the consultation, which I have found many clients find valuable, it is best to stop the music before you begin recording because the resultant backdrop creates a diversion from what the client should be listening to at a deep level, may obscure what is being said and breaks copyright laws. I have found that the time when the client is selecting their cards offers a good chance to turn my music off.

Position any tape recorder as unobtrusively as possible any so that wires are not likely to be tripped over. If you are using battery power, ensure they are fully charged beforehand. Try to avoid large microphones pointing at the client, as they immediately put them off saying anything. Do not make a fuss of the recording, simply turn the machine on when you wish to and then leave it. Test when setting up your room that it will pick both you and your client up clearly. Decide on the length of tape you need and suggest this to your client when arranging the booking.

A final note on recording consultations is to decide if you or the client will provide the tape. You will find that the continual provision of tapes gets expensive and clients are happy to provide their own tape. It is still a good idea to have one available however, for those clients that will forget.

You should always give the client the option of having the consultation recorded, if you wish to pursue this practice, rather than insisting that this be done. It is surprising how many clients have a consultation without the knowledge of their partner, for many reasons and so do not wish for the evidence of a tape. If this is the case, they may prefer the option of a pen and paper to hand, on which to make their own notes as you talk. This can distract from the effectiveness of the consultation however, but key words, phrases or sentences are good to jot down to jog the memory.

Some clients may wish to make notes a well as having the consultation recorded and I do recommend the availability of pen and paper to jot down any specific advice such as names and addresses of other therapists, book titles and so on. I would not recommend lending your own books to clients, unless you are happy not to see them again, as this does happen, even unintentionally.

Returning to the subject of your household, where the consultation room is in your house, you must ensure there are no interruptions from children, animals or other members of the household and that all unavoidable noise is kept to a minimum, in particular that of the television. Pets must be kept under control and it is wise to ensure they have no access to the client at all if possible, as clients may have allergies, phobias or fears connected to the animals you may view as your best friend. This can apply to caged as well as free animals. Some animals, particularly cats, seem to display an inherent curiosity when it comes to activities of this kind, so a degree of discipline may be appropriate!

Another part of your preparation worthy of some attention is your own appearance. Whilst there is no intention to dictate or suggest in any way what your appearance should be as a Tarot Therapist, some forethought may be beneficial. You may consider that a white coat, tunic or other uniform may be required to reflect your status, though do consider if this may alienate you from your clients at all, or make you appear detached or 'starchy'. It may be however, that you need to wear the above kind of clothing if you combine your Tarot work with some other kind of therapy. This practice increases the range of Tarot Therapy enormously and is explored further in Chapter 9 of this volume.

The traditional image of the 'Tarot reader' is still that of the gypsy with headscarf, replete with bangles and jewellery about her person, muttering incoherently about dark strangers crossing your path and so on. Clearly the image of the Tarot Therapist does not fit this scenario and I feel that a rather more modern feel is called for. With regard to jewellery, do consider its 'rattleability' as the clinking and clanking created sounds terrible on tape, if you record consultations. I would recommend avoiding baggy sleeves as I have found that these tend to drag cards along with them when you reach across the table and can create a fire hazard if you have candles nearby! Male therapists may fell that a suit and tie is appropriate, whilst others may decide this is too formal. Whilst being important that you are comfortable and relaxed, your appearance should generally suggest that you are professional yet approachable and have respect for your work.

As Tarot Therapy work is sourced from esoteric levels the complete process of a consultation can be viewed as a ritual. We have examined the necessity and importance of entering your inner self and connecting with guides and so on. Many people involved in ritual on a regular basis have a robe or cloak they adorn when practising their 'art'. Whilst this is not appropriate for Tarot Therapy work, you may like to have a special piece of jewellery that you put on to signify this to yourself, if for no other reason. This can have a surprising effect, once a mental and emotional association with the significance of this jewellery has been constructed, as soon as you put it on. This can be an excellent means of adopting the professional persona required for your work. The power of symbolism should be now clear to you in this respect.

Having organised yourself, your attention must now turn to your room. The table or surface on which you conduct your consultations is important as it acts as a focal point not just of your room, but your whole work. Its height should be easily accessible for you, and so for the majority of your clients. It is preferable if this is the only activity that occurs on this table, for this helps to retain the special energy and aura around it.

Size, here, does matter. Your table should be big enough to accommodate the largest of card layouts you are likely to use, without making your cards look messy or cluttered. Equally, you must take into account the size of your room, so the table does not look out of place. The typical dining table usually provides an acceptable solution, some offering the added benefit of having drop leaves which you can utilise for extra space when needed. Office desks are another option, but some may find this too official. The stability of your table is important too, as it will get kicked and knocked by both you and your client, also signalling that the prized antique table should remain as a display piece.

The chairs you and your client sit in are also important. Armchairs are not good as they do not encourage active participation and will soon leave you with backache as you strain forward to see the cards. Posture is an important consideration for you if you are likely to spend considerable time working, sometimes for long stretches of time in one day. I have found that the standard, modern office chairs are good as they allow for a reasonable posture, offer adjustable height and can move about easily. They are also cheap to buy and are usually available second-hand on searching the local newspaper adverts.

Many people choose to cover their table with a cloth, additional to that on which they lay their cards. This can be for practical and aesthetic reasons. You may want to protect the restored surface of your table (as in my case, which I mention for this being an unusually successful practice for me!) or hide any unsightly marks that will not come off. If using a cloth, check that it does not move freely as it will get pulled around during a consultation, with two people leaning on it, and it will take its contents with it. Ensure that the pattern is not a distraction from the cards. Check that the cloth does not hang too low over the edges of your table as this will make it much easier to achieve the objective, as it seems sometimes, of carrying out the trick of removing the cloth leaving the table as it was! It is all too easy for the cloth to settle under the clients, or your, foot, without noticing, then pulling everything off. Your own special cloth can easily be bought and sewn to the required size. This will also have the effect of imbuing it with your own energy, following the ancient edict of all 'magical' materials being constructed by the user.

The same applies to the cloth that you lay your cards on. You may find the perfect cloth ready-made, or you may like to decorate it yourself. It is good if this cloth is not patterned as you must be able to see all cards clearly. The silk you may wrap your cards in is not recommended to use for this purpose as it will not be heavy enough on your table and will slip about. Creating the right cloths to use can be an exciting thing to do when setting yourself up as a Tarot Therapist and lends the practice your own unique touch.

The silk cloth traditionally used to wrap cards in is chosen for the natural protective properties of this material. It is often written that black is the only colour to use for this purpose. This is so because of the ability of this colour to absorb energy that comes to it, so protecting your cards. However, I have a tendency to use a coloured silk that I feels blends well with the individual cards for each pack I work with. This, combined with the wooden box, another natural and protective substance, lends more than adequate protection for my working cards. Ready-made and many coloured options of silks are easily available in many places where cards are now sold. Having removed the thin and easily broken cardboard boxes most cards are supplied in, they can be carefully wrapped in their silk and placed in their own little wooden home for lasting protection, from both seen and unseen damage.

The range of wooden boxes available is wide, or you can obtain a blank box from a craft box and decorate it yourself. Placing a beautifully carved or painted box on your table can add to its attraction and pull the clients attention to where it needs to be for the consultation. The psychological aspect of keeping your cards in a box and silk should be mentioned here, as it shows that you have a special respect and regard for your cards. They are not left for all and sundry to play with. Rather they are set aside for this specific purpose. You should ideally treat your cards as you would your client, with care, respect and love. It is inevitable that your cards will suffer from spilt drinks and/or food, sticky child hand syndrome, if given the chance, so these measures are wise to take.

This brings me to the subject of food and drink, which can have a role to play in the consultation process. Clients may have travelled some distance to get to you and may welcome a drink, both for refreshing purposes and because it may help to relax their nerves a little. If tired the stimulus of coffee or tea may be useful (though the majority of us are too addicted to caffeine to notice its effects now). If giving the clients any kind of drink, a tip I recommend is not to fill the cup too much as this will give you more chance of not having a mess to clear up when the client kicks or knocks the table leg! You may decide that a glass of water placed on the table is enough at this stage. Water is certainly less damaging than a hot drink when spilt!

Certainly you will be doing most of the talking through the consultation and will welcome something to soothe your throat, particularly until your vocal chords get used to talking for this length of time. It can appear uncaring and rude if you have a drink available and your client does not!

Your last act prior to beginning your consultation is to ensure that you will not be disturbed by the 'phone. An answer phone is to be recommended, but if not, it is essential that the 'phone is taken off the hook, as there is a law that ensures it will ring during your consultation! A telephone for the Tarot Therapist is essential for booking clients and I advise an answering machine so that you can decide when you wish to be available for your clients. I have taken calls unwittingly from clients as early as 7 am and as late as midnight and may get little sleep without my answerphone! Once installed, I suggest however that you only turn it on when the client arrives as they may need to call you to inform you they will be a little late or to ask for directions to find you, having got lost. Lastly, if possible turn the volume on the 'phone down as there is no more distracting noise than the 'phone ringing and not knowing who it was!

It should have become clear that setting the scene for a consultation is a personal thing that the therapist must please themselves with, while trying to avoid the likelihood of causing offence to a client. The guidelines given above will hopefully make this deceptively difficult task an easier and more pleasant one. It can be a deeply satisfying experience to have created your consultation room and observe your clients reaction when they enter. Lastly here, remember that your room says much about you and reflects the way in which you work.

The colour and general decor of your room should therefore be of importance to you, though this may be dictated by the positioning and general level of light the room receives. It is obvious that you must like your room as you will spend much time there and since choice of colour is a purely individual and personal thing, it is best to choose a colour that suits you. There are esoteric ascriptions to colours that you may like to follow if you wish that are too complex to enter into here.

This lengthy diatribe is now finished but its subjects are all too often ignored at the expense of the quality of the consultation. All is then prepared and we simply sit and wait quietly the arrival of our client. This is not a time for suddenly remembered activities or for taking other 'phone calls. It is a time for relaxed patience, in which I usually sit and watch the comings and goings of the natural world outside my window, until I hear the knock at the door.

THE PRACTICALITIES OF CONSULTATIONS

The structure and format of your consultation offers further pitfalls and opportunities to enhance its delivery. In truth the consultation begins before the client arrives, as you undertake the ritual of the preparation of yourself and your room. By the time the client arrives you need to know that all is ready and waiting and you are in a calm and untroubled state.

Especially at their first meeting with you, the client may be nervous and even a little scared. If this is their first experience of the Tarot they will be unsure what is going to happen and will want and expect you to take the lead, just as you should do. The need to put the client at their ease as far as is possible is therefore paramount if you are to achieve the feat of allowing them to be open and honest about their deepest feelings, fears and thoughts, as is often necessary for the successful consultation.

This process begins with your greeting, which should be warm and friendly, without going over the top. A hand shake can be appropriate, a smile is essential, as is eye contact, indicating trust, openness and honesty. Use of their name is also recommended, especially if you work from your home, as the client may be unsure if they have the right house! This also indicates that they are expected and identified.

The question of 'how are you' as the usual opening gambit to a conversation is best left until consultation stage. Rather casual conversation about the weather or their journey to you is better suited as this takes their mind of the unknown events ahead for them and demonstrates friendliness and personability on your part. You may also discover useful information to adjust the instructions or directions you give to clients about getting to you. Perhaps strangely, this can help you appear 'normal'. First-time clients may be unsure what kind of person you are and may base their assumptions on the plentiful horror stories they have heard about weird and wonderful characters reading the Tarot in dark and dingy surroundings. That you make the same chatter as the ordinary folk in the street somehow acts as an indicator of normality and may help to remove their fears.

You will need to direct them to the room and invite them to take a seat where you wish them to be. If you take their coat from them, it should remain in the room so that they are assured nobody will interfere with it. The client may be suspicious and wary of you and your conduct and all opportunities to demonstrate openness and trust help.

Where you sit the client can have an effect on your consultation worthy of consideration. You may feel that the traditional positions of either side of a desk is too formal and create a barrier between the client and yourself, yet sitting next to the client may be too intimate and even threatening to some. Some therapists seat their client at the end of their table. This can help the client to view the cards but can make the client uncomfortable if they cannot get their legs underneath the table. It is very important that the client can view the cards, so although the practicalities of my room dictate that the client sits opposite me, I often lay the cards at right angles across the table, so that we can both see them. I also verbally inform the client they are free to pick up and examine the cards if they wish.

Sitting opposite the client does help a great deal in making eye contact easy. This can be an important means of establishing contact with the clients' deeper self or soul, allowing for your own intuitive reaction to be sourced from here. It is important to do this during your preliminary conversation, before you begin the consultation proper.

A Tarot Therapy consultation is a two way process and getting the client involved and communicating is important. This is begun by the opening conversation and asking direct but non-confrontational questions eases them into talking, preferably about themselves. Your conversation will, with experience and practice, gradually and naturally evolve to the consultation itself. The client will then not allow any nervousness or fear to well up when you pick up the cards.

Explaining to the client that they are free to examine the cards is also important in helping the client to achieve their own insights, which are often the most powerful ones. The most satisfying and rewarding consultations are often the ones in which the clients does their own interpretation, based on what they see in the cards. This is the ideal indication that you are looking for as therapist, to indicate that a realisation has occurred that itself demonstrates the beginnings of a shift and flow at the energy level of their being, where all change must originate or reach if it is to be lasting and effective.

You will require more than the direct 'what do you make of this card' approach however. Your experience and skill as a Therapist will teach you the process of outlining themes you detect in the selection of cards before you and by a process of reflection, discussion and a little of both intuition and analysis, you can arrive at the deepest layer of what the cards are saying. Tarot cards are multi-layered things and as you gradually peel off these layers through the consultation, or over several consultations, the deeper significance's uncovered do not negate those already revealed.

Wherever they sit, observe the client to ensure they appear reasonably comfortable. Observation of the client during your opening conversation also offers you the chance to learn more about them. This is again a process that comes with experience. Rather than slipping into the realms of cheating, as some may accuse you of, this is simply allowing the natural instincts we all have and use unconsciously at all times, to become conscious and mastered and used on behalf of the client, as you strive to help them as best you are able.

The opening conversation referred to here is the time for your explanation of how your work is constructed and what the consultation entails, as general guide. I ask my first-time clients if they have consulted the Tarot before, the question being appreciated, as they can then know and trust you will not assume something they are not familiar with. Your explanations should always be full at all times regardless of the clients' familiarity with the cards. Your view of any one card or cards may differ greatly from theirs, both being of value. It has been said with some justification that a good Tarot consultation should be like a lesson in learning about the cards.

This is the time for ascertaining if the client has specific themes, questions or subjects they wish to look at or perhaps giving them the option of allowing the consultation to be 'open' and letting you take the lead. Some clients prefer this and even state that they will not tell you anything as they want to see you demonstrate your psychic power, to know that you are genuine. This is the province of the fortune teller however and so a gentle explanation is required here. I inform clients that my work is different to this method and that whilst the processes of intuition are utilised and highly valued, the consultation can reach a deeper level if they are open and honest. The more information I have, the better an interpretation I can give, much the same as a full description of symptoms assists the medical doctor in their prescription.

The client should also be given the opportunity to ask any questions they may have about any aspect of the consultation before you begin working with the cards. It is impossible for you to cover everything the client may wish to know and you need to avoid sounding as if you are reciting a script for each person. Rather let the procedure be natural and flowing. The more experienced you become, the better this will sound and if you have connected to you guides or deities this will occur naturally to the necessary level. Individual clients have different concerns and questions. Some of which you will doubtless not expect or envision.

Whether your cards are removed from their box ready for use before your client arrives is another choice to make in your practice. I have found that the act of taking them out from their box and unwrapping them when the time arrives in the consultation for using them acts as an excellent focal and turning point. This indicates the preliminary conversation has finished and the cards will now be consulted. In time you may well use more than one pack in your work and consequently may not decide which ones to use until after seeing and talking to your client. This makes the decision for you. Your handling of the cards should demonstrate the value you place on them, yet be open enough to invite the client to feel comfortable enough to pick them up. Though special, they are only pieces of laminated card. It is what they represent that is sacred.

The consultation itself then follows, which although largely a matter for personal preference will benefit from some analysis of its stages and unfoldment. You will need to establish an initial process for your consultation that will then be adapted as you progress and learn more about your work. The intricacies and methods of the consultation are observed as we now witness the therapist in action.

AFTER THE CONSULTATION

Concluding the consultation can be a difficult and awkward thing if handled incorrectly or inefficiently. How long it lasts is something you may feel the need to establish at the booking stage or be clear about on your promotional literature. If you set a finite length to your consultations it is important that you stick to this, perhaps having a timer set to remind you when this has been reached. You may find that such a definite end is difficult to determine for what can often need to be an open ended process until a natural conclusion occurs. It is as well to be sure the client knows the approximate length of time the consultation is expected to last, in case they are being collected, met or have transport to catch at a certain time. You may decide to make it part of your practice to ask the client if they have to leave by a particular time.

Finishing the consultation can bring into play many of the psychological aspects of therapeutic work. Some clients will take almost open advantage of a willing nature and will continue to ask any questions they can think of to get their monies worth. In actuality this has the tendency to belittle the value placed upon what has already occurred. It is then up to you to take the lead, as you should at all times, and declare that the end has been reached. Clients always accept this as they know that you are in charge.

Experience will be the best teacher, as with so many aspects of this work. This will tell you when and how it seems appropriate to conclude the consultation. The client should again be offered the chance for questions, but do guard against simply covering ground you have already trekked across, in a different language. You may well need to repeat yourself once or perhaps twice, but if the consultation is recorded, more is a waste of both person's time and energy. A gentle prompt, referral or reminder to the client will suffice.

Do not shirk from suggesting that further large subjects require a further consultation. Again this will have become apparent as the consultation progresses but the actual stating of it can be awkward. As long as you are honest and know that you are not taking advantage of your client by trying to illicit more money from them you have no fear of reprisal in suggesting or recommending this. I try to work with the client with regard to follow-up consultations, encouraging them where possible to take responsibility for their own evolution by doing so. In the early stages, you may need to set a suitable interval between consultations yourself.

Neither should you hesitate to recommend to the client that they reach a certain stage in the development or work you have uncovered during the consultation before the next one will be effective and so appropriate. You need to guard against the possibility of the client becoming dependent on either yourself or the Tarot and here the need for effective supervision and authority becomes clear. This is an individual determination however and one that only the Therapist themselves, knowing the client as they will, can determine, Some will need close and regular consultations for a time, for others their therapy may take the form of an annual 'check-up'. Your aim as therapist should always be to encourage the client to take responsibility for their own being, development and evolution and your working practice should reflect this. By sticking to this edict, dependency will be avoided.

An awkwardness can arise in the clients actual leaving and knowing when the consultation has finished and a concluding conversation begun. You may decide that offering the client a drink does this effectively, but this can be interpreted as an invitation to stay as long as they wish and creates a potential crossing of boundaries between client and therapist. During the conversation that may follow a consultation it is important not to be drawn into further work, as it should be clear this has concluded. An excellent method of indicating this time has been reached that the client will notice is simply to shuffle your cards and put them away whilst you are exchanging concluding pleasantries. I have found this to be both subtle and effective and not likely to cause offence to the sensitive client. You can also extinguish any candle you may have burning and turn your music back on. All these are subtle and gentle ways of overcoming what can become a difficult time during your work.

Taking payment should also follow and you should have no qualms about requesting the balance of payment. You should mention that you have received a deposit and ask politely and clearly for the remaining sum. You need to be clear if you accept cheques and I recommend taking clients card number and so on, following the usual security measures in shops. If booking a further consultation, you may also need to obtain the deposit for this.

I feel that the appropriate time for payment is following the consultation. Some clients are all too eager to pay you and will present the money as soon as they sit down. You can simply lay this aside until afterwards or tell them you do not take money until after. Others will genuinely forget or will wait until you take the lead. In your dealings with money, do not be embarrassed, vague or coy. Be open, honest and polite, following a straight forward approach that is always respected by the client and this often grey area is avoided.

Remember to check that the client has all their belongings with them before they leave and perhaps ensure they are not having to walk through a dark area, putting them in a vulnerable position. When they have left you need to return to your room and finish your business.

You should take time to give thanks to any guides, deities or other beings you have invited in beforehand, whether you have been aware of them or not. This should be done simply and sincerely in your own, usual language. It can also be helpful to perform a brief relaxation, to centre and still yourself once more and adjust back to the everyday, outer world. This should not be a lengthy procedure but should be a short method of 'grounding' your life force energy back to your physical body and the world around you. Another way of achieving this is to take a drink and snack, which helps the contact at this level re-establish itself. If you have another client following this one, you will need to take time to relax and switch off, perhaps getting some fresh air to clear your head.

As we have seen, everything that happen, happens also at an energy level. The realisations and revelations that can occur during a consultation can have a powerful effect on clients. Some may react to this immediately, with others it may take some time and repeated listening to their recording before something 'clicks'. Immediate reactions may manifest in the form of tears or other emotions, which are a good indication of energy flowing and shifting, releasing what has been prevented from expression. You should not flinch from client's strong language on occasions because of this! Expressions of energy, in whatever form they take leave a residue in the surrounding area that contribute powerfully to the atmosphere in your consultation room. Regardless of whether another client is expected shortly, this needs to be cleared.

There are several methods of doing this. A mental process can be effective, by visualising any energy expressed from the client being absorbed back down into the Earth and a cleaner flow of energy coming into the room. Concentrated thought is more than adequate for this, following the esoteric principle 'energy follows thought'. Your thoughts may however be tired and unfocussed by this time and so it is good to have a physical practice of esoteric cleansing too.

The most effective method I have found for this is the Native American one of smudging. This involves a stick of twined herbs, available from many places (see Appendix 2). The herbs used vary, but sage is the most common for space clearing. An alternative is cedar, but this has a more uplifting effect than is required for these purposes. Once lit, the smoke is wafted around the room, often with the aid of a feather, but your hand will suffice. Any feather should first be held in the smoke to cleanse it and make it fit and effective for its purposes. Some like to fan smoke to the four sacred directions first too, to acknowledge their presence and power.

Beginning by the door, walk around your room, fanning the smoke as you go. Pay attention to corners as energy does tend to gather here and under tables and chairs. Return to the door and blow the smoke out from it. Lastly place the tip of the feather on the ground to 'Earth' the energy that will have accumulated in it. Extinguish the smudge stick (carefully and safely) and your job is done.

A cleansing practice of some kind is therefore required after every client, to retain the sanctity and purity of your room at the esoteric level, just as regular cleaning does the same on the physical. An alternative to smudging can be the use of Tibetan bells. These are two small bells, joined by a thread. When knocked together the vibration of the usually high pitched sound cleanses the energy. These can be sounded to the four directions, in the four corners of your room and is very pleasant and effective. Your room can then be safely left, awaiting your next client who will enter a room prepared for them and them alone.

By following this attitude, your room effectively becomes your Temple, existing at both the physical and esoteric levels. Within it you are the High Priest/ess of the Tarot. Let your conduct whilst in these hallowed walls be always worthy of this grand title

EXERCISES

The questions and exercises that follow are designed to guide you through the process of constructing your own consultation room. Obviously they cannot cover every eventuality, but will cover the general decisions and choices that must be made, as they are indicated in the main text of this Chapter. In your answers be honest with yourself, in particular for your answers to question 7.

1. Design a 'Booking Form', or write a checklist that you can use when taking bookings from clients. Include on this all the information you think you will need so that you can be sure you will not miss anything and can present a professional approach. Obtain a diary to take bookings in.

2. Write out clear and as simple directions as possible to your home or place of work, or if possible and it is easily understood, copy a map that shows where clients need to go to find you. Consider any instruction you may need to give with regard to where they may can or must park.

3. Decide how much you will charge for your consultations, based on an honest assessment of what you feel you are worth. Perhaps ask around to get an idea of the current 'going rate' in your area and fix your price based on this. Consider if you are going to operate a reduced priced policy for those on low incomes and what the reduction will be. Also consider the level of deposit you would like and whether you are willing to give the occasional free consultation if requested.

4. Decide on the maximum number of clients you feel you can truly and correctly manage to see in any one day and also per week. You may also need to decide the length your consultations are likely to take in determining this. You can then plan your preferred times when you will make yourself available to clients. If you feel it necessary, write a list of these figures.

5. Consider your own need for therapy and try to establish some means of receiving the support you feel you need, whether by way of exchanging sessions or finding a therapist you feel you can work with. In discussion with them, decide if a regular visit is required and plan for this, allocating time where necessary in your diary.

6. Look out for Introduction to Counselling courses in your area and see if you can enrol on one as part of your training for Tarot Therapy. Perhaps find a book on counselling and read this also. Adult Education classes usually run regularly.

7. Work through the following list of qualities. Give yourself a rating out of ten for each one, as an assessment of the degree to which you possess that quality. Add the figures together and divide by 16 to discover your average mark. Ask someone who knows you well to award you marks for each quality and calculate the average too. Compare the results and consider honestly what this tells you. Examine

any areas that you scored particularly low on and see why this may be so, thinking about ways you might be able to improve your rating. There is no 'average' score, but your reaction to your own average will be a good indication of whether you are aware of your need to improve or not.

Empathy, Sensitivity, Diplomacy, Objectivity, Honesty, Tact, Gentleness, Compassion, Love of people, Love of the Tarot, Intuition, Saying No, Observation, Assertiveness, Sincerity, Open-mindedness

8. What are your beliefs regarding deities and guides and do you wish to request or enlist their help in your work? Try to decide what your feelings and beliefs are in this area as you may well be asked your views by clients. If you decide you will work with such beings, try to discover and implement a regular practice of contacting them.

9. Consider beginning a regular practice of meditation if you do not do so already. At the very least practice a relaxation technique that you can utilise before you consultations and do this so it becomes familiar, easy and effective for you.

10. Examine the lighting in your consultation room and make any changes that become apparent, experimenting as indicated in the text. The same applies to candles.

11. Examine and experiment for the heating in your room in the same way.

12. Decide if you wish to use incense in your preparations and experiment to discover those fragrances you like and find beneficial.

13. Repeat the above with regard to music, remembering that you will probably wish to acquire a variety of selections over a period of time.

14. Decide if you wish to offer the facility of recording consultations and obtain the necessary equipment to do so. Carry out experiments to ensure sound levels are adequate and the set-up is as you would wish.

15. Arrange your table and chairs in the best and most pleasing way possible in your room and again experiment with different arrangements.

16. Obtain a box, silk and cloths as you decide you require for your consultations, remembering that if you decide later that you dislike your choices, changes can always be made.

17. Decide if you are going to offer your clients a drink, of what and at what stage in the proceedings. If taking drinks into your consultation room, make sure they can be placed as safely and conveniently as possible

18. Consider the necessity of an answerphone for your activities or add to your checklist a reminder to turn the 'phone down and/or take it off the hook before starting your consultation.

19. Decide on the decor and colour you would like your consultation room to be and make any changes you feel are necessary.

20. Lastly consider your own appearance and what you may like to wear to work in. Does this impart a message that you are comfortable with to your client

There is a great deal of work in these questions and exercises and some that can involve not a little expense. It is not a necessity to spend a great deal of money to become a Tarot Therapist and many items can be purchased cheaply with a little thought and effort Any initial expense now can save unexpected payment later and do bear in mind that I have tried to list as many possibilities as I can think of, from my own experience. You may well not need them all. You should also take as long as you need to get things as far as possible the way you want them to be and spread any cost out. All this will help to add to the professionalism of your set-up and in the long run make you feel good about what you do.

CHAPTER 8 - THE THERAPIST IN ACTION

The complexities of the Tarot Therapy consultation demand some exploration, prior to an analysis of the cards themselves, which constitute Volumes 2 and 3. This volume concerns itself with the theory of Tarot Therapy, giving the practice over to the other two books.

It is impossible however, to cover every eventually and nuance that may occur during a Tarot consultation. As has been stated before, it is an individual process, wherein the characteristics and foibles of both therapist and client dictate how it is carried out. Despite this, some guidance and suggestions can be given that will hopefully provoke an inquiring attitude amongst potential therapists so that they are motivated to explore and discover the most appropriate approach for them. As before, the suggestions given are done so in a spirit of openness and encouragement, rather than any attempt to instigate laws or rules. In this and the previous chapter, I write from the perspective of my own experience, as both therapist and client.

COUNSELLING

As has been previously mentioned, the methods of counselling have more of a role to play in the work of Tarot Therapy than the fortune tellers predictions. Here we enter a vast array of differing approaches, traditions and genres, each offering something that contributes to this vast field. It is certainly not my intention to dissect and explore this, as it is too large to do so here, has been done before anyway and I am not sufficiently qualified to do so. What can be done however is to illustrate the basic areas and techniques used in some counselling methods that may be of benefit to the aspiring Tarot Therapist. This does not constitute a substitute for official and recognised training and it is recommended that the reader pursue this as a part of their training for Tarot Therapy.

It should be made equally clear that Tarot Therapy is not simply counselling with a few cards being selected in addition. Counselling is a specific approach, as is Tarot Therapy, the two differing in their tools and methods. The one may influence the other but the distinction is clear. We have seen that the Tarot is formed from the very structure of life itself and as such concerns itself with matters of this nature. Its view of the human being is therefore of this inclusive nature, using the holistic paradigm as its basis. The outworking of this way of using the Tarot is by nature a holistic one too, that embraces the concept of instinct, intuition and spirituality as a part of that holism. Counselling sets no such precepts. As the Libran I am, in the interests of peace-making, I would point out I am not trying to infer in any way that any of these is better than the other.

One of the keys to be aware of here is communication and all that it implies and entails for us as human beings. Communication can justifiably be seen as the art of counselling. The word itself implies an exchange of information, but in reality is much more than that. A Tarot Therapy consultation relies on effective communication for its success, however this is measured.

We cannot rely or expect the communication we receive from the client to be exactly what we would wish, by way of a step by step guide through their difficulties. It may well be that problems with communication in some form are what have necessitated their coming to us in the first place. For all of us, when we are in the middle of any problem or situation we find troublesome, we find it difficult to express the crux of the matter to another. If we can achieve this we are able to share the essence of our problem and something of ourselves. This is a deeply moving moment and one that opens the door to healing, through the expression that takes place.

Remembering that we are dealing with the energy level of reality as we know it, the expression of what we think and feel, as the continual flow of that energy is vital to our well-being. The alternative is to become stagnant, polluted and eventually physically ill, as the only remaining form of expression available to the energy. By instigating a new communication both to and ideally from the client, the Tarot Therapist is able to offer the client the opportunity to realise anew their need for release.

Skill in communication, perhaps employing some of the methods used in counselling can therefore be a powerful spoke in the wheel of Tarot Therapy. Effective communication requires some exploration of our motivation to listen to the client, listening being seen as a participatory event, as opposed to simply sitting and waiting while the client talks.

Listening is therefore active and there can be many blockages to its successful action. The majority of these stem from a desire to fulfil our own needs, rather than those of the client. Looking at what listening is not can tell us much about what it is. As Tarot Therapists we do not listen because it helps the client to like us or to ensure that the risk of our being rejected is lessened. The therapist must be bigger than their personal feelings in a consultation and the clients' right to reject what we say must be respected and accepted.

In listening to the client we hear everything they say, rather than focussing only on one aspect we happen to understand. This means that we do not seize on a weakness we might spot in their 'argument' or presentation, then triumphantly explain why this is wrong. Like the proverbial customer, the client is never 'wrong'. There is no room for manipulating the client to ensure we get the response we would like to see, to make our job easier and make us feel good or get us out of a difficult question. When asked why others had acted badly towards a client of mine, when they had only been positive towards them, the response I gave was a sympathetic 'shit happens', indicating that sometimes there are no reasons or explanations we can give, no matter how good a therapist or how enlightened we are.

We do not therefore, try to be 'nice' or anything other than what we are, simply listening and responding as seems appropriate to what we have heard. Being distanced gives the therapist the ability to remain cool and reflective to the client, whilst trying to show them that you understand, respect and support their position, whatever this may be and together try to find ways to help them. It is at this stage that the Tarot enables a quantum leap to be taken away from and above that of counselling. The Tarot brings us to an awareness of the energy that the client needs to express and it is this level that it is essential to reach. The difference is energy!

We are required to allow the client to take the time that they need to communicate in the way they choose. In doing so we should not prepare our next comment in advance, since this may be usurped before we get to speak and no longer be appropriate or relevant. Neither do we pre-empt what we believe is going to be said and interrupt on this basis. If you feel the client is simply repeating themselves however, there is certainly merit in pointing this out and directing them to consider why this may be so, but always without butting in, which is not conducive to or part of effective communication.

Listening means just that, hearing what is being said, then responding. We listen fully and try to indicate that we are doing so. This is achieved through the body language we impart, that should also be observed from the client. As an aspiring Tarot Therapist you will need to observe the posture you naturally adopt when seated at a desk or table, as this can be an unconscious process that may well give off the wrong messages to the client.

There is no 'correct' posture of course this again being a matter for personal preference. The value of clear eye contact cannot be underestimated, not only because in the traditional view it helps to identify with the client, show them our honesty and become close to them, but because the eyes are truly the window to the soul. When we look into someone's eyes and communicate with them we can speak directly to the soul, as well as hear from them at that level. Since in Tarot Therapy we are attempting to access and cause changes at this level of reality and the clients being and reality, eye contact should be made and continued through the consultation. This is not done in a deliberate or forced way however, for if we are open and honest, dedicating ourselves to our work and the client before us, the tendency and instinctual urge will be to connect with them in this way regardless. Experience will allow the good therapist to 'go with the flow' of this and the many other processes that constitute the Tarot Therapy session.

Our body language reveals much about us and communicates with the client at a level that is arguably more important than what we consciously put across. Folded arms or tapping fingers are two obvious ways to demonstrate you are not actively listening, but the angle at which we sit can give just as powerful an indication. Try to remain reasonably upright through your consultations! If you are truly involved in what the client is saying and doing your body language will take care of itself.

Humour in a consultation can also be a difficult area, for what one finds amusing another does not. The main edict here is to ensure that you are laughing with and not at the client. Pointing out the humour in a situation that the client may not be aware of, since our observation is very different from the centre of a difficult situation than on the therapeutic side-line, can be a helpful and welcome relief however. This will need to be done gently and sensitively when appropriate.

If we get it wrong, we have not failed. As Tarot Therapists it is important that we dare to be wrong, allowing ourselves the freedom of following our intuitive urges and instincts. When we are correctly and fully connected to our guides or sources of information, including our own beings. Our flow of energy ensures that what we say and do is largely correct. This demands that our own lives and selves are taken care of, but there will be times when matters must remain unresolved until after a consultation. If we do not feel we can carry out a consultation effectively, it should be postponed. This may be rare for the practice of professionalism will enable us in most cases to obtain the objectivity required. However there are always occasions when we are not quite as good, however this is measured, as we know we can be. At such times we should not reproach ourselves for being wrong, but should have the strength to admit this and communicate it as necessary. It may be that by doing so you feel that you cannot charge the client or that you suggest they return at another time.

Prejudice has been responsible for many wrong doings in our history. Each of us has our prejudices, some at a collective level, endemic to our society or country, others instigated by our upbringing and family, with still others formed by our opinions and judgements, based on our own experience. Whilst we cannot hope to remove all prejudice from our feelings, thoughts, speech and actions, we can at the very least attempt to become aware of them, in so doing taking some notable steps to preventing their adversely influencing our work as a therapist. An exercise is included at the end of this Chapter to help you in this task.

Possibly one of the greatest strengths and abilities available to every therapist, whatever the tools of their trade, is that of empathy. This difficult to define but powerful trait lends a support to the client that can be everything from the prop they require to literally, get themselves back on their feet, to the feeling that there is just one other person in the world that knows how they feel. Empathy helps the client via the old adage of a problem shared being a problem halved. This does not mean that you take the burden of the problem for them, but that you understand and identify with it, thereby acknowledging and supporting them with it.

The 'ability' or technique of empathy demonstrates to the client that you are alongside them, sharing their changing patterns through a situation from moment to moment. Once achieved the collective identity of empathy enables a stronger energy to be focussed towards the core of the problem or situation that the client faces, since the 'forces' of both client and therapist are united through it. Empathy can be viewed as the goal of the therapist, from where the last push to the finishing line can be taken hand in hand with the client.

The achievement of empathy with the client depends to a large degree on the personalities of both parties and the subtle interplay between them, which however objective one or other is being, cannot be ignored. Usually, the client will have been or is being, subject to their feelings in regard to their difficulty. As therapist and with the clear and essential aid of the Tarot, we can help them to recognise what those feelings are, if necessary exploring what their sources are and the reason for them. Once identified in this manner, the client is gently encouraged to allow their feelings to surface, empathising with the pain this may bring with it. Such repressed or suppressed feelings are allowed final release and expression, in turn letting the energy that trapped them go too. The client is able to take a deep breath and move forward as the energy dissipates from around their being. The new energy, that of their potential future, is then attracted and so they move forward.

CONSULTATION PROCEDURES

We have examined the preparation for a consultation and seen something of its process, as well as what is required after its conclusion. We now turn our attention to the consultation itself, beginning at the point at which it begins properly, in the sense of the cards being consulted, after any opening conversation and preliminaries have taken place.

This switch can be a tricky one to make for it is easy for an hour or more to pass in background conversation, it being unclear what constitutes the consultation itself. The principles of counselling tell us that everything that is discussed once the client is present forms part of the consultation and bearing this in mind you may wish to begin recording the session from its very beginnings. This may seem unnecessary, but you may not realise the significance of what is said until later in the consultation and the client may come to value having this to hear again in this context. This can also be a good indication that you have moved from chat to consultation.

Another method of achieving this awareness, for both therapist and client, is the time when you reach for your cards. Taking them out of their box or cloth indicates this very well without being showy or obvious about it and can be done while conversation continues. If you already have your cards out of their container, you may decide to pick them up and start shuffling them. I usually do this while the client and I continue to talk and often use this time to explain the methods of reading the cards that I utilise.

Shuffling the cards also demonstrates to the client that there is no possibility of certain cards appearing and that their selection is random. Should the client be nervous or apprehensive of the cards or the Tarot in general, as a surprising number are (due largely to the misrepresentation that has occurred concerning them) a good tip is to shuffle them by dealing them out into three piles, face up. Continue to talk to the client while you do so and leave the client to take the chance of having a look at the cards, familiarising themselves with them a little before the important act of making their choice comes.

How long you take to shuffle your cards is entirely up to you. Some feel that once or twice is enough, while others shuffle habitually, without even noticing they are doing so, in which category I now fall, after years of practice. Your shuffling ability will need to be practised, which can be done while watching television. You should appear confident and capable in handling your cards. The majority of Tarot cards are bigger than playing cards, to which you may be used, so your hands will need to adjust to shuffling bigger cards. Different packs have different sizes and you should be adept with every pack you use.

Your client will usually comment that they are too big and have difficulty if they shuffle them which is another choice you must make for your consultation process. This is not a necessity, for there are no rules to follow. The advantage in letting the client handle your cards to shuffle lies in getting them involved, indicating trust towards them and offering further proof of randomisation of choice. The disadvantage can be in their being dropped on the floor, risking damage, increasing your feeling of losing their sanctity and generally being handled roughly or without the respect you give them. The choice is yours to make.

My own practice that has evolved now involves my shuffling the cards, then spreading them out in a horizontal line, face down, for the client to make their selection from. This offers a middle ground between the above polarities. The client has the whole pack at their disposal and I simply leave them to select as they wish. Some hold their hand over the pack, waiting for a feeling, intuition or energy reaction that tells them which card to choose. They can shuffle them on the table if they wish, but do not have to pick them up to do so.

At this point I turn off any music playing and remain silent. Some clients expect you to be silent while they choose their cards as they recognise the importance of this act. If they follow the 'sensitive' method of selection outlined above, they may desire silence to do so, in order to concentrate.

They may talk, perhaps nervously, to which you should of course respond. Allow them as much time as they wish to make their choice and for this part of the consultation, let them take the lead.

Of course how many cards they choose is dependent on what you are doing in the consultation and your choice of 'spread' (another disagreeable term!). This in is turn dependent on the question you are answering or subject you are dealing with. It may be that you have no question or subject and are giving a more general consultation. The client should be given the option of setting any subject area prior to the cards being dealt.

Some clients have a definite and set agenda they present and have no wish to explore anything outside of this, despite what you may discover during the consultation. You may feel most strongly as their therapist that a certain issue is being presented by the cards, but you must respect the clients' wishes and need not to face this at that time. It may be that simply by making mention of it the client is fuelled enough to spend time considering it, then dealing with it further at your next consultation. In this respect you should always be 'client-led' in your work.

The opposite extreme to the rigid one above is the client having no idea why they have come. It may be somebody else booked for them and they have simply come to please their well-meaning friend. You may have received or sensed some information during your preparatory meditation, or all may be a blank for you, even while you deal the cards. In this case you are acting blind, with no leads to follow or target to aim at. Though this can appear daunting, it does offer the Tarot the full scope and chance to speak, communicating what it will.

In giving the client chance to dictate any subjects or questions, the option of no questions should also be given. Many will choose this path, thinking that your psychism will be tested appropriately to see if you come out with what is on their mind. In Tarot Therapy, it is different, of course. If setting no subjects or questions I usually explain that this gives the Tarot the chance to focus on what is most important at that time, which is often not what we consider to be most important. The many veiled and secret levels and layers of the human being we have created as we live our lives is a many splendoured beast and one which is full of tricks and deviousness to make life more pleasant and easy. The avoidance of pain and suffering is one of the many games played to prevent the hard work of progressive evolution we all must achieve at some point.

If your client gives you a specific question or subject area, the cards chosen should be interpreted in the light of this, which can give some limitations to what you can deduce from it. You may notice something apparently unrelated to what the client has asked, but that to you seems important nonetheless. At any point in the consultation, it is the clients' choice to accept or reject what you say and this applies here too. It is perhaps best simply to mention what you have seen, as an addition to the consultation and judge by the clients' reaction whether it is appropriate to continue down this avenue.

Since adjusting my work with the Tarot to the therapeutic approach, I have found that there is usually a good reason why the client has been prompted to book, bothered to send a deposit and motivated enough to turn up, even on the coldest, wettest night. They may well not be aware of this reason and often nor am I, until the end of the consultation or after it, but I work with the assumption that there is one, in particular when the client does not have pre-determined areas they wish to look at. This may not be the case in subsequent consultations, but is certainly my preferred scenario for the first time I work with a client.

Taking this underlying theme and working with it can be the key to a powerfully transformative session, primarily of course for the client, but also for the therapist. The fulfilment and satisfaction that results from this work must be experienced, for is beyond descriptive speech. It is an act of sacrifice and service with the paradox of offering a reward that motivates you to continue. It cannot be manufactured and is usually spontaneous and often unexpected. It is for me, something of the essence of poetry and all beauty in the world. It is a humbling experience to witness what can be a major turning point in somebody's life that they will look back on as a pivotal moment. Such times are sacred and prized in the memory.

It has been said that those of us who choose the path of the therapist do so really because this is what they need for themselves. I have found that clients come to me presenting similar areas, difficulties or themes over any one period of time. It has often been only when I realised that I had a similar need or difficulty and begin to listen myself to what is being said in a consultation that things have shifted, both for the client and myself. This synchronous process is a mysterious one but does show us the need for continual observation, supervision and therapy for the therapist.

By offering the Tarot the full range of its ability, depth and meaning by setting no questions, restriction of interpretation is removed. Any one Tarot card has many different possible interpretations and the permutations offered by the different combinations possible are beyond number. Having a 'blank sheet' presented to the therapist by the client opting for the general consultation affords the chance for anything and everything to appear. This process of consultation, as a two way one between therapist and client ensures that what is most relevant and significant will be what is eventually focussed and acted upon.

The only possible method of teaching the intricacies of Tarot Therapy, in particular this aspect of the work, is on a personal basis. The pages of a book offer the optimum chance to explore and outline the theory, but the actual practice, being a thing of some subtlety when it comes to card interpretation, must happen on a personal basis. It therefore requires a tutor to be present with the aspiring therapist, who is then left to practice what they have learnt on willing, 'would-be' clients. I have attempted to give what guidance I can for use in consultations, but there can be no substitute for your own practice and experience.

The same is true of the actual meanings you give to each card. These are the subjects of volumes 2 and 3 of this work, for the Major and Minor Arcanas respectively but a brief note is relevant here. The analysis of the cards I will present in those volumes will not include a section that tells what each card means and what to say when it occurs in a consultation. Rather by dissecting the card, examining its symbolism, mythological and other associations and its cultural context we shall discover the ideas, themes and relevance it has. From this analysis, you will be directed through the use of exercises and questions, to arrive at your own interpretation of each card.

This may be a unique one, drastically different from any that has preceded it. There are no rules or laws that direct you to say what a card must mean. Your interpretation can and should be based on your own assessment and judgement, which will arise from your own character and experience, both from your current and previous lives, your soul and conscious and unconscious mind; in short your whole being. In Tarot Therapy card meanings are personal things, often unique to the therapist.

Even then, the interpretation you give to each card forms but the basis or skeleton around which additional meaning and understanding is given for each client for whom it appears in a consultation. It is as well to record occurrences and further meanings you discover for each card as you go, as some may well be profound and need to be shared with others and at the very least recorded so you do not forget. It has long been a vision of mine to see a specialist magazine on the

Tarot in existence and the above process may give rise to some excellent articles!

So the massive permutations possible from a single card become clear when we realise its own multi-layered structure, which is then combined with the additional permutations possible from the cards it is selected with in any one consultation. Clients are also individuals of course and it is true to say that an identical set of cards chosen in consecutive consultations with the same therapist would result in different things being said.

The workings of intuition are our best explanation for this strange seeming phenomena that is surprisingly frequently queried. The power of symbolism as we understand it now, has revealed to us the way in which the human eye is led towards a certain aspect of any one card in a consultation, or towards one figure, colour and so on. When we are open to allow ourselves to be led by the cards in this manner, letting the workings of our instinct and intuition guide us, we find that subtle but powerful differences emerge in our interpretations of cards from one moment to the next. This also reveals the necessity for a clear and direct connection to be made with our source of guidance and inspiration before a consultation.

Constructing your interpretation for the cards is a long and ongoing process that demands a great deal of work. It is something that can never be mastered, because like ourselves, the cards are constantly adapting to the changing times and society we create. This amazing ability, leaving the Tarot as true today as it has always been, shows that the Tarot acts as an excellent reflector for the collective and individual conduct of humanity. As we have seen, it is this that makes it such a powerful and useful therapeutic tool. As we uncover more of ourselves and the Universe of, which we are a part and live in, so we can learn to relate to the Tarot in new ways, learning more about what is encapsulated in each individual card and the pack as a whole. There can therefore be no such thing as an expert on the Tarot, only those with work in progress. Each time you use your cards you are contributing to the sum total not only of what the Tarot is, but of what it says about the human race. This deserves our highest respect and conduct.

Just as the process of interpreting cards is a personal one, so is the means by which you arrange your work. This applies to the majority of the different aspects of a consultation. Having dealt with the preparation for and examined the dynamics of interpretation, we now turn our attention to the actual laying down of the cards. As with the other portions of the consultation process we have seen, there are different options from which to choose, both in terms of the actual cards you work with and the way in which you do so. This brings us to the matter of dealing the cards.

Much has been written concerning the ascription of two distinct meanings to each card, being indicated by which way up the card faces when it is dealt. The idea here is usually to interpret the card as being 'reversed' or negated when it is dealt the wrong way up, as it faces the 'reader'. The implication of this procedure is that the original meaning of the card, given when it faces the correct way, is changed to the negative view of this interpretation. This means that the client is subject to such a negative force as is described by that particular card.

Such negativism has no place in therapeutic working. The use of reversed cards assumes that the meaning of the card is distinctly positive or negative, dependent on how it is dealt. Reminding ourselves that the cards are acting as a reflection of the client and their life, we are implying that they are under an entirely positive or negative influence from the realm of that card in its area of influence. My experience has been that life is very rarely, if ever, all good or all bad. There is usually never one without the other, such is the polarity of our world and all things in it. For me, this negates the need for reversed cards, giving us instead one central, basic interpretation to each card that encompasses all its aspects, range and possibilities. Some, or even just one of these may apply to any individual in a consultation, as determined by both therapist and client.

In addition, if we are saying that a card is positive or negative, we are implying that this is a clear influence on the client that they are subject to. This contains a deference that the client is the weaker of these forces, when the purpose of a therapeutic consultation should be to encourage self-responsibility and control of the client's life with the suggestion that they are the ones that can shape and dictate the forces and energies that shape their lives.

I feel too that those artists and creative souls who create Tarot cards work hard and with definite purpose in heart and mind to express a concept for each card, usually with great care and attention to detail. Everything that is on a Tarot card should be there for a specific reason. To then turn the card upside down so we cannot see it correctly or clearly seems at the least an insult to the creator of each work and at the most an insult to the Tarot itself (and therefore the sanctity of life), since each card is a part of the life of the Universe that the pack represents. We have also seen the necessity, power and importance of allowing symbols to do their work by making association with and between them as we observe the spread of cards before us. This is lost if the card is upside down.

If however you choose to utilise the double meanings associated with reversed cards, as you are completely free to do, I urge care in your method of dealing cards. You will obviously need to shuffle the cards in such a manner as to ensure that they are turned on their heads occasionally, in order to offer full possibility to which way each card faces. When dealing out cards to your table, if you hold them in your hands to do so, you will need to ensure that you turn them over by the sides rather than the end as this immediately reverses which way the card faces, making something of a mockery of the point of reversed cards.

On the subject of negativism, we must always be sure we are not slipping into the dark traps that can beset the pressured therapist in their work. Whilst the difficult and negative areas of the cards should not be ignored or even diminished to give the client false hope, we need to approach their situations with a positive intent, so as to create the same in them. It is surprisingly easy to sound negative about something you have identified when faced with a client that is all too aware of the hardship they are dealing with. Indeed it is for this very reason that a positively aligned therapist is necessary. The need for separation from the therapists own problems is also made clear here.

Should it become apparent that the client faces a difficult struggle to turn a situation around or achieve their stated aims, this should not be avoided but ways sought out by which the client can best help themselves and you can be of best use to them through the time of the consultation.

The subject of the forces and energies that we are subject to brings us to the area of fate and destiny. This is something about which much controversy rages, especially amongst those active in this field. Whatever you decide is your view it is important in your work as a Tarot Therapist that you neither impose it on your clients nor allow it to restrict the interpretation possibilities of the cards. Clarity of opinion is required, as the client may ask you for an explanation, since this is a related area and they may expect you to know all there is to know.

When asked it is best to give a brief explanation of your view, but be clear that this is your opinion only and has no relevance to the consultation. The same may apply to other related subjects, in particular that of astrology. There are many and close relationships possible to draw between the stars and the cards, which it is helpful and useful to be aware of in your work as a Tarot Therapist, but this does mean that you must or need be an astrologer or have a need to know the details of your clients birth chart. It may be that you choose to gain a qualification in this subject and combine it with your Tarot Therapy work (an aspect covered in the next Chapter), but unless holding or working towards an appropriate qualification, it is not advisable to use knowledge of other subjects in your work.

The subject of fate and destiny returns us to the area of future prediction and its place in Tarot Therapy. In the past the Tarot has concerned itself greatly with the nature and workings of the past and the future. When we use the Tarot correctly, we are accessing a level of reality which is beyond time as we know and experience it, in a liner fashion. This system of organising one second after another, one minute following the last, one hour after the last and so on is unique to our Earth level of life. Our intrepid and growing number of space explorers find that Earth time moves slower for them at their higher altitude. At a higher level of life, that can now be scientifically labelled as the quantum one, time per se, does not exist. At this non-physical realm, there is existence and in that moment of existence all is present in each moment.

When we open ourselves to this aspect of reality, through means such as meditation and/or the Tarot, we can obtain information that tells us about the past and the future. The Tarot Therapist however, must bear in mind that this information is true only for the time at which it is obtained and is subject to change determined by the emotions and thoughts of the client on whose behalf it is obtained. The result of this truth is that when we predict futures, we are seeing only one possible future of many.

This should be made clear to the client, in addition to the edict contained in the Code of Ethics, Conduct and Principles that declares we must consider if such knowledge is in the best interest of the client for them to have. Whilst it is advantageous and helpful for the clarity of our work to be definite about our own views regarding fate and destiny, we must work within the confines of this flexible view with regard to the future we may predict for the client. Therapeutic work involves assisting the client to (re)gain control and command over themselves and their lives, encouraging them to fashion it as they would wish and in the most positive way for them. Ultimately this means we help them decide their own fate and destiny; we help them to help themselves.

We are now faced with a choice of 78 cards from which we must make a determination regarding our client. We have previously dissected the pack to examine its component parts, these being firstly two halves, one of which is further sub-divided into four quarters. Though we have seen that the complete pack is whole and inter-dependent, the option of utilising only one or more parts of the whole in a consultation is open to us.

Throughout this work I have stressed the unity of the whole pack and emphasised the relationships that exist between the Elements on which they are based. For this reason I would suggest and recommend that the whole pack be used for Tarot Therapy. Many previous Tarot practitioners have suggested that it is possible to split the pack so as to use, for example, the suit of Cups when answering a question regarding emotions, or Swords for a mental based question, Rods for career related subjects and Pentacles for those concerning money, with the possible addition of the Major Arcana or any one other suit should it seem appropriate.

To divide the Tarot firstly represents a split in the view and approach to life the therapist has. Just as life is not wholly positive or negative at any one time, so it is very difficult to compartmentalise the clients life into distinct areas of money, work, emotions and thoughts. Part of the positive and successful life is to integrate it towards a wholeness of expression and action, based on an understanding of the way in which one area effects all the others. In Tarot

Therapy a holistic approach is required, that necessitates the whole pack be used, so as to ensure no aspect of the client or their life is being neglected.

Should it be revealed by a selection of cards that there is a predominance of, say emotional considerations affecting the client, this will become apparent from the number of Cups cards they select. This may require further investigation, which is best achieved by examining the cards chosen in the light of this information. It is this process that allows for the deeper and sometimes hidden layers of the cards to be revealed and one that shows the power an effective consultation can have.

When beginning your interpretation a good place to begin is a brief overview of the cards selected. This requires some swift addition and careful observation. You should note the number of cards present from each suit and the Major Arcana as well as the numbers of the cards, seeing if any number is duplicated, tripled or vary rarely, quadrupled. If so, this will indicate more power and energy being active and received by the client in the area covered by that suit or number.

You should also look for progressions of numbers and noteworthy multiplications, such as 3, 6 and 9, a most powerful and welcome conjunction in the light of the energy of the number 3. Aces can be particularly important as they can indicate turning points, moments of crisis, catharsis or catalyst that the client may need to know about. What follows and precedes the Ace is therefore important and needs to be addressed.

Equally a repetition of 10's implies the end of a phase for the client or reaching a point at which something must and needs to give way. Preceding cards will again point the means by which this can occur and the following cards the release and direction that can follow.

The cards that surround the Major Arcana cards are also significant as they indicate how the deeper aspects of these cards are being worked out in the everyday aspect of the client and their life. Recall the analogy here of the Major Arcana being the puppet moved by the strings of the Minor Arcana.

These intricacies also add weight to the necessity of the presence of the whole pack to choose from in a consultation to allow for the accuracy to be made and for the links to be constructed. It is a favourite saying of mine that the 'art' of interpreting the Tarot lies not in knowing what individual cards mean but in forging, observing and then explaining the links between them. It is how the cards relate to each other that creates the story that forms a consultation. The chief players and characters in the story can be met and known intimately by discussion, sometimes using some carefully phrased questioning on the part of the therapist. Each card is a chapter in your story and by following this analogy to its conclusion, of which I am fond, you can view yourself as presenting to the client part of the story of their life when you hand them their tape at the end of the consultation.

Explanation of card meaning and interpretation is a difficult art, again taking experience to gain confidence and surety in. One way in which sometimes obscure sounding ideas and principles can be made clearer to the client is to use experiences and stories from your own life. However there are dangers involved in this practice of which you should be aware.

The client has not come to hear you talk about yourself, no matter how amusing or apt you feel your story to be, or how strong an impact it has had on you. Whilst illustrations of this kind can be good adjuncts to the investigation of a particular card, remember that it is how it relates to the client that is important. You will also need to take care that you do not give away the identity of anyone involved in your story, as it may just be someone your client knows and an embarrassing or difficult situation may result. It can be a remarkably small world!

Another potential mine set to disarm the therapist is the use of significators in traditional Tarot reading. The significator is a card pre-selected from the pack, most often a Court card, to represent your client. Which card is used is dependent on the sex, age and appearance of the client, amongst other possible sources. This card is then placed down beside any spread you may be using. The exact reason for this is unclear, unless the client is not physically present. If the client is with you, it seems a strange policy to select a card to represent them when you have the real thing but a couple of feet away!

Though sounding facetious, this is a serious point, but one that does offer an opportunity to use the method but in a different and arguably more therapeutic manner. If I am using a constructed layout, I often place the first card chosen by the client, for this purpose, where a significator would traditionally have gone. It is then referred to as the Theme Card. It is taken as showing us the overall and genuine theme prevalent to the clients' subject or question, which is the only time I use such layouts. It is stressed that this is not any more or less powerful or important than any other card in their selection, but gives us a starting point from where we can lead with purpose and intent into the main body of the layout.

It is an interesting addition to this process to note that since its influence is seen as covering the whole of the layout, it is often referred to again once the main body of cards has been dealt with and re-examined in the light of what has been uncovered. This often shows a new and as yet undisclosed aspect to the subject at hand. You may well find that the theme with which you began has changed greatly by the time you have finished, since the nature of Tarot Therapy is to allow an organic process to occur in consultations that leads you down an unknown path often in the dark. You are accompanied by the best of guides in the Tarot however, with the light given by the client to help you in this respect.

Coming at last to the actual consultation of the cards, there are two basic divisions we can make. First, we can work with a pre-determined 'spread' or 'layout' as is preferred and second, we can work without any arrangement or layout at all. Both will be examined so that you are empowered to make your own choices. An open approach is recommended, so that you are able to use the method of approach you feel is most appropriate for each individual that is your client. This may differ from consultation to consultation, the flexibility for which should be retained.

WORKING WITHOUT CARD LAYOUTS

Since it has become my preference and usual practice to work without the aid of the 'safety net' of the calculated layout in recent times, I will begin with an exploration of this method, which I feel is best suited to Tarot Therapy. The reasons why require some explanation which will follow but first an outline of the method.

Traditionally, the client will have shuffled the pack and returned them to the reader, who then deals out from the top the required number of cards for the 'spread' they are using. In Tarot Therapy a more open approach is required, to allow for the full range of possibilities and interpretations to occur. As previously explained this method is preferred largely because it provides for the necessity of drawing forth deeper and often hidden, unresolved areas of the client and their life.

The process used is one that is very simple but very effective. Whatever methods of shuffling chosen having been employed, the pack is fanned out across the table, face down and the client is simply invited to select as many cards as they wish for their consultation. This is an initial selection only, having the option of adding to these cards as becomes necessary through the consultation.

The majority of clients choose between 3 and 10 cards, though you may finish with more than this number of course. Some clients will demonstrate a certain reluctance or nervousness, which can indicate their approach to their current situation. The manner in which they choose the cards can reveal much about them and is worth observing, as should all aspects of their conduct and behaviour throughout the consultation.

Those clients that draw their cards without hesitation, drama, speech or apparent thought usually have a direct and straight forward approach to life and will require a solution to their predicament that reflects this. The cards selected will confirm this and dictate the style of the consultation for you, if you allow yourself to be led intuitively.

In contrast, other clients will question the process, requesting confirmation of how many they should choose, ask how many most people choose, nervously push just one or two cards forward a little from the fan and then ask you if that is OK. Neither approach is better than the other, they are simply different and indicate differences in the character and current state of the individual. In this case, the client is likely to need a sensitive approach to their situation or problem, requiring reassurance and encouragement in 'facing and embracing' it.

Most clients will fall somewhere between these extremes and will utilise many and varied, sometimes intriguing methods of selecting their cards. What follows the selection method is the procedure of interpreting the cards and uncovering their relevance to the client, their life, circumstances and any question they have set. This 'open' method of consulting the cards is suited both to working with or without specific questions or subject areas.

Whether working with or without these guidelines, the overall selection of cards should first be examined, as explained previously noticing the number of cards from each suit, duplication of numbers, Major Arcana cards and so on. Another relevant aspect at this point can be which cards have not been selected, as much as those before you. The significance of all this analysis will be affected to a large degree by the number of cards chosen in the first place, but this will become apparent as you proceed.

Should the client have no cards from any one suit, this often indicates a lack of involvement from the area governing that suit. By example, should there be no Swords cards, the client may not be considering their situation from a mental level, operating perhaps solely from their emotions. Many people can be divided into one of two groups, a huge generalisation, being those that operate predominantly from the heart and those that work from the head. The preferred approach is one that utilises both, thereby arriving at a more intuitive and balanced perspective.

My experience is that clients' card selections show you which group they are currently in, as it can change according to their need to respond differently to different situations. Given that a balanced approach is the one that will lead them towards a balanced and more truthful solution or means or progression, pointing out the suit or portion of the pack that is missing can play an important part in a consultation. This method provides a subtle yet effective means of drawing the clients' attention back to what they may have chosen to ignore, often unconsciously, or be unaware of. The realisation that can result from this awareness can be enough by itself to bring about the shift of energy spoken of before and which is one of the main aims of a Tarot Therapy consultation.

The absence of any one suit indicates the absence of attention towards that area or an attempt to proceed without its inclusion. A lack of Rods cards can show that the client is attempting to force themselves to do something that their heart is not in, in the sense of having little or no real motivation to do so, as they have no real contact with the subject in their soul or spirit, this being the realm of Rods. Far better then, to examine what their true motivation is and explore the possibilities of this together.

An absence of Pentacles cards can often show the client who is unable or unwilling to act, preferring instead to be making plans or be the emotional dreamer, the preferences for which will be shown by the number of Swords or Cups cards in their selection. They may be the person who has plans and ideas but lacks the organisation or willpower to see them through, so this may be the area you can focus on together in the consultation. It becomes clear here that in all your work, the aim is to restore the client to a wholeness that begets the completion of their expression of who and what they are, within themselves in their character and persona and without themselves in their life and its tasks.

An absence of Major Arcana cards is also relevant, but indicating that a different focus to your consultation is required. The Major Arcana cards chosen in a consultation will indicate the deepest level and underlying concept to the client and their current predicament, problem or need that they must focus on. They may or may not be aware of this and it can be part of your task as therapist to gently draw them to an awareness of this, using the art of interpretation combined with your tact and skill in communication. Once outlined, the realisation of the meaning and relevance of the Major Arcana cards in a clients' spread can trigger them to a hitherto unobserved awareness of their difficulty. This alone can also provide the shift required to give them their solution that may have eluded them for so long, such is the power and ability of the Tarot.

Should there be no Major Arcana cards in their initial selection, the tendency indicated is that the client is refusing to acknowledge or accept the truth of their situation or they have taken a (possibly unconscious) decision to ignore what they know to be true. My experience has often been that at the close of a consultation the client comments that it has provided a confirmation for them of things that they sensed were probably true but could not consciously access or admit. Having the Tarot put it into words or just images for them that they could relate to has helped them to a place of realisation and so energy shift. The rest, as they say, is easy. Such a comment or conclusion is a good indication to me that the work of the consultation has been achieved. What remains is a matter for the client to put into practice what has been learnt or realised, but even here the Tarot can help those clients who may still have some uncertainty. An examination of the Pentacles cards, with others, will point the way towards the best path of action.

Major Arcana cards point out the deeper themes and causes of the point of attention for the client. Should there be none, the task is to discover why they may be ignoring or avoiding this by an examination and exploration of the cards they have chosen. With this approach the therapist will be lead to some indication of what the deeper general area may be. A further card or cards can then be selected to give the details of this deeper level. By analysing the number of cards the client feels drawn to select or seems appropriate to add to the initial selection, the cause of a problem can be uncovered and the client assisted in their attempt to deal with it as they are able at the time.

Just as the absence of cards can indicate certain factors, a predominance of certain cards can have an equal indicator. If a client is in balance their selection of cards will reflect this. This is not usually the case of course, for if they were in balance they would not require the assistance of your services and be consulting the Tarot. An over emphasis of cards from any one suit therefore shows an unhealthy attention is being paid to the area of that suit.

Should the weight of cards swing too far in favour of the Major Arcana cards, the indication is that the client is deeply involved in their situation and may be too caught up in the significance and importance of it in their lives to see it clearly and objectively. Exactly how this is done will be shown by the actual cards chosen. How many cards constitute 'too many' will of course be dependent on the total number of cards in that selection. A surplus of Major Arcana cards can show that the client is aware of the burden currently upon them, but needs to focus their attention more on the result of their action and on the everyday aspect of the situation rather than what it symbolises. This can be likened to the process of the person who looks so deeply into their reflection in water that they lose awareness of where they are and fall in! Along comes the therapist to offer the hand to fish them out again!

With the cards fanned out across your table and the clients selection turned up the process of interpretation and analysis follows. It is at this point that the therapist is on their own and certainly through this medium, little direction can be given. The therapist must now utilise their knowledge of the cards, their experience both of life and their work and their skills of communication.

Working without a structure to the layout of your cards enables the therapist complete freedom in their interpretation. It can be worthwhile to note the order in which the client chooses their cards, beginning with the first one chosen, seeing this as the starting point of your consultation and the beginning of their situation. From here you can work your way together through each card, taking the first, and following with the second and so on until all have been examined.

This linear method is a good way to begin the interpretation you give to the cards before you. Deeper levels of meaning and significance to the client can be revealed by the links you can now forge between them in the light and knowledge of what has already been uncovered. This process of review is when you sit back a little and allow your eyes to be led to the symbols or cards that have seemed prevalent in your first look. This will allow associations to be made with other cards in the selection that you have not considered so far, which takes the consultation to a hitherto unknown aspect in the client too.

At this stage questioning the client as to their view and opinions may be necessary so as to ascertain which of your ideas may be correct. Intuition will guide you a good deal of the way, but particularly in your early days as a Tarot Therapist you may welcome some feedback at this point. This also serves to keep the client involved and active.

As you continue this processes you are free to follow apparently random associations that may help you and the client to uncover aspects they did not know or believed existed, showing us one of the most powerful abilities the Tarot possesses. Because it encompasses the whole and complete human being in its structure, the Tarot is able to address itself to the dark, neglected and unknown areas of those who consult it. In the hands of the sensitive and effective therapist, the compassionate light of the Tarot is both a healing and revelatory one.

What these associations may be and what they may reveal is unique to each consultation. The depth they may reach is dependent on both client and therapist and requires some experience and at the least confidence on both parts. It is a wonderful thing to be witness to however and again the rewards when enlightenment appears in the face of the client is really beyond measure. An often ignored part of this process can be that which the client plays. Having listened to your opening interpretation and view of the cards they may well feel emboldened to make their own observation, which should always be encouraged at any point. In particular having heard your opinion, they may be able to use this for their own interpretation and so you continue to work together towards a point at which it is clear the cards conclude.

It is at this stage also that additional cards may need to be added, to reveal what lays beneath the meaning of any one card or cards. There are no rules or limits to follow here, save those of your own promptings and dependable intuition. In this take care not to lose the power of what you have done so far, as too many cards in a consultation will belittle their power. The cards, if allowed, have an ability to make this clear to the sensitively attuned therapist.

Whilst little has been said here about the addition of further cards to a consultation, their significance should not be underestimated. The succeeding layers of blockage can be stripped away card by card until the truth is revealed. Each card added takes us a little nearer our goal. The success of this procedure entails our proceeding cautiously and checking after each card is added whether the end has been reached, either to this stage or the whole consultation.

This association procedure and deeper analysis should be allowed to continue until a natural conclusion has been reached or the time limit has come. By this stage a summary and recapitulation may be needed, in order to clarify for yourself and the client what has been learnt and what the next stage may be. This is also the time for arranging any further consultation agreed as necessary and appropriate between both parties. If you keep records as therapist now may be the time to jot the salient points down and to give the client their tape, if applicable.

WORKING WITH LAYOUTS

Tarot Therapy is in part an instinctive art and one that responds to the moment, in accordance with our earlier definition of empathy. Utilising this approach results in their being little room for definite rules for the therapist to follow. The consequence of this is that the therapist must take an adaptive attitude and embrace the openness of approach that demonstrates a trust and surety in the tools of the trade, in this case the cards.

Such openness may bring us naturally to the above method of consulting the cards, but this may not always be the case. Even with the flexible spirit in which I have tried to present the approach of Tarot Therapy, there will be exceptions. Tarot Therapists may find that in the early days of their career, they require something of a structure on which to base their consultations, until they feel strong and confident enough to fly from this particular nest, letting the freedom the open approach gives guide their wings.

The structures that Tarot Therapists may choose must be adapted to the specific goals of this approach to working with the Tarot. We have seen that for the purposes of Tarot Therapy, a defined spread can impose limitations not in the spirit of this method. This does not however, fully negate their possible use and effectiveness.

For first-time clients and perhaps for those who expect to see this more traditional and accepted way of using the cards, it may be more appropriate to use a layout of some kind. If the client expects to see something, it may be that this is the only way they will come to accept what is being said in their consultation. Whilst I do not advocate 'pandering' to the clients wishes throughout the procedure of Tarot Therapy, there may be occasions that it is wise to capitulate, in the interests of best serving their needs and building them up. It may be that this is more necessary in the earlier consultations of the many that can often constitute a complete 'treatment' of Tarot Therapy. Allowing the client the structure they need may be one way to instil the security they require and need to see from you before they will take to their heart what is revealed and suggested. Exactly when this is appropriate is something that must be determined by the therapist at the time.

It is in this context that I offer for use the following layouts, that I have constructed for use with Tarot Therapy and that I have found to be effective over the years. There are a great many 'spreads' available and almost every book produced on the Tarot will have a chapter concerning their use. I recommend that as an aspiring Tarot Therapist you avail yourself of those books that appeal to you (there is a comprehensive selection given in the Bibliography and more seem to appear constantly) and plunder them as you deem fit.

In doing so I would remind you that every Tarot book, including this one of course, is written from the perspective and degree of unfoldment of its author. This is not said to belittle anyone's work, for all has something to offer. The spreads included in each book equally have a different approach that will suit correspondingly different people. The task as Tarot Therapist is to sift through those available and select those that you are attracted to and resonate with.

There are many spreads that are seen as being standard and accepted, chief among these being the so-called 'Celtic Cross'. This and many other spreads are really the province of the fortune teller. Those that lend themselves more naturally to the work of the Tarot Therapist may or may not be those that appear involved or complicated, In selecting the layouts that you choose to work with, the 'less is more' approach can often be applicable.

There are many Tarot readers that utilise almost the whole pack in one half hour reading. Such approaches cannot possibly hope to do justice to the deeper layers and relationships between cards that constitute the backbone of the Tarot Therapy consultation. Do not underestimate the power of the simple layout, using perhaps just three cards. The most beautiful and most profound truths are usually the simplest ones. Spiritual advancement is not dependent on mental intelligence or the measure of someone's intellectual grasp of any one or number of books, theories, prayers or pack of cards. There have been many, many occasions when the client has attested to what has been presented in their Tarot consultation as being obvious and staring them in the face all the time. In these wonderful instances of realisation and progression, the Tarot has acted as an effective therapy by revealing what has become obscured to the client. This rarely requires the complicated procedure, clever apparatus or technical wizardry attempted in many Tarot readings.

The layouts I present here try to retain both this simplicity and the necessary structure to lead the aspiring consultant towards the therapeutic use of the Tarot. The majority of layouts give a different placing for the differing areas of a clients life, such as the past, present and future, influence of 'loved ones', hindrances, work, home life and so on. In Tarot Therapy we concentrate on the client as the focal point of their lives, examining what occurs both within and without their own being, while seeing the reflective relationship between the two.

We also link into the present as the result and cause of the past and future respectively. Taking the open plan approach, the influences of the past and future can be determined as appropriate, as the consultation unfolds. Should it seem to be required, the past and/or possible future can be investigated as an additional aspect of what has been uncovered. The present moment, being the outworking of the clients thoughts, emotions and subsequent actions is where effective change must be sought and so is where the consultation looks to first and foremost.

The layouts presented here also include the holistic view of the human being, as it consists of body, mind and spirit as inter-linked parts of the whole. This structure is intrinsic to all the layouts given here, as we shall see. These layouts form a complete set of themselves, or can be used individually. The intention is that they have the capability of forming a complete and thorough Tarot Therapy consultation, but can of course be used in conjunction with others of your choosing or as an opening to the open-plan unstructured method.

HOLISTIC HEALTH LAYOUT

We begin with a layout I have entitled 'Holistic Health'. The placing of the cards are as shown here, showing what is a deceptively simple and easy format. The first card, to the left of the main body of cards is the Theme Card, being the first one selected in the consultation. This is placed to the left in this illustration but can be put anywhere you feel is best, since its influence is unlimited in the layout.

The remaining cards selected are laid out in order of being chosen in the following pattern:

	1	2	3
T	4	5	6
	7	8	9
	10	11	12

Dividing the client into their holistic components, as they relate through the structure of the Tarot itself, this layout takes the fourfold division of the human being derived from the Elements, in its four horizontal levels. We have seen that the Elements constitute the human being as well as the physical world in which we live. This makes them the perfect skeleton for a layout, on which the flesh is constructed as we interpret it with the client.

The top level, cards 1, 2 and 3, show us the condition and influence of the clients' spirit, based on the Element of Fire. This is viewed as their inspiration, their spiritual make-up, which is distinct from and irrespective of, individual belief systems they may or may not have. This includes their motivation and level of get-up and go, perhaps defined as that which stimulates their body to wake up each morning, should the client be an atheist. How you choose to define spirituality is the definition of what these three cards tell you about the client at the time of the consultation.

The second level down of the layout concerns itself with the mind of the client, being their thought processes and their influence on their holistic health, based on the Element of Air. The mental level is often a powerful drain on an individual's well-being, so shows us their state of mind and its effect on their overall level of health. Those who work physically, say as builders, carpenters and so on are always seen to be hard workers. Those who work in offices or in study can work just as hard however, with an equal drain on their resources from the levels of pressure they face, usually exerted mentally by concentration. For health to be present all four Elemental levels must be in balance.

The next level down, cards 7, 8 and 9, show us the workings of the Element of Water, related through the clients emotions. As with the mind, the heart can cause a drain on our well-being, either through powerful feelings at any one time or through a more gradual deterioration, often via worrying over a situation or person. This will act to siphon off one's life force energy as we are gradually depleted to the eventual outcome of physical disease or illness. These three cards show us the clients' emotional condition, as it relates to their overall health.

This leaves the bottom level, cards 10, 11, and 12 to be the condition and influence of the clients Body, as the Element Earth. This shows us their physical health and matters relating to their body, but also their everyday life, as what they are doing with their body, since this contributes greatly to our overall health. Overwork is very common in the modern world and imbalances here will be shown in this line.

The interpretation of the cards should follow the format and structure of the open-plan approach previously described. An initial examination should reveal the numbers of cards and their duplicates as well as multiples of suits, Court and Major cards. As well as these observations, the therapist should look for where the cards are to be found. Should there be a predominance of any multiple or types of cards on any one level, the likelihood is of there being a point of stress or friction at this area in the clients' life. This can also apply should there be an emphasis of Pentacles on the Body level, Cups on the Emotional level, and Swords on the Mind level or Rods on the Spirit level.

Looking then at the vertical lines of the layout, the therapist is introduced to the idea of a flow of events, progression and succession in the consultation. Card 1 acts as a starting point, showing us where the situation began and something of what is at its roots. Working down from card 1 to cards 4, 7 and 10 shows what has past and what the client needs to put behind them and move on from; what needs to be released.

Equally the middle vertical row will explain what the client is involved with at the time of the consultation and will indicate where their energies are being taken at this time. This leads naturally on to the last line, cards 3, 6, 9 and 12, being the energies yet to be received and those being created by their current actions, thoughts and feelings. This is the possible future created by their position at the present time. Examination here, interpreted in the light of the middle line of cards, reveals what the client may wish to control, take charge of and bring about effective change in. Your interpretation can show them how.

The layout should not be interpreted in a linear fashion, following the order of cards they are selected. The numbers in the above layout refer to first, second, third and so on, without any implication of order. It is the way in which correspondences and relationships between the cards are revealed and understood between client and therapist that unleashes the potential and power of the Tarot Therapy consultation.

Additional cards can be added to the layout at any area that appears to warrant further investigation. This may take the form of asking the client to select one card, to add depth to one that seems to contain a turning or focal point in the layout. This will often reveal a similar message, but one that relates to a deeper, often unacknowledged level in the client or their life.

Further cards can also be added to a complete line in this layout, whether horizontal or vertical. Should the cards in that line show a significance unparalleled in the rest of the layout, an additional line of three cards may be added to explain what this significance is. By example, there may be three Swords and one Major Arcana card on the mental line. This would immediately draw attention to this line and could demand extra investigation by way of four additional cards, since they demonstrate that the point of attention the client is showing requires closer examination. It may be however that your exploration of the initial four cards is sufficient. The key to what they require will be found if eight cards are selected, as they relate to the complete picture of the clients holistic health.

An interesting adjunct to the interpretation of this layout comes from the tradition of the Lakota Native American Indians. In their view, the four levels of consciousness of the physical, emotional, mental, and spiritual, as depicted in this layout, are related to the unfolding of the four stages of life. These are childhood, youth, adulthood (maturity) and old age respectively. The four horizontal rows can also be viewed and interpreted in this respect, beginning from the bottom upwards in the order given.

DEEPER LAYOUTS

Another option open to the therapist is to deepen their investigation still further by focussing another, additional layout solely on the level revealed as the focal one. This gives us four further layouts, presented here, one each for Body, Emotions, Mind and Spirit. It may be that the client presents specific areas of concern to you, requesting that you focus only on this. In such, admittedly unusual but no less important circumstances, you have the option of selecting one of the four following layouts which is closest to the area requested.

In building on the information discovered from the initial Holistic Health layout, each of the following layouts follows the same structure, so as to allow for correspondences and relationships to be made between them. This adds a further dimension to their use in one consultation, enabling the therapist to observe progressive influences from related areas of influence through subsequent layouts.

In all of these four 'follow-up' layouts, the Theme card is utilised in the same manner as with the Holistic Health layout. The card can however, be specifically selected from the original ones chosen, should there appear to be a key card that appears to demand further investigation, in the appropriate line. During interpretation of any layout, all cards selected are there for a reason and have something to impart to the client. However, it is true to say that the attention of both therapist and client will inexorably be drawn to certain cards, usually two or three in number, through the

246

interpretative process. It is often from these focal and catalytic cards that the Theme card for subsequent layouts may make itself apparent for use. The remainder of the cards for use in the four investigative layouts are selected in the same manner as before.

BODY LAYOUT

The first of these we shall imaginatively call 'Body', using similarly inspired names for the other three. The workings of the human body are many and varied and there are an equal number of options available for a layout based on such information and knowledge. In investigating the influence of the 'Body' as the everyday level of the human being, as it continues from the Holistic Health layout, we look towards its constituent parts, turning our attention to that from which it is derived. It is here, at what we have termed the 'energy level' of the human being that the causal level is found and it is at this level that the Tarot Therapist can be most effective.

The layout for the client at the everyday level is therefore comprised of the way in which the individual utilises and disperses what energy they have. This can be categorised in three broad areas, giving the following layout. For clarity, this is also illustrated here and since it also applies to the following two layouts.

	1	2	3
T	4	5	6
	7	8	9

Beginning with the top line, as the first cards selected, the levels of this layout are;

WORK
The active use of one's energy, what is required for one's positive existence and how it is distributed. Our choice of

work can tell us a great deal of how we express the energy of our being. In a world where the career path is often seen as the most important, whether we are content with our work indicates to a considerable degree if we are content with ourselves. The three cards chosen here will give information regarding this level of contentment and if the client is expressing their energy in the appropriate field of work. With the material pressures we face in our current society's structure, it can be all too easy to fall into a job, as opposed to our chosen career. The interpretation of cards at this level can help to alleviate the pressure created by an unwanted but necessary job, by bringing about an understanding of the energy process at work in the client.

LEISURE
Adults are seen for these purposes, as perhaps they always should be, as big children, who have a need to play in just the same way as our smaller counterparts. For the purposes of energy, how the client chooses to practise their leisure, and perhaps if they do at all in any noticeable or significant way, indicates the manner and level to which they are allowing a free flow and expression of energy through their being. As we have seen, the energy that we comprise needs to be expressed and these three cards show us if this is being done sufficiently and appropriately through our chief opportunity to do so.

REST
Just as energy requires release, we must also ensure that we regenerate sufficient qualities to enable us to continue this expression. The major form that this takes is of course sleep. The unbalanced person often finds that their sleep pattern is interrupted, creating an additional drain on their well-being. The level and type of activity we experience while asleep also indicates any possible energy drain here. The three cards of the bottom line of this layout show us how the client obtains the energy they require for their own balanced life and indeed, if they are doing this.

EMOTIONS LAYOUT

The Emotions layout is used when further attention and investigation is deemed applicable from the cards shown on the second line up from the bottom of the Holistic Health layout, or when the clients' subject or question is specifically and exclusively emotional in nature.

The layout also requires three lines, following our familiar pattern thus:

	1	2	3
T	4	5	6
	7	8	9

In this layout we begin as usual with the Theme card, possibly selected from those we already have or as the first card chosen for this layout by the client. The remaining cards are laid out following our established pattern. The interpretation follows the same established pattern in this inter-related series of layouts, created so deliberately, to allow for and show clearly progressions of issues, causes and possible consequences.

The significances of the three lines follow the nature of emotions, as they are perceived and integrated into our being. Whilst it is acknowledged that emotions of themselves can be complicated beasts with an equally involved effect, their introduction into the human system can be grouped into the following three areas, which give us the corresponding lines in the layout, working from the top down.

EXPRESSED
The first level of emotions relates to those we are conscious of, those emotions that we feel and which can dictate our

actions. These are the emotions that are noticeable by others as we express them freely.

REPRESSED
The second level of emotions and of our layout are those which we may be conscious and aware of, but seek to control. It may be that we have identified them as inappropriate or that they are too painful for us to acknowledge in the immediate time. We therefore seek to repress them, trapping some of the energy associated with them, which the therapist can help us with, by guiding us to a place where they can be expressed in a non-destructive manner.

SUPPRESSED
The bottom level of emotions are classified as suppressed. We are rarely conscious of these feelings, since this is usually our immediate and instinctive reaction to them, as soon as they enter our initial awareness. The causes of this can be many and varied, but are usually because of any pain we associate with them, perhaps arriving from a trauma or memory we seek escape from. By filing them in the bottom drawer of our heart, so to speak, we find a surface release from their causes. There they lie, awaiting an escape as surely they must, as is their nature. Like energy, all emotion must flow and be expressed. From this level possible physical dis-ease can result, dependent on a variety of influences. Should the therapist access locked in emotion at this level, the task is to work with the client in first seeking its acknowledgement, then proceeding to a point   of release and expression, probably through further consultations.

MIND LAYOUT

The layout derived from the second level down of the Holistic Health, is equal in many ways to the Emotions layout. It follows the same system of classification for our thoughts as with our feelings, as there is often a correlation between the two. Indeed it may sometimes be appropriate for these two layouts to be interpreted in tandem, such is the relationship between these two levels of the human being. The layout is therefore identical to that above, following the same ten card selection procedure, inclusive of the Theme card and all interpretative methods.

The difference between the two layouts is of course that the first is concerned with emotions, the second with thoughts. The groupings for the level of our mental processes are as follows:

CONSCIOUS
What one believes or knows to be true about oneself and acts on as acceptable. These are the thoughts and their influence that we work with in the everyday aspect of our lives and living. This is an indication of the clients' logical processes and free operation, that they are comfortable and familiar with.

SUBCONSCIOUS
One's instinctual nature, with several layers: suppressed, unrecognised, desires, guilt's and urges, inherited tendencies and innate predisposition's. These are the thoughts that may be currently troubling the client, that require some objective input to help process and integrate to a comfortable level of understanding. This level of our mind notices and records all things we encounter and is exposed to and decides whether the conscious mind needs to be informed or if the data can be retained in this retrieval system for any later use that may be required. The mind is a vast operation and resource that is still largely untapped and

utilised and it is this level that keeps a great deal of Knowledge never used or inspected. These can be the thoughts that the client seeks to keep in check and under control, perhaps because their force appears too strong to be safe to them. Their expression can often precipitate a creative inspiration.

UNCONSCIOUS

This level has also been referred to as the cellular level, as the intelligence of an individual cell in the body, displaying instinctive knowledge, adaptation and memory. This is the level of our 'fight or flight' response to external stimuli. A defensive or aggressive reaction kicks in, seemingly without our control. The reflexes and drives we contain in this 'basic' mind dictate our mental condition to a surprising degree and though their inspection may reveal some long-stored painful memory, the benefits gained from this can be stronger. Like the corresponding level of emotions, the 'primitive' thoughts we have can often reveal a simple survival instinct that is non-judgemental in its motivation, thereby releasing the client from any guilt or blame they associate with it. The acknowledgement of this however, may still require the client at some point to 'face and embrace' the source of their pain. The value of a sensitive and empathic therapist in this process cannot be too high.

For those familiar with the Jungian view of the mental processes of the human being as outlined in this layout, there exists the option of adding a further, fourth level of cards. This will act as signposts to a still deeper realm of thoughts influencing the client. Familiarity with the concept and workings of the Collective Unconscious as defined by Jung is helpful to investigate this line of cards, but it can be added in the instance of a client still being troubled by what the above three lines of cards may show. This principle in fact applies to all consultations when one additional card may be required, as a last resort if the client feels they have received little help or clarification from their consultation. A helpful procedure in such cases as this is to lay the cards selected before the client and invite their response, before giving any of your own. Their reaction will demonstrate the crux of their problem or difficulty.

The Collective Unconscious is that level to which we all belong, without knowing it. Certain ideas, concepts and symbols are universally or collectively understood as having a certain or particular influence or effect on the human mind, because they 'mean the same the world over'. This concept is used to a sometimes alarming degree in the modern, technological world as larger and larger companies seek to communicate their message in the cheapest yet most effective way. A symbol acts beyond a level requiring language yet communicates a great deal of information associated with it, often shown by advertising. This is the realm of the collective unconscious, where things are accepted without our noticing, yet still having an impact upon us. The ability to investigate these influences therefore requires a good appreciation of the implications of such a power, acting without restraint and due regard for its recipient's welfare. Equally, what a line of cards representing the collective unconscious influence may reveal can be equally empowering for the client.

It is often those clients who are engaged in some form of spiritual activity who are more prone to or affected by influences of this kind. This is because they can act at a level of collective awareness or even (spiritual) responsibility, thereby opening them to the necessity of forces affecting us at this level of our beings. Such occult activity is not for the untrained person, and so should it be for those acting as therapists for such people.

SPIRIT LAYOUT

The subsequent layout for the line representing the clients Spirit from the Holistic Health layout is again based on the same structure and principles. As before, the same interpretative procedure and selection technique should be followed. It should be made clear to the client that investigation of this level of their being does not constitute an investigation of their beliefs or the strength of their conviction concerning them. The clients' individual beliefs are not a matter for concern here, rather a supportive exploration of their effect upon their overall being.

```
            1    2    3

            4    5    6

     T      7    8    9

           10   11   12

           13   14   15
```

As can be seen from the above layout there are two additional lines of cards here, to illustrate the broad groupings and workings of the spiritual procedures of the human beings. As with all layouts included in both this book and all Tarot books, they are not set in stone (or even card!) and should you feel the spiritual process is a different one, you are free to adjust this layout accordingly. I ask only that you remain true to yourself and that you are thoroughly familiar with your reasons for allocation of cards, for equal explanation to clients.

The design of individual layouts is always to be encouraged, though not advised until some experience has been gained in Tarot Therapy, for obvious reasons. Since they are based on one's individual and unique workings with the cards in this manner, your own layouts are likely to be the most effective you find, following the principle of Tarot Therapy being as individual as the therapist.

The Spirit layout, as I have used it for some years, consists of the following levels of interpretation, working as always from the top line down.

GUIDED

The top line reveals the specific content of what is given to the client directly from their guide(s) or any deities they acknowledge. Information from this level is given in such a form that it enters the edges or highest level of the consciousness. It is then dependent on the awareness, spirituality and motivation of the individual concerned as to how long a period of human time passes before this information is received and acknowledged consciously and so acted on in the appropriate way. Spiritual guidance and information always seeks to assist us with our growth, development and evolution, but can be open to human error. Investigation of this level can act as a key to the unlocking of a powerful revelation for the client, often resulting in their declaring with a relieved sigh that they can now put into words and action that which they thought was true but could not quite bring themselves to believe. Guidance may be received immediately by the client or it may take several years before it becomes conscious to them. This line of cards may accelerate this process, but if this is necessary and appropriate it will become apparent. As with all aspects of Tarot Therapy, tread carefully and sensitively in your interpretation with the client here. In summary, we can view this line as being above the clients' consciousness.

INTUITIVE

Following the investigation of what spiritual information the client needs to focus on, we look to their intuitive awareness of it and to their initial response to it, as indicated and begun at this level of their being. Our intuition can be seen as a combination of our thoughts and emotions and this line can therefore be deemed to be a combination of the middle two lines of the original Holistic Health layout. This line of cards will give indications as to how aware the client is of the guidance and inspiration coming to them, at the periphery of their consciousness. This line is equal to the highest level of the clients' consciousness and awareness. They may be partially aware of its contents and meaning for them, but with the addition of the understanding of the higher, first line of this layout the client can come to view a new significance and possibility from the consultation, from the fuller awareness that results.

SENSED
We have discovered previously that the human being can be broadly and basically split in two, for those that work from a mental basis and those that work from the emotional. This line subsequently shows us which of the two groups the client falls into, as it tells us of what they sense, as an inner awareness in their body, what they feel within to be true for them. This may be termed as what the client knows they must do, whether they actually want to or not. A reluctance will often be present, showing the therapist that this is the root of the problem or difficulty they are having. Clients will often see this as the 'correct' thing to do in their situation, as the one that demonstrates maturity or sensibility. However, they may not feel like being mature or sensible and this should be honoured. As therapist it is your task to outline the interpretation of this information and assist them in making their decision as to what they feel they must or need to do. Because it exists does not mean that the spiritually correct way of action must be carried out at this time and as therapist you must be able to rise above any feeling that prompts you to direct the client to do so and without judgement on your part. The objectivity of the Tarot Therapist becomes clear here.

PROCESSED
The penultimate layer of cards for this layout concerns itself with the manner in which the client is currently processing

what is represented by the above three lines of cards. This may be before any action or decision has been taken, but what is currently in mind or heart for them. The client will often be aware of this, but be unsure if they are correct. Exploration of these cards can therefore assist them in coming to a firm and clear decision, with the added value of understanding of the reasons for their decision, the power of which can be very strong.

EXPRESSED

The final level of cards tells us about how the client either needs to, has or is currently likely to express their spirituality or higher aspect to their being. This may be the manner in which they follow their spiritual beliefs in the everyday world, their preferred method of expression towards the deity they acknowledge and the effect of this upon their life. The integration of one's spirituality in the day to day life can often bring problems, be they ones of embarrassment, suspicion, or ridicule, from or to the individual concerned. I have found the requirement to point out that people often ridicule that which they have no explanation for, as spiritual beliefs can often be termed. Proving in one's mind that something is rubbish is an excellent method of finding comfort when it is beyond comprehension, logic or fits in with our accepted view of the world and all things. This is a very common trait of behaviour, the definition of which can lead to a great advancement for those on the receiving end. Interpretation of this line between therapist and client can bring great rewards in the spiritual or belief field.

CHAKRAS LAYOUT

The layouts we have examined above are concerned with the client as the focus of their life, taking the life force energy that is the origin of both as the subject matter for the cards. The esoteric structure of the human being and its place in the world, as the outworking of that energy and the concern of the Tarot, provides the above layouts in its structure, as they relate to and are formed from, the Elements. This can be viewed as a general or collective view of energy working in our world.

For a personal viewpoint that the Tarot adapts itself to wonderfully, we can turn to the esoteric structure of the human being itself. We know that the way in which an individual receives and processes the life force energy it inherits at the Elemental level is key to their well-being and health. The energy level of the human structure is comprised of levels and 'organs' that can be explored in a consultation for an in depth investigation of the clients complete well-being. The following layout can be seen as an alternative to the Holistic Health layout or can be used in conjunction with it. It should however, only be used by those Tarot Therapists proficient in the knowledge and operation of the chakras upon which it is based.

The term chakra is a Sanskrit one in origin, meaning wheel. Each chakra point of the body marks an area of intersection of the meridian lines, the vessels which carry the life force through and within our physical bodies. Where several such lines cross an 'energy vortex' is created, which is the chakra. They are points of reception of energy of differing qualities and vibrations into the etheric/physical system from the aura that surrounds and interpenetrates the physical body.

CARD	CHAKRA	GOVERNS
1ST	BASE	SECURITY, STRUCTURE, STABILITY
2ND	SACRAL	DESIRE, PLEASURE, SEXUALITY
3RD	SOLAR PLEXUS	WILL, POWER, ENERGY
4TH	HEART	EMOTIONS, LOVE, COMPASSION
5TH	THROAT	COMMUNICATION, EXPRESSION
6TH	BROW	PERCEPTION, INTUITION,
7TH	CROWN	UNDERSTANDING, CONNECTION

The structure of the layout follows the same pattern in order to enable this integration and to provide for the complete picture required of such a large working. The layout consists of seven lines, one for each of the main and most widely acknowledged chakras, with the usual three vertical lines created for the flow we are now familiar with.

```
                1       2       3

                4       5       6

                7       8       9

    T          10      11      12

               13      14      15

               16      17      18

               19      20      21
```

The format we follow is the usual one, by way of allocation of chakras to cards and interpretation. The total of knowledge we currently possess regarding the chakras has filled a great many volumes, the basics of which the Tarot Therapist should exceed before they make use of this layout. Bearing in mind too that the explanation of the chakras warrants at least one book by itself, so vast are their correspondences and importance to us, I will give only the chakras and the very basic role they play here, to provoke those unfamiliar to discover more, to avoid those same people using the layout before they are reasonably able and by assumption that this information is all that will be required by those already qualified to do so.

The interpretation of this layout opens up vistas of information available to the therapist and client. The chakras relate to every aspect of the human being and their welfare, so it can be no exaggeration to say that anything is possible for the client, through the open, complete and thorough Tarot Therapy consultation. The same guidelines apply in the interpretation as before and it is through the utilisation of layouts such as this and doubtless others that already exist and will be devised, that we can begin to glimpse the full force of Tarot Therapy and so begin to see how it can take a hallowed place in the therapies of the Aquarian Age.

EXERCISES

As Therapists we need to be aware of our motivation in listening to the client. There are four identifiable areas for this, based on our intention. These are:

- to understand the client
- to enjoy the client
- to learn something
- to give help or solace; to serve

Consider your own motivation in this context and rate the above from 1 to 4, with 4 being the highest. Having done this, consider what you may need to change about the way you listen to bring each score to 4. How might you implement these changes?

Try to write a definition of empathy in your own words. Once you have done this to what degree do you think you possess it and how might you increase it?

How can being wrong help?

List all the qualities you can think of that constitute a successful Tarot Therapy consultation. From this see if you can arrive at a definition of a successful consultation. What does this tell you about your own concept of success in this field of work and are you content with this? Consider if you need to make any changes here.

List all the ways you can think of that prejudice manifests itself and consider which of these might apply to a Tarot Therapy consultation. We all have some prejudice, so which are yours and why? How might you alleviate yourself from them?

What do you consider are the skills, qualities and practices that you need to achieve the quality of empathy in your work? List everything you can think of, then consider which of them you truly possess now, which you do not and how you might work towards them.

The main and most required exercise now is practice. Familiarise yourself thoroughly with the methods of working both without and with layouts, by practising them many time. You can do this with willing 'guinea-pig's or imaginary people and situations. You should always explain to your volunteers that you are only practising. Make a list of the stages of a consultation, from its very beginning, then practice and experiment with the options and layouts open to you. Try to reach a stage that you feel comfortable and confident with, both in your procedural methods and your interpretation. This is an ongoing process, so do be patient with yourself. Competence, rather than mastery should be your aim, the rest will take care of itself, with experience.

CHAPTER 9 - THE TAROT IN THE AQUARIAN AGE

Chapter 2 of this book concerned itself with the Evolution of the Tarot, tracing its possible origins and seeking to show how the body of knowledge the Tarot represents is alive of itself and so adaptive to the circumstances of the existence it reflects. This existence includes the human race, the very subject and outworking of the knowledge contained in the cards. At this juncture in our history the human race runs into another lap and is entering a New Age in its own evolution. Since it is primarily concerned with the individuals participating in that race, for its continued evolution and adaptation, practitioners of the Tarot must discover what that New Age is and where and how it fits into it.

The subject of the 'New Age' is one met with much derision and scorn in a good many circles, as it can be seen as the realm of 'air-heads' and those for whom the concept of the dirt and grime of the street has no place next to the fluffy clouds of their existence. Whilst it is not my place to judge another's view, we must accept that there are many realities, each one subject to the view of its owner. The various practices and therapies of the New Age are often seen as incomprehensible, non-effective and/or a swindle, fuelling the opulent life style of its designers. It is very much hoped that the approach of this book does not allow any room for the Tarot to be included in the above scenario.

To discover the niche into which the cards will fit snugly, it is necessary to give a brief examination of what the New Age actually is. There are many prophecies, visions and stories that speak of such a 'golden age' beginning at or around this time. Spanning the globe from the Mayans of South America and the various nations of tribal North America to the works of Nostradamus and others in between, we read of the 'dawning of the Age of Aquarius'.

In referring to the 'New Age' as the Age of Aquarius or Aquarian Age, we give it a more correct and accurate term that tells us a great deal of what it means, sufficient for our purposes. The various sources of teaching inform us that the evolution of humanity is subject to differing influences at various junctures in its development, changing every two thousand years or so. The last such change occurred around the time of the birth of Christ, when our present yearly count began. However, there are differing views as to the time of the birth of Christ, seen as the beginning of the Piscean Age and out of which we are now emerging.

If Christ was born, as if often proposed, sometime after 25th December in the year 0, this may mean that the 'official' beginning of the Aquarian Age is dated correspondingly later. This is one of the reasons posited for the confusion surrounding this new chance for humanity. Other dates for its dawning are formed from the tradition of its origin. In the case of the Mayans calculations are made by use of their calendar. This gave rise in 1987 to what some consider the start of the Aquarian Age, with a famous event called Harmonic Convergence. The theory here was that if enough people of like heart and mind gathered together, sufficient energy would be created to enable a shift to occur that would carry us into the Age of Aquarius.

Another theory follows astrological circumstances that cause the necessary energy to flow to humanity, for use by those open and ready to receive it. The planetary alignment required was later put into the words of a song from the musical Hair: 'when the Moon is in the seventh house and Jupiter aligns with Mars'.

Other theories propound that we are presently in the midst of a two hundred year transition time, with the Aquarian Age not truly in place until the year 2035 or 2062. Whether one of these ideas or suggestions is true is open to much debate. What is clear from the evidence of the changes apparent across the globe, from environmental, political, social and technological changes at an unprecedented scale, is that something is happening. Whether the idea of the new age is accepted or not, the evidence of radical change cannot be denied. Humanity must learn to adapt and embrace the new principles and methods coming into being as a direct result of the changes across the world.

These principles are in direct agreement and alignment with those of the Aquarian Age. We are told in the prophecies that these offer us a chance to instil a new era of peace in our world. History is replete with conflict, which continues unabated in various parts of the world today. Because our media do not inform us of smaller conflicts does not mean they do not exist. We hear of (some of) those we are involved in, but no more. The prophecies also tell us that if we do not take charge of our destiny and manifest peace at this time, we are in danger of destroying ourselves. Certainly we have the technological capability to achieve this.

If not by military we could also destroy ourselves by ecological means. Humanity has sought domination over nature since the time of the Industrial Revolution, when we lost the awareness of the need to live in harmony with our surroundings. Now we are offered the awareness, through the disasters and problems we have created to learn to adapt our way of life to integrate rather than control, nature. If we cannot learn this vital lesson, we risk the event of the Earth cleansing the cause of the pollution from her body: humanity. If we do, we can enter a global time of plenty for all, as the Earth has always had abundant resources to provide.

Along with the above scenario of peace and plenty, which it must be clear are not fanciful dreams, but possibilities we have the potential to manifest ourselves, come other principles in keeping with the astrological sign of Aquarius. The zodiacal calendar is one of these cycles, humanity evolving in accordance with ever higher turns of the spiral pattern created, just like the DNA in our bodies. At this time, one of the larger cycles, that which changes every two thousand years or so, is bringing a new influence at a collective, global level to our hearts and minds.

It is this influence that each individual must seek to embrace to truly 'move with the times.' As each person accepts the new energy coming to them from the constellation of Aquarius, so they become attuned within the very fibre and make-up of the being to its methods. It is with these methods that we are here concerned.

Aquarius brings us understanding, communication, sharing and equality. When these principles are applied to global concerns it is easy to see the changes that are required in our world. These must occur individually to occur collectively. This work begins with a new realisation occurring in the heart and mind of each one open and willing to seek and find it. Here we can draw an easy analogy between these brave souls and the Fool. One of the effects of such a realisation is the onset of a new awareness of the nature of reality. Part of this reality is the truth of the spiritual or esoteric world. It is here that the Tarot can administer its teaching.

Aquarian principles include those of the acceptance of a new awareness of what the human being is. This includes the idea of a spirit, the human as divine, in accordance with the particular beliefs of each person. To bring this new awareness into being in a measured and practical way requires guidance. This is the realm of Tarot Therapy, where it can fulfil a much needed role for a great many people. Many things are necessary for the manifestation of the Aquarian Age at a practical level, from political negotiation and environmental management to spiritual guidance. Each is equal in importance if we are to be balanced, both individually and collectively.

There are many methods of guidance and therapy available today, many assisting with the work of bringing into being a higher reality that is now offered to us. As we open to the new knowledge of awareness of who we are, we need new techniques first to bring about this understanding and second to integrate it. New diseases require new medicines and new methods of healing. The last half of the twentieth century has seen the birth and growth of a great many new diseases, from the plague of AIDS to so-called 'Mad Cow Disease'. It is in the complementary and natural therapies that we will find the cure to such Aquarian illness, since they originate from an Aquarian origin; that of inclusiveness of body, mind and spirit of the individual and acceptance of our being part of the natural world, from where such cures are to be found.

The advance of such methods of healing as aromatherapy, homeopathy, acupuncture and herbalism has been astounding. As we learn to accept that in its ability to provide enough food for all of humanity, so we can learn to accept that the Earth can provide cures for all our ills too. It is hoped that in the reading of this book you will have gained an insight into why and how the Tarot can be used as a therapy, now in accordance with the principles and reasons outlined here. At the present time, many of the above types of healing work in isolation, each attempting to effect a total cure for the client.

Many times a wonderful cure is indeed effected, often without the need for surgery, drugs or intervention of this kind. What can sometime be seen as lacking in the methods of such treatments is an insight into the causes, at a higher or esoteric level, of the dis-eases we create for ourselves. With our advance into the Aquarian Age we must accept that we create our own reality, both individually and collectively. This brings a powerful realisation of responsibility that again needs guidance. This is offered as a general principle here and there are many associated areas of debate necessary, that are not the province of this book.

If we can accept this principle, we accept that we create the illness we have at any one time. An insight into the causes of this, while it may not always be possible, can be an enormous boost in bringing about an equal cure and of course, preventing it re-occurring. The mental needs of those suffering from illness can often be addressed by the Tarot, an area that, as mentioned above, can be lacking in some cases. The Tarot has already shown itself to be a wonderfully adaptive thing, by virtue of its continued existence and also by the links made with such therapies, techniques, methods and understanding utilised by many complementary and natural therapies. I am sure that further advancement will be made in this area by those who work with the Tarot in years to come, as has been the case throughout the twentieth century. By opening the work of the Tarot Therapist to include other therapies and vice-versa, we can arrive at a more complete and truly holistic method of healing. Each link covered in this Chapter is made in this spirit, again by way of suggestion and offering. Some require the reader to have an open mind to new approaches, but it is likely that if you have read this far, you have this regard for the Tarot. It is but a short step to extending it to what follows!

COLOUR

The Tarot is, like all things, an expression of energy. Moreover, the Tarot is an explanation of energy. When we realise that all things that exist are an expression of energy in some form, we open ourselves to one of the basic tenets of the Aquarian Age. As we learn more of the ways of energy enormous possibilities open up to us, in many fields, not least that of medicine and healing.

The nature of energy is to vibrate. Different speeds of vibration create different forms of energy. One of the strongest means by which we perceive these energies is by colour. Though a scientifically complicated procedure, one of the most effective and beautiful illustrations of this principle is the rainbow. Our bodies are also energy, again at differing levels and speeds of vibration. Each part of our being vibrates to its own particular rhythm which creates and maintains its physical structure and well-being. When something happens to cause an interruption to this rhythm the energy is disrupted too and we experience a resultant physical disease, based around that organ or part of our being. By creating a corresponding vibration we can bring about a re-alignment of the energy of the diseased part.

Many natural and complementary therapies utilise this principle in their different methods. Colour is one of the most readily available and accessible forms of healing, that we use daily in the choice of colours we wear, foods we eat, decor we surround ourselves with and so on. All the colours we encounter have an effect upon us, principally mentally and emotionally, but also at a higher and purely vibratory level.

The workings of Colour can also be seen biologically. We absorb colour through our skin and eyes. What we observe is passed to our brains via the Hypothalamus, described as a 'neutral control centre' at the base of the brain and which regulates our automatic functions via the glands. One such gland, the pineal gland, synthesises and secretes melatonin and is subjective to light or energy and therefore colour. By introducing specific colours into a clients being, in one of several forms, the necessary chemicals are stimulated within the body to effect the cure required at this level.

Every good Tarot card is designed specifically to reflect and create certain ideas and truths. A strong and basic means of the expression of its truth and meaning is the colour given to the card. As with the symbols seen in a selection of cards in a consultation, the eye of both therapist and client is instinctively led to certain colours, perhaps observed as a continuation of colour across the cards chosen, as one concentrated in a particular cards or the colour(s) occurring on the card that makes itself known as the key card in a consultation.

By adding the vibratory principle and effect of these colours to the interpretation and discussion of the consultation, the Tarot Therapist is able to offer suggestions or perhaps the practice of colour therapy or healing. We are all sensitive to colour, even or perhaps especially, those of us who do not have physical sight. Clients will often make mention of the colour(s) on a card, whether in a positive or negative context. These should be investigated by a process of discussion between therapist and client. The influence of colours revealed in the cards can be surprisingly strong and offer a means of addressing the imbalance of the client.

Before some suggestions of the ways in which colour can be used in healing as a consequence of its realisation in the consultation are given, it is necessary to examine the principles and nature of different colours, by way of a basic introduction to this process. The Bibliography includes titles that contain much greater and detailed information concerning colour, which it is useful for the Tarot Therapist to become familiar with.

There are seven main colours in our spectrum conforming to the rainbow colours and matching the significance of the rainbow. It is these colours with some significant additions that are mentioned briefly here, as fuel for further learning. These colours also conform to the Chakra system, mentioned in the previous Chapter. Our well-being is dependent on the unblocked and unhindered functioning of the chakras that can also be affected by the use of colour. The chakras can also be linked to the annual round of the wheel of the year, covered later. The integration of these factors give us a complete system for development of body, mind and spirit, teaching us a great deal else in its wake. This can form a complete system of integrated healing, the subject of a book yet to come.

The seven colours included here contain the complete spectrum, with red as the densest colour, containing black with violet as the lightest colour, containing white. From this spectrum a healing can be effected that is specifically geared to the individual concerned by the use, in whatever form, of a specific shade and hue, derived from one of the seven basic colours below.

RED
This is the Spirit of Life and is seen as the colour of passion, life-blood, courage and anger. It is linked with the physical nature, strength and vitality. It is the colour of aggression and the fire of the will. Red can be used for treating fear, worry and depression and anything related to the blood and circulation.

ORANGE
Orange is the Spirit of Health and Purity and is the colour of energy and enthusiasm. It is related to the sexual urge and the reproductive system. It is linked to the Sun and its regenerative power. Orange is good to use for problems of an emotional nature, for overcoming depletion of energy, tiredness and depression.

YELLOW
Yellow is the Spirit of Knowledge and Wisdom and is the colour related to the conscious or lower mind, governing the activity of the left brain. Yellow is used to aid the digestive system, to help the nervous system and to encourage the client to mentally realise what they require to help themselves.

GREEN
Green is the Spirit of Evolution and is acknowledged as the colour of the heart and of love. Green is a traditional healing colour, being associated with nature and its predominant colour in our lands. It is seen as a colour of compassion, generosity, humility and kindness. It can also be the colour of envy. Green is used to bring the client back to balance and harmony and is also good to treat shock, neuralgia and heart and lung conditions.

BLUE

Blue is the Spirit of Truth and relates to the intuitive faculty of our minds, governing the right-brain functions. It is therefore the colour of the higher mind and communication. It is associated with devotion, religion, faith and trust. It is used for throat conditions, for calming the mind and the nerves and to cool down generally. It is good to slow bleeding and for shock.

INDIGO

Indigo is the Spirit of Power and Knowledge and is the colour of the faculty of psychism and inspiration This is the colour of the visionary and is used to treat the client at a deeper or higher level than the physical. Indigo can also be used as an aid to the hypnotic state and for the general growth and development of the body.

VIOLET

Violet is the Spirit of Sacrifice of High Ideals and is the colour of the mystic and those with awareness of other worlds. It is a colour of idealism and divine love. It has a highly creative feel and can be used to stimulate these higher and creative faculties in the client. This colour can be used to unite the physical with the divine, realigning the client to their own sacred awareness.

GREY	Fear and conventional formality
BLACK	Can be seen as unmanifest light and relates to that which is hidden; potential. It also gives power to other colours. It can be seen as nurturing and offering safety and refuge.
WHITE	The brother/sister hood of humanity. Purity and potential, containing all other colours.
SILVER	The colour for the feminine. movement, awareness and adaptability.
GOLD	The colour for the masculine, strengthening, building, forming and mending.

Colour is of course, in use at all times and often unconsciously. We use colour to help express ourselves, in our choice of clothing and the colour of our hair if we change it. The colours we choose to decorate the place we live in are the colours we need. The foods we are drawn to can also be because of the energy they give us in the form of the colour they are, the most obvious example here being the vegetable known as 'greens' and oranges!

However these effects can be amplified when used consciously and with specific and deliberate intent, afforded us by the principle 'energy follows thought'. With the power of intention and focus, the energy of the colour is increased to create a directly focussed healing energy to the object of our requirements. Apart from the uses outlined above, there are several ways colour can be used for therapy.

Clothing is a very powerful means of absorbing colour, particularly those worn next to the skin. A cloth or piece of silk could be lightly tied around an arm or leg or even carried in a pocket, by way of a talisman, when it is of the colour we need at any one time.

It is now possible to acquire a great many different coloured light bulbs, or they can be easily painted the colour we need, to effect its hue in a room. Sitting calmly in this room will enable us to absorb this colour. We can charge water with colour, by either covering it with a cloth and leaving it in the sun or day light for absorption, then drinking it. This takes the energy within our bodies, particularly when done with reverence and thanks. We can create a complete meal featuring foods of the colours we need, applying the maxim 'you are what you eat' to its fullest extent!

Using the breath and meditation are two excellent methods of employing colour for healing. Once calm, the necessary colour can be imagined as being absorbed into the body as each inhalation is taken. With the addition of a comfortable rhythmic breathing for the individual, this form of 'coloured breath' is very effective. In meditation the colour we use can be visualised, surrounding our entire being with it, then allowing it gradually and gently to seep into every fibre of our being and our bodies through the pores of the skin.

AROMATHERAPY AND HERBALISM

The healing art known as aromatherapy is one of the complementary/natural therapies that has found a place alongside the mainstream, accepted forms of 20th century medicine. In aromatherapy, the essential oils of a plant or flower are extracted and applied in a number of different ways. The active chemical constituents of plants treat various forms of disease in the body and can also act on emotional, mental and spiritual levels. Oils can be made into a massage blend, when added to a base or carrier oil such as sweet almond or avocado. Oils can be added to a bath, used as a steam inhalation or simply in a burner, as well as a number of other ways.

In Herbalism plants are used on the same basis, but are more often prescribed as a tincture, in capsule form or applied as a poultice. The professional approach to aromatherapy and herbalism, being the only one that the Tarot Therapist should concern themselves with, requires a detailed knowledge of the tools of the trade and a degree of sensitivity in dealing with clients. In this respect, there is an immediate overlap with the Tarot Therapist.

Different oils or herbs are used for a particular disease, the actual choice and combination of oils really being a matter of personal preference on the part of the therapist and personal taste (or rather smell!) for the client. The plants from which oils are extracted have featured on Tarot cards for many years and in many different pack designs. One of the packs to feature plants, including roses, lilies and irises, though not obtrusively, is the Rider-Waite deck. However, the pack of the Aromatherapist and herbalist par-excellence is the Herbal Tarot (see Appendix 1). This pack blends the underlying meaning of each card of the Tarot deck with a herb that matches its properties.

It is my suggestion and understanding that Tarot cards blend so well with the plants and flowers used in these professions because they share the same root (if you will excuse this pun!). This is a deep integration and basis in the natural world. We are returned once more to our awareness that 'all is energy'. The natural world is an expression of energy too, albeit at a larger, planetary scale. With this understanding comes a recognition that both plants and the Tarot, being an explanation of the form this energy takes in our world, share the same essence. It is this essence that is applied in aromatherapy, herbalism and Tarot Therapy.

As such it constitutes a powerful, optional aid for the Tarot Therapist. The close relationship between the cards and plants/herbs is an astounding one that can be utilised to great effect here. To gain a thorough understanding of this relationship I refer readers to the Bibliography, wherein can be found books dealing excellently with this subject in the necessary detail. Volumes 2 and 3 of this work constitute a detailed examination of the Major and Minor Arcanas respectively, in the light of Tarot Therapy, which include the oils and herbs associated with the cards.

By the use of a pack such as the Herbal Tarot, some important clues can be gained as to the ascription and use of herbs that may aid a client in dealing with a disease, problem or situation. Whilst it should be made clear that it is recommended that a Tarot Therapist who is not a qualified herbalist does not prescribe herbs for use, recommendations can be made on referral to an (open-minded) herbalist. It may even be that such a Herbalist or Aromatherapist utilise the Tarot in their work or that the Tarot Therapist gain a qualification in this subject to add to their work. Care should also be taken when working with herbs, as some utilised in the profession are poisonous or have psychotropic effects.

Whilst these can be a help one needs to know exactly how to use them.

Herbs and oils can also be used as aids to some of the inner processes described below, with particular emphasis on meditation and the Tarot. This deceptively powerful form of therapy can be boosted still further when, in the context described below, an oil is burnt (vaporised) in the room, or applied to a client's body, before undertaking their guided meditation. Some herbs can be used to 'smudge' or cleanse the clients aura or energy body prior to their inner working or taken as a tincture. These methods are also another way for the client to continue their therapeutic work, after the time of the consultation. This takes us to the need for ongoing treatment, in the form of subsequent consultations that can often be required for a difficulty, situation or disease to be fully cleared or worked through.

HOMEOPATHY

There are many other complementary and natural medicines and methods of healing available, many of which can be easily and comfortably combined with a Tarot Therapy consultation to provide a more complete form of treatment. This is because many of these methods utilise the same techniques based on the principles of nature that the Tarot is also based upon. They each seek to restore a balanced well-being in the client, taking into account their holistic requirements, aiming to treat body, mind and spirit.
The principles of such workings are broadly similar to the above. Once an area of need has been identified it is then a matter of how best to address the underlying cause, as opposed to only the symptoms. This causal approach is another one common to both the Tarot and natural therapies.

By way of example, a homeopath bases their prescription on a thorough analysis of their client, which could be aided and abetted by the Tarot, enabling a still deeper diagnosis to be made. Though I have only a basic knowledge of this subject, I am sure that correspondences could be made between the medicines and the cards. Homeopathy takes as its basis the principle of 'like cures like' It is easy for the Tarot Therapist to realise that this can be applied to the cards selected by the client as they reflect or are 'like' their state of being at the time of the consultation.

BACH FLOWER REMEDIES

In recent years there has been a veritable explosion of remedies derived from flowers, from ever more exotic parts of the world. The original and quite possibly still the best of these flower remedies are those introduced by Dr. Edward Bach in the 1930's. These treat the "personality disorders' of the client, rather than the physical condition, as of course, does the Tarot. This offers an excellent means by which the Tarot Therapist can easily and effectively suggest an ongoing method of treatment, based on the consultation.

Flower remedies are non-invasive and gentle, are non-addictive, have no side effects and are harmless if wrongly prescribed. With such a reliable safety-net the Tarot Therapist is quite safe in 'prescribing' one or more remedies to their client. The remedies may be taken individually or in combination, which are used being best decided upon by an objective observation, such as a Tarot Therapy consultation!

Because they treat the client at a level deeper than the physical, it is easy to determine which remedies are applicable because the Tarot Therapy consultation process will make this plain. It is relatively easy to become familiar with the thirty-eight remedies available, as they are based in seven groups. Once the basic group(s) to which the clients' condition belongs has been identified, easily achieved by the cards, more specific determination can be made by discussion and observation of the cards. Those cards which show themselves to be particularly significant can be married to a remedy or remedies, since each has more than one area of influence.

If this task appears too daunting we have been helped a great deal by the consistently admirable work of John and Caitlin Matthews who have presented their own Combinations of the Tarot and Bach Flower Remedies. These are presented in Appendix 2 of their 'Arthurian Tarot Course' (see Bibliography) and constitute a comprehensive reference list. Whilst it is recommended that prescription of remedies is a process best done individually, the Matthews' work is always of sufficient quality as to be recommended for this practice.

Use of a remedy is best continued until it is felt that it is not required any longer. Exactly when this occurs may be indicated by a variety of means, from outer, physical or practical changes or inner, more subtle ones. It can often be the case that use of a different remedy becomes necessary as further levels of imbalance are uncovered as a healing progresses. This process, akin to that of ongoing Tarot Therapy, allows for a review to be made at subsequent consultations. When a client receives their next consultation after what is deemed the most appropriate interval by both parties, it may be that an alternative remedy is suggested. This may be necessary in order to take account of different cards being chosen, indicating a different quality of energy being processed by the client. Healing can be an instant thing, but is more often a gradual process, to be truly whole and complete. The combination of Bach Remedies and the Tarot offer an excellent means of achieving such a state of completion, balance and wellbeing.

HEALING

Just as there now exists a plethora of flower remedies there seems to be an equal number of hands-on healing methods. Whatever the particular method used, the age old practice of 'laying on of hands' uses the transference of energy from healer to client to effect a cure. Since it works at the same energy level of reality, healing can be combined with the Tarot Therapy consultation to bring about a more thorough cure.

When attending for healing, the client will present problems or conditions that they may not know the cause of. The Tarot can be used to ascertain the underlying reason for their malady, the mental realisation that follows then being combined with the physical, emotional and often spiritual healing permitted by the transference of energy.

Though described here as the 'laying-on' of hands, healing of this type often does not involve physical touch at all. This is because the healer works in the aura or energy field of the client, affecting change at this level. By doing so they become attuned to and aware of the holistic condition of the client. They may receive impressions regarding any aspect of the client while treating them. Such impressions can be shared with the client and investigated by use of the Tarot.

Healing can work in tandem with the Tarot, using either as the initial diagnostic tool, and the other as the investigate method. Healing given in this from is nearly always a pleasantly relaxing experience at the very least and can be a profound and revelatory one. Following the sometimes stressful experience and hard concentration required during the Tarot consultation, healing can be warmly welcomed by the client, giving them a chance to lie down and relax, which in itself, allows for absorption of the material covered by the consultation. Remembering that this takes an energy form, the relaxed client will more readily and easily absorb what has been offered to them by the cards.

Because energy operates at what we call the 'subtle' level of reality, the client may not realise at the time the significance of what has been said during a consultation. As previously pointed out, it may take a period of time before the realisation occurs in the client to enable to them to make use of what has been said. Healing given during a consultation can certainly assist this process, also enabling a smoother and less traumatic transition to be made when it does occur. Change can often be an uncomfortable thing, causing insecurity in the client, when the foundations of their being or life are moved. Healing can allow for this to be as positive an experience as possible. A healing ability should therefore be seen as a valuable addition to the repertoire of the Tarot Therapist.

PHYSICALLY BASED HEALING

There are a great many natural therapies that are more physically based than those mentioned above. This does not make them any less effective than any other therapy of course. In the case of methods such as acupuncture and Shiatsu, the healing is still applied at an energy level, being based on the free flow and direction of the energetic structure of the physical body.

The 'etheric' body as it is known is the blueprint for the physical body, the energy framework on which the blood and bones of the physical body hang. The physical organs and systems of the human body have their energy equivalent in the form of the meridian lines that flow through it. To the practitioners of the Eastern methods of therapy, energy must flow freely along each of these meridian lines for health to be present. When blockages occur at any point along a meridian line, an imbalance occurs which in turn creates a disease. This may be caused at a physical, emotional, mental or spiritual level. The acupuncturist or Shiatsu practitioner uses their 'art' to free the blockage in the meridian and so health and balance is restored.

In techniques such as reflexology and acupressure, pressure is applied to specific areas of the body, for the same reasons and ends. In reflexology the soles of the feet are seen as maps of the body on which each of the vital organs and areas of the body have their place. When pressure is applied, energy is focussed to its corresponding place in the body, so ensuring the freedom of energy associated with it. In this way health is maintained or restored.

In acupressure, the same principle applies, to the specific points on the body held by the therapist. These points are usually those at which meridian lines begin or end or at some point where they cross. These places create a more powerful focus of energy, increasing the possibilities of malfunction. Where several meridian lines intersect, the energy vortex that is a chakra is created.

As with the other therapies explored so far, there is ample opportunity for the Tarot Therapist who is proficient at their technique, to include its use in their consultation. The Tarot can again be used as a diagnostic tool to aid in the treatment given by the bodywork therapist, of whatever method. Alternatively, it is possible for a layout to be constructed that reflects the path of the meridian lines of the body and its energetic structure as a whole. When laid in this manner, the Therapist is supplied with a method of analysis as well as their usual diagnosis.

Such a layout could be combined with the chakra layout suggested previously to create a full analysis of the energy of the client at a physical level. This requires a good deal of investigation and then more space than is appropriate here, but I look forward to the implementation of such a method as this.

One of the objectives of this work is to introduce the idea of the Tarot as a therapy, over and above its current use and image. It is hoped that as a consequence of this new view and regard for the Tarot, others will be inspired to work with the cards and produce ever more effective and complete methods and forms of treatment. What has been presented above is but the briefest outline and introduction of this process, focussing only on those areas I am personally aware of, usually though my own experience.

As we move into the new millennium with all that this symbolises for the possibilities of advancement for humanity, it is heartening to reflect on the new understanding that will be achieved in the hitherto unexplored field of energy. As the discoveries made are applied to the field of healing and therapy, there is a very exciting future for the Tarot. This full awareness of the structure of the human being is yet to be achieved. As we move closer to it, the Tarot will be able to assume an ever more relevant and important place as we realise the measure of what it represents.

As part of this process, detailed and investigative work on the many areas mentioned here is required, carried out by those with deep knowledge of their specialist subject, possibly in combination with the Tarot Therapist. I have no doubt that the pioneers required are those souls already or waiting to be incarnate on the Earth. I hope that I may meet and even work with some of them and serve the spirit of the Tarot in this way a while longer.

ASTROLOGY

Though not always seen as a therapy, astrology can be a powerful means of self-realisation, understanding and development, thereby coming easily under the umbrella of therapy. It should be stressed at the outset that the astrology referred to is not that of the daily newspapers and the generalised predictive outpourings based on the 'sun signs' only. The astrology required alongside Tarot Therapy is that of the qualified or at the very least, knowledgeable astrologer, able to apply the personal birth chart, transits and progressions of the client to their Tarot consultation. In this field, there are many possibilities that open up, for both therapist and client.

The Tarot and astrology share a long and varied history, varied in the sense of the correspondences made between the cards and the signs, planets and houses of astrology differing, according to the approach and understanding of the individual making them. Here the reader will need to familiarise themselves with the basics of this subject prior to making their own choices, these, as ever, being the ones that will work best and most effectively for them. This is in itself a huge task, owing to the many and varied books available on both subjects.

However, a brief guide and introduction here may help to alleviate matters somewhat. The Tarot and astrology can be used together in different ways, further complicating an already complex procedure. Here, two approaches will be considered. The first is that of the calendrical approach and the second is the interpretative one.

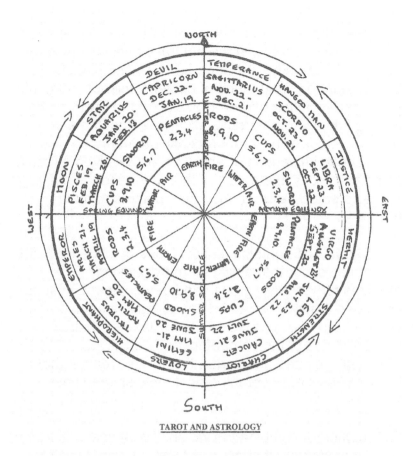

Tarot and Astrology

The calendar offers us many opportunities for personal and spiritual development through a process of self-observation, as we each progress around the spiralling pattern of the wheel of the year. Each year places us on an ever higher turn of the spiral if we are following a conscious path of evolution. There have been many attempts to produce a calendar that sticks to various formulae inherent in the yearly round of nature. Nature however, always retains an unpredictable element, with so many factors influencing it, that it becomes very difficult to produce a definitive, stagnant calendar by which to regulate ourselves and lives.

One of the strongest factors influencing the manifestation of a great many occurrences in the natural world, including the procedures of humanity, is that of the stars and planets. In the view of astrology and much of esoteric science, humanity and the wider evolution and progression of the Earth and all it entails, is subject to energetic influences from the stars and planets as our own Earth processes through the heavens. These influences or energies are received by each according to the circumstances of their birth and the placings and angles created between the stars, planets and the Earth.

As an individual's life unfolds, critical times of influence from these energies occur that assist them by causing opportunities for learning, growth and development. Just as we have seen that the Tarot can depict the influence of these underlying energies, so can the science of astrology, when in the hands of the competent and sensitive, therapeutically minded astrologer. It is for this reason that the Tarot and astrology combine as deeply as they have done.

The first method of combination we shall examine is that of a fixed calendar system, that does not seek to adapt itself to the ongoing annual evolution, but rather purports a typology of its own. This is to divide the year into 36 equal divisions, around the 360 degrees of the annual astrological map of the heavens. By ascribing one Tarot card to each of these 'decans', basic psychological types are established. This working is based on the seminal work 'Tarot and Astrology' (see Bibliography).

This method is of principal use for the Tarot Therapist as specific cards occur in a consultation. We have seen that frequently in the course of a consultation one card in particular presents itself as being of prime significance, for a variety of reasons. With the additional analysis afforded us by the decan in which the card falls, basic character traits can be applied that may well have a further bearing on the relevance of this card.

For a full appreciation of this relevance, readers will need to familiarise themselves with the book 'Tarot and Astrology', but a brief analysis here will assist. In this system, the Minor Arcana cards from the two's to the nine's only are used, seen as 'potentials' within the client. Each one is ascribed a 'decan' of ten days of the year, over which its influence extends. In addition a Major Arcana card is seen as governing one of each of the twelve signs of the zodiac, thereby also overseeing three Minor Arcana cards. For Tarot Therapy purposes this process adds a further dimension to our analytical and interpretative consultation procedure.

The second method of combining the Tarot with astrology is the more traditional one. This forms correspondences between a card and the similar interpretations and influences from a planet, sign or house. As a consequence of this process and in keeping with the individual nature of both subjects there are various different opinions as to which astrological emblem or influence belongings to which card. These correspondences are based on the understanding of the individual forming them of both the signs of the zodiac, heavenly planets and the house system of division in use (there being different ones available). These will in turn be dependent on the experience, development and history of the individual.

Use of this method therefore requires the Tarot Therapist to have their own working knowledge of astrology in order to combine its procedures with their consultations. However, to aid the achievement of such an understanding, I will include the astrological correspondences most generally agreed upon in my analysis of the cards in Volumes 2 and 3, as they apply to Tarot Therapy. In the meantime, the Exercises for this Chapter include directions to begin this work.

GROUP THERAPY

The general field of Personal Development offers many tried and tested methods for the understanding of the self, based on mental or psychological approaches, emotional ones or a combination of both. There are many techniques available, practised within a broad category of therapy, such as counselling, which are of value in Tarot Therapy, such as having a pillow and bat available for the client to hit, as a release of anger, tension or pent-up emotion. For this to be effective and reach the required depth, it is helpful if the 'offending' emotion is identified prior to the act. This is the province of the Tarot consultation.

The practices and therapies we have examined so far have all been based on a one-to-one approach. This can be viewed as the optimum technique for Tarot Therapy, but the possibilities and options for therapy to be conducted in a group also offer many benefits that should not be ignored. Though not necessarily therapeutic by definition or even by approach, the effects of the act often result in an enlargement of consciousness, deepening of understanding or gentle release of emotion that can certainly be considered a therapeutic one. It is in this broader regard that the following methods are explored, to fuel the reader with ideas and inspiration for their own ways in which they may practise Tarot Therapy.

The marketplace is currently full of workshops and courses, often costing a good deal of money, promising wonderful revelations and results. At risk of perhaps adding to this list, the subjects covered here are ideal for the workshop environment. It should be borne in mind that such events need not cost the earth, for a group of like-minded souls can often be gathered quite easily, for little more than the cost of a small advert in the local newspaper or shop window. With a little organisation and determination it is quite possible to establish a group to conduct its own Tarot Therapy. In such a context the material that follows, and the Exercises for this Chapter, are ideal.

We begin with the simplest approach to group therapy, that of a discussion group. This may be undertaken to explore and study the Tarot, perhaps using this, or any other book on the subject as a guide. A piece can be read aloud at each evening, or studied by the group members prior to the gathering and ideas shared at the meeting. An easy and most effective way to establish an agenda for the meetings is simply to select one card per meeting. With weekly meetings the complete pack will have been studied in depth in approximately 18 months and an excellent understanding of what the cards represent achieved.

The success of such a group depends on the efforts of not just one 'leader' however for each member must play their part, contributing to the whole as they are able. Experience has taught me that the best means of achieving such a unity is to ensure that the workings of the group are dedicated to the highest good and development of the individuals within it. It is helpful to then determine the responsibilities of being part of the group, in such areas as each member feels fit. The dynamics of group work are many and varied and can be quite complex. I will not therefore endeavour to examine them all here, but simply recommend an open-minded and patient approach. Once achieved, a committed group can establish a series of friendships that reach far deeper in a few meetings than years of one-to-one work can sometimes achieve. The shared beauty of tender moments of understanding, companionship and communication must be experienced to be appreciated.

In the examination of the card the discussion group may invite an open floor, perhaps allowing each member in turn to put their views for five or ten minutes. An allotted person could make notes of the salient points, noting disagreements and shared views. They may then share the summary with the group at the end of the evening. In this or any similar process a further dimension may be added by an examination of the reasons for each individual's views and opinions. The cards always retain the ability of reflection of the inner self. Once a good rapport and understanding has been established in the group, with the stated aim of honesty (with sensitivity), other group members will be in a good place to offer objective observation as to the reasons for the views expressed towards a certain card. Careful and again sensitive questioning can prompt an individual to the same kind of realisation possible in a consultation.

In this situation, it may be that the realisation prompts an equal release of emotion. In these circumstances the group must be careful to allow time for this energy to be released and to be supportive of what is felt and said for the individual concerned. The therapeutic power of the Tarot should not be seen in a shallow light, but the healing and beauty of such times should always be remembered.

A powerful additive to this group scenario is meditation. Previous Chapters have included meditations regarding the Tarot in general but here we enter a different realm of possibilities afforded us by this ancient art. Meditation enables its practitioner to reach a transpersonal level of the subject, if there is one. In this case the subject is a Tarot card, as it applies to the individual approaching it. In the group setting, one person may be elected (voluntarily, or nominated by the gods by way of lots) to guide the rest of the group through the meditation.

In encountering the card at this level, understanding of it can be achieved that is above and beyond that possible by the conscious mind alone. Again, this must be experienced to be understood, for it is the experience itself that grants the understanding. The fruits or realisations of a meditation can be explained and shared with others and this is certainly of use, but particularly in the case of Tarot meditation, experience is all.

Following the 'energy follows thought' principle, the thought forms focussed on this card by people over the years of a cards history create what is in effect, a living being that is the card. This level of reality can be experienced through meditation and the card can quite literally come alive to the meditator. Events should be allowed to unfold in the meditation, as the card will quite often appear to dictate what is experienced within it.

The scene on a card can be entered into in meditation and an active role played in it by the meditator. Events should be allowed to unfold as they wish, for the dynamics of this practice are such that 'going with the flow' is the best approach for the fullness of the experience. A figure in the card may speak to the individual, or they may sense words or feelings coming to them in their consciousness, while in the meditation. These communications may be universal in nature or may apply only to that person at that time. Whichever applies, the material received should be recorded on coming out of meditation, lest it be lost. It is easy to feel that one will remember the contents, but these details are like dreams that disappear like the morning mist as the consciousness clears. Once written down, they are grounded in the physical reality to which they apply.

Meditation on the Tarot is a very powerful means of therapy but should only be entered into once a basic familiarity of both subjects is achieved. The Tarot reflects reality as it truly is, not as something that is always gentle, kind, sensitive and understanding, for life is not always like this. As such, the experiences possible in meditation may not always be of this nature so a basic awareness of the depth to which the meditator can experience, coupled with the energy represented by the card they are meditating on should be present. This will allow the individual to expect at least something of what may occur. This is not to say of course that Tarot meditation is always unpleasant, The most beautiful and indescribable feelings are certainly possible through its practice.

The possibilities of Tarot meditation are enormous and can of course be used both in the one-to-one consultation and group setting. Both are effective but may be preferred by different individuals. Having established the most significant card or perhaps two (at the most three) cards from a consultation, they can be entered into via meditation, with the Tarot Therapist acting as guide. This can be a beautiful way of following the mental realisation achieved by the consultation interpretation through to a therapeutic conclusion. The level reached by the meditation can ensure that the effects of the consultation are lasting and positive for the client.

In a group setting, meditation can be a collective means of enjoyment at the very least, but at the most can provide for shifts in consciousness from which the group progress to a new understanding and dynamic in their operation and communication. Tarot meditation should be entered into with a positive regard and open-mindedness that will surely be reflected back with the rewards granted that are beyond ordinary comprehension.

There are two approaches to this subject that are possible. The first is to enter into the cards, by way of playing an active part in it and allowing events to unfold as they wish. This requires a greater degree of depth on the part of the meditator but can offer a return from an equal depth within the individual. Also required is an open-minded approach as to what may occur and what feelings it may bring up.

The second approach is that of attempting to make a contact with what is essentially the spirit of the card and allowing this to communicate as it may. This could be by way of direct words, heard as if inside the ear as is usual with such forms of communication, or by way of feelings, symbols, images or the precious rarity of a full blown vision.

Whichever is your choice, or perhaps what choice is made for you by the card, meditation on the Tarot is an excellent and powerful method of therapy. It is recommended that the meditation experiences are discussed with the therapist, or group, following the experience. This is not in an attempt to analyse it or decipher the meaning of what has been communicated. Rather, this is to ground the energy of the meditation into a more physical reality, so as not to forget or lose the essence of the experience and what may have been realised from it.

What is realised or learnt form any one Tarot Therapy meditation may not be known at a conscious level for some time, if at all. This does not invalidate the meditation or mean that its worth has been lost. The workings of energy, as the underlying but strongest reality we have, are what ultimately matter. It may well be that the individual needed to have their experience in meditation so as to allow opportunity for the energy shift to occur that in turn causes a change at the outer, practical level, without the person's awareness of it. The nature of energy is to move, it cannot be static. Our conscious comprehension is a secondary matter and so is the case with Tarot meditation. Sometimes it can be enough simply to visualise a card or figure from it in meditation for the most profound revelation and learning to occur. This simplest things are often the most striking and true.

STORYTELLING

An area of therapy afforded a unique opportunity by the Tarot is that of story-telling. The telling of stories was the main method of learning before the ability to write was widespread. The use of allegory and myth, wrapped in the tales of heroes and ancestors, was easily and wonderfully capable of imparting the knowledge required in the world. Now we have largely lost the art of telling stories that are based on the imagination and ability of the teller.

In days past the magical ability and worth of the story teller was recognised and they were richly rewarded, with gifts freely given. As the mental talents required for the strength of imagination needed have faded, many of us find it difficult to conjure up tales to spark the light in the eyes and the open mouthed stare of the listener, even if they are a child. The Tarot gives you the chance to achieve this magical state, in both teller and listener, by doing much of the hard work for you.

The magical potency of stories to bring about shifts at the same energy level as meditation and the other practices we have examined is not in doubt. There is ample evidence available, although most of our modern stories are told in film or on the printed page. For the child who has not yet learnt to distinguish fully what is fiction and fact, the characters of a story are alive and vibrant, the places of a story real and alive to them. This is magic.

That magic can cause changes. It is those changes that are the same as those brought about by therapy, in its many forms, as they occur at the necessary energy level we have identified. The art of storytelling can lie in the creation of believable characters and the settings they are placed in. With the use of the Tarot for your stories, this is done in what can be a breath-taking way.

There are many options available for Tarot story telling. It is not necessary but certainly preferable, for this to occur in a group. If alone, the individual can simply select a number of cards at random and create a story from them. This could be written down but is preferable for it to be recorded. In order to unleash the transformative potential of the imagination and the potency of the symbolic art encountered, it is better if the story is spoken aloud and simply made up as it goes along. It may be surprising how similar this can be to the interpretative process of a consultation!

In the group situation the story could be recorded, so its fruits are not lost. The short stories created could well be useful and therapeutic for others, this being an excellent subject for the Tarot magazine I mentioned earlier!

In a group setting, as with the individual story teller, it is especially helpful to create a mood and atmosphere to assist the story and its teller. The lights can be dimmed and candles lit, appropriate music played, incense burnt, decorations hung, even scenery created. All these help in bringing a story to life and in the case of dimmed lights, remove any embarrassment or self-consciousness felt by the teller! Perhaps the ideal setting for a story is around a fire, wrapped in a blanket, (optional hip-flask/pipe by your side!) beneath a starry sky. By staring into the fire, the effect is one of scrying, which of itself awakens the inner faculties.

Speaking aloud can be a daunting process for some particularly direct from one's imagination, for some. It is therefore worthwhile to mention that a story is not measured in terms of how 'good' or otherwise it is by means of the quality of the words used or how sensible it is. Rather the quality of a story is in the quality of its teaching. As any Klingon from Star Trek worth their bat-leth will tell you, a good story can be told many times and not lose its power.

If you feel fraught or nervous when it comes to your turn to speak and tell your story, a little 'Dutch courage' may be in order, by way of a sip or two from the mead jug. This will help you to relax and may assist in getting the imagination a little looser too! It can add to the complete experience if the mead jug, or whatever, is passed around the listeners while the story is being told. Not too much should be taken however!

There are several options for how the Tarot is utilised in the telling of stories. The first depends on who is doing the telling. If one person is selected to tell the whole story, the remaining members of the group may like to select cards, for any reason. It may be because they feel that particular card has something to teach them, or the teller. The teller may like to select cards themselves, at random, or perhaps one card to represent each member of the group. Cards can be drawn unseen, leaving the process in the hands of 'fate'. Another option is to draw only one card at a time, continuing with the story until it seems to pause, when the next card is turned over.

For the more adventurous of spirit, all can participate in the story, each adding their own particular slant to the tale. This process requires the order of tellers to be selected, by any preferred method and then one card chosen per person, again by whichever method. The story begins and continues until the first person feels the story of their card is told. The story is continued with the next in line and so it goes on, until an end is reached.

Exactly how this process is therapeutic is difficult to explain, for like meditation with the Tarot, one needs to experience it to know. The lessons learned may be in what one hears or what one says, what one feels as a result of a tale, or what is realised from its telling. This may not be while it is being told or at its conclusion. A story may just be a pleasant thing to be a part of (listeners being as important as tellers) and only months later the 'message' it contains is realised.

A group may feel the need after a story is told to examine it to see what has been learnt and what exactly has been said. Whilst this can be a useful process, it is easy to lose the spirit of the story in dry analysis. The process of reflection is perhaps better carried out alone and in silence, sometime after the event in one's own company. If in a group that meets on a regular basis, say each full moon to tell a story, insights from the previous meetings story can be shared and the learning realised afresh.

Whatever the outcome, Tarot story telling remains a largely and sadly unexplored art. It is hoped that this changes as we learn again to utilise the Tarot for something more akin to its intended purpose. At the very least we may gain some memorable evenings and establish some important, deep and wonderful relationships as a result. This in itself is therapeutic and helps to fulfil the need for harmony within humanity.

ROLE-PLAYING

For brave souls, the practice of role-playing can extend the therapeutic process of storytelling into a further dimension. Many people fear being made to take part in role playing, while the frustrated actor in others relishes the chance. With the addition of Tarot into the process, much of the fear can be removed yet none of the transformative power.

Many of the fears associated with role-playing come from a fear of having to 'perform', or of looking silly in front of a group. Examined more deeply, this can show that the fear is one of not having a firm basis on which to work, no material to base the role on. With the Tarot, the cards provide a structure for you and the rest is easy!

In Tarot role-play, the options are much the same as with story-telling. If in a group setting, the ascription of cards can be done by all the methods described above. It may be that an individual in a group feels that they should represent a card or character that is challenging, rather than comfortable for them. In this way the card may be allowed its best opportunity to teach its lesson to that person.

Perhaps the most effective form of Tarot role-play is that where the cards used for each person's character have been previously revealed to be of significance to them. Here they are able to directly confront what that card has to say to them, by doing so themselves. This may require a willingness to 'face and embrace' the object of one's fears, but this can be a powerfully transformative experience when approached positively and non-judgementally. This positive approach is one where there are no expectations for a person to 'perform' or reach a certain standard, just as with story-telling.

An individual may well be unaware of the significance of a card, being aware only that it is significant in some way. The practice of Tarot role-play can enable them to realise the message of the card. Discussion, both before and after may be a useful adjunct to the role-play itself, considering why individuals feel drawn to act a certain way in response to their card and how they felt about doing the role-play itself. As with story-telling there are other options that participants can utilise to assist and enhance their experience, such as costume and scenery. This takes us neatly into a process that dovetails with role-play, just as story-telling does before it.

DRAMA

Drama, in its many and varied forms, can also be a therapeutic process, for both participants and audience alike. At its best it is a profound and spiritual method of teaching, learning and enjoyment. This borders on the more ancient practice of sacred drama, to which the Tarot is ideally suited.

The performance of ritual plays and mythological stories is being explored once more, the esoteric nature of such activities beginning to be recognised and valued again. We have seen that the subject matter of the Tarot is a sacred one and as such sacred drama comes easily within the boundaries of Tarot Therapy.

Again, the details of a play or ritualised drama can be determined by chance or by careful and purposeful selection of cards. It may be that the use of one suit or other particular choice of cards is appropriate for the theme of an evening, festival or gathering to which the drama belongs. The selection of who plays which part also offers much by way of therapy. With the addition of appropriate scenery, which need not be costly or extravagant, a piece of Tarot drama can communicate the most striking spiritual truths in a wonderful way. The audience may not even need to be aware that the source of what is imparted is the Tarot, or the message can be broadcast by having enlargements of the cards as a backdrop to the drama. With a little creative lighting and perhaps some incense, an atmosphere of transformation can be constructed that allow the Tarot characters a chance to shine through the participants in the drama.

The form a Tarot drama may take is best left to those motivated enough to give it a go. The ideal scenario described above is just that, but just as powerful a piece can be played out between just two people in a living room, with nobody else present. It is only for the participants and the spirit of the Tarot to know the mysteries that may be revealed and the truths imparted on such an occasion.

Sacred drama can also lead us the creative possibilities afforded and inspired by the Tarot. Because its subject matter and structure is the very nature and material of life itself, there are many good stories, principles, illustrations, depictions and situations that can be brought to life by way of a movie or book. As humanity seeks to embrace more of an awareness of who and what we are, so it is likely that our creativity and art will reflect this interest and awareness. The Tarot is yet again ideally placed to offer inspiration and guidance.

Given the right funding (as seems to be the first requisite) an excellent and epic film could be made depicting the Seekers Quest, or story of the journey of the Fool. This need not be a direct telling of the tale, but one by way of allegory, as for example, with Terry Gilliam's recent telling of the ancient story of the Fisher King, in the setting of modern America. Indeed the modernising of the Tarot is something that may help a great deal in placing it once again in a respected position in the field of medicine, healing and therapy. I therefore look forward to one day settling into my local cinema seat and watching the Hollywood blockbuster 'The Seekers Quest'!

Music is another creative form that the Tarot can give of itself too, the therapeutic effects of music being a matter of personal taste but undeniable in their existence. With a little careful construction and study the music of the Tarot can be created and a voice given to the spirit of the Tarot. A piece of music can be created based on a particular card or its theme or on several cards forming a group. There have been attempts made at this, some more successful than others, but again I anticipate listening to what could be the most beautiful and therapeutic sounds (see Appendix 2).

RITUAL

Creativity takes many forms and there are other forms that the Tarot can give inspiration to. The dividing line between what is entertainment and what is a sacred or ritual act can often become blurred, both in the creation itself and its later performance. The possibilities of Tarot Ritual are as enormous as the numerical permutations of combinations of the seventy-eight cards.

The subject of ritual is one that participants should be familiar and aware of before they attempt to perform any ritual or ceremony, either for themselves or in a group. There are many and widely varied approaches and methods to ritual and like the options available in the various creative disciplines above, the Tarot can be used in an equally varied number of ways. Rituals can be structured for a definite purpose, each participant perhaps being given a card to reflect their role in its working. These can again be selected by lots or specific selections made with a clear purpose in mind. Whatever the decisions made, it is important that each is clear as to the reason why they have the card they do for the particular ritual they participate in.

The therapeutic purposes of Tarot Ritual are largely confined to the group setting, since it is within the safety offered by the sympathetic and supportive group that one can learn much through its practice. Solitary ritual certainly has its place and whilst one can learn a great deal, release of emotion and revelatory thought brought about by a ceremony often requires the reflection and objectivity of the Tarot Therapist for its full appreciation. This is just the same as with the conventional consultation.

It is again difficult to write of ritual and express its true meaning for it is another subject that must be experienced to be understood and appreciated. Its power and effect lies in the energy raised by the workings carried out during it. There are a great many methods of achieving this, often dependent on or dictated by the tradition one is working in. A ritual based on or following a Druid tradition may take quite a different form from that of the Egyptian ancestry. Each is valid and powerful and though the effects may be similar, the practice can be different.

The same is true of ritual based on the tradition and structure of the Tarot. There are certain basics applicable to any and every ritual, such as the necessity for protection and recognition and honour of the sanctity of the circle as scared space. This book is not an attempt to guide the reader through ritual, for this takes a book in itself, of which there are many already in existence (see Bibliography). My purpose here is to point out the possibilities of Tarot Ritual for therapeutic purposes.

In the therapeutic group it may be decided that a ritual or ceremony is an appropriate means for expression of what is happening within it. The purpose of the ritual should be clearly defined and understood by all those participating, with the non-judgemental option not to participate retained for any who wish. They can perhaps be involved by the writing of scripts if required, decoration of robes and the circle or room, provision of refreshments following and so on. The importance of this role will be understood at the time and will be certainly appreciated.

Once the theme or purpose has been decided, it falls to the therapist in the group to allot roles in the ritual. This is where the Tarot plays its part, offering a ready-made structure. Perhaps the ritual will take the form of the enactment of a rite between the Magician and High Priestess or Empress and Emperor, or of the wider dynamics between families of Court cards of one suit. In this case the roles and cards can be allotted by chance or deliberately, as determined by the therapist, for a known or unknown reason.

The actual structure of the ritual should then be a matter for the participants or in some circumstances may be strongly recommended by the therapist, if they have one that is tried and tested for the purpose or object in mind. There is a sufficient variety of approaches possible here that it is impossible to offer more guidance than what seems appropriate for your purposes. The guidance offered by one's intuition or instinct is the best available for this section of a ritual.

Once the middle working of your ceremony is done, allowing in this space and time to 'adlib' from any script you may be following, it is necessary to carefully disassemble what has been constructed, in terms of both your circle and the energy within it. Energy will have been raised or injected with potency and power during your ritual whether you are aware of it or not and since the nature of energy is to flow and move, it must be released and directed to a suitable destination. Once this has been done the participants are free from the constraints of the sacred space to celebrate its working with food and drink, also used to ground the participants to the everyday realm once more.

In the working of Tarot Therapy, a full and potent possibility is afforded by the cards, since a ceremony can provide the perfect framework for energy to flow. As mentioned previously in this book, each Tarot card has about it an etheric body of energy created and developing since its original inception many ages ago. Such an ancient body of energy contains a store of wisdom and power waiting a suitable opportunity to unleash its transformative potential. The well-constructed and carried out ritual is the perfect chance to achieve this. Tarot ritual should therefore not be entered into lightly, but reverently. It can then be a quite astounding therapeutic practice that not only assists the participants in their evolution but that of the Spirit of the Tarot too.

THE WHEEL OF THE YEAR

An option for the dedicated Tarot Therapist and equally dedicated group, is to perform a series of eight Tarot rituals, one each on the festivals that mark the turning of the natural cycle on its annual round, known as the Wheel of the Year. I have mentioned this previously as being linked expertly with the Tarot by the recent work of Chesca Potter and Mark Ryan in their 'Greenwood Tarot'.

The wheel of the year offers a well-rounded method of observation and spiralling forward development for both nature, ourselves and the connection between the two. With the advent of the clarity and perception of the Greenwood Tarot, we are now able to extend that link to include the Tarot. By focussing on the card(s) associated with each particular festival, we are able to construct rituals and ceremonies that open us to the natural energy of the time, thereby assisting us in our highest evolution and purpose.

The Tarot and the Wheel of the Year follows the workings of the Universe at its energetic level and frequency, as applied to our Solar System and focussed around our home planet. As dwellers on that planet, each of us receives and is imbued with Universal energy from which all things, from physical objects to emotions and thoughts, are formed.

301

When we are able to align ourselves with the rhythm and nature of that energy we are assisted immeasurably on our evolution, both individually and collectively.

The nature and character, or type of energy we receive changes as humanity and the Earth evolves. This follows many cycles, the most immediate and accessible being the annual one. As part of the natural system and aspect of the Earth, humanity is inextricably linked to its energy system. Depending on where we live on the planet, we receive a different intensity of energy from the Sun, from the Moon and the other planets, as our Earth revolves and move on its path. By opening ourselves through ritual and ceremony at specific points in this annual cycle we can bring about a connection to what, how and why we should be doing with our lives to fulfil our potential and evolution. We can also become aware of and remove that which blocks or prevents us from doing so at any one moment.

Following the pattern of Potter and Ryan, we are able to plot the Tarot cards to work with for each Festival, as well as those suits to which the seasons are aligned. This offers us a multi-levelled and multifaceted approach to the wheel of the year. The different levels of our existence are slowly becoming more understood and appreciated by those at the forefront of such fields as particle and quantum physics (and possibly the writers of 'Star Trek'!). As we learn more of how our Universe works and is constructed, so its levels and layers become clear to us.

FESTIVAL	CHAKRA	SEASON	MAJOR ARCANA CARDS	COURT CARDS	MINOR ARCANA NUMBER CARDS
IMBOLC	SOLES OF FEET	WINTER/SPRING	HIEROPHANT, STAR	PENTACLES KING, SWORDS PAGE	ACES
SPRING EQUINOX	BASE	SPRING	MAGICIAN, CHARIOT, JUSTICE	SWORDS KNIGHT & QUEEN	TWOS, TENS
BELTANE	SACRAL	SPRING/SUMMER	LOVERS, TEMPERANCE	SWORDS KING, RODS PAGE	THREES
SUMMER SOLSTICE	SOLAR PLEXUS	SUMMER	EMPRESS, EMPEROR, SUN	RODS KNIGHT & QUEEN	FOURS
LUGHNASADH	HEART	SUMMER/AUTUMN	STRENGTH, TOWER	RODS KING, CUPS PAGE	FIVES
AUTUMN EQUINOX	THROAT	AUTUMN	HIGH PRIESTESS, WHEEL, HANGED MAN	CUPS KNIGHT & QUEEN	SIXES, NINES
SAMHAIN	BROW	AUTUMN/WINTER	DEATH, DEVIL	CUPS KING, PENTACLES PAGE	SEVENS
WINTER SOLSTICE	CROWN	WINTER	HERMIT, JUDGEMENT, MOON	PENTACLES KNIGHT & QUEEN	EIGHTS

Tarot and the Wheel of the Year

It should be stressed that the information in this diagram is presented in a linear fashion, but represents a multi-layered structure. There are several points that need to be made for the successful working of ritual at the festivals.

1. The Fire Festivals, of Imbolc, Beltane, Lughnasadh and Samhain, mark the turning point from one season to another. The two seasons given in the table are the ending of one and beginning of the other in the order given. The Solstices and Equinoxes are therefore the mid-point of their season.

2. The Chakras given for each of the Festivals are the chief means by which we receive the energy spoken of above. Work can be done during a ritual to open the respective chakra, and focus on the reception of energy and direct it to the purposes of the ritual. As we orient ourselves around the wheel of the year so we climb through our bodies through the tone and quality of energy we are receiving.

3. It is to be noted that the Major Arcana cards of The Fool and the World are missing from the table. Following this system, these two cards operate a place at the centre of the wheel. The Fool therefore becomes the ritualist themselves, while the World is the circle in which we make the ritual.

4. It is to be noted that the Fire Festivals contain Court cards from two different suits. This is because of their being junctions of the seasons. Each suit governs a season, so the turning points require a reflection of this.

5. The Equinoxes are given two numbered cards from the Minor Arcana. This is because they are points of balance between dark and light in the year. Each of the numbers included therefore balance each other, one being a multiple of the other.

There are ample opportunities for effective and therapeutic ritual from this table. By use of the Major Arcana, Court and numbered cards a large working can be constructed with easily a dozen participants. This might include one person for each card (making 9), one officer to represent the season, perhaps even a Fool, free to play the traditional Jokers rule and disrupt proceedings as they may! The possibilities are endless here and the effects to be wondered at. I cannot do justice to the subject of Tarot ritual in one section of one book, it deserving an additional volume of its own, but for curious readers I would recommend the work of John and Caitlin Matthews (again!), as detailed in the Bibliography, as a good place to start.

NEW TECHNOLOGY

The advances made recently and doubtless to be made shortly can also offer opportunities for the Tarot to prove its adaptive ability. As I have tried to illustrate throughout this book, the Tarot has always been able to make itself relevant to the times and the changing technologies humanity sees fit to employ. It is unlikely this epoch in our history will prove the exception.

One of the principles of the Aquarian Age is communication, where new forms will come into use. The lightning speed of the spread of the Internet suggests this is one such form, in particular given the name of the 'World Wide Web'. In many shamanic and tribal cultures the world is seen as a web, each of us and the stars in the night sky hung on its threads.

One of the possibilities arising from the Internet and the use of e-mail is the Tarot consultation given across the world. The selection of cards can be carried out by the client and then mailed to the therapist sitting at their computer, wherever they may be. An interpretation can then be mailed back and questions relayed as appropriate, complete with suggestions and recommendations for exercises resulting and so on. Whilst not being as preferable as being present, the dynamics of such a consultation are intriguing.

The spread of computer games has also been an astonishing, though perhaps not surprising one. From my own vantage point, it seems that the majority of CD ROM games concern the field of science fiction, complete with unlikely aliens, all bent on invading Earth and killing us all. The use of violence as a method of teaching, which such games with their predilection towards young people have, is deplored. However, there are opportunities here for the sensitive and inspired person to design a game with more therapeutic qualities as the goal. As we have seen the progression of the Seekers Quest or journey of the Fool, offers an excellent structure for a compelling, challenging and rewarding game. I am sure some bright spark will avail themselves of this opportunity.

The teaching opportunities of CD ROM are also directly applicable to the Tarot. The amount of information the Tarot can carry is a huge one and so firmly suited to such a medium as this. With the benefits of interaction that can be utilised, an on-line teaching system could also be devised that allows the cards to speak for themselves!

Clearly the Tarot will not be left lagging in the human race. As humanity evolves so will the Tarot, for we are each a part of the other, based on the same ingredients, each when used mixed in ever more wonderful ways. This recipe creates by turns dishes to delight and revolt the palate but each is a necessary part of the meal. Likewise Tarot consultations may not always be a therapeutic or healing experience, but their nature will move inexorably towards an acknowledgement of the Divine, Great Spirit whom they reflect.

EXERCISES

What colour do you imagine yourself to be? Base your choice on the brief information given in this Chapter, but more on your intuitive reaction. Answer this question in meditation. What does this tell you about yourself? What colours would you like more or less of ? What colours do others think you are and what colour do you think they are? Experiment and discover if you agree. What colour do you like the least and what does this tell you?

Examine your Tarot pack, in particular noting the colours this time. Make notes with regard to what you see or feel within about the colours of the cards. Add these to the other notes in your collection.

Try to familiarise yourself with one of the therapies covered in this Chapter. It is not necessary to become qualified in one of them to be an effective Tarot Therapist, for the Tarot can stand alone in this respect quite capably. It is however, useful to have a basic knowledge of one or more of the therapies to which it readily blends, although the Code of Ethics dictates that you cannot prescribe unless qualified. You may choose in time therefore to achieve qualification standard in one therapy to use alongside your specialism of the Tarot.

Since astrology can have such a strong correspondence with the work of Tarot Therapy it is helpful for the Tarot Therapist to familiarise themselves with the basics of the subject. This need only include a basic knowledge of the properties of each sign, planets and house and the fundamental workings of the birth chart. Please see the Bibliography for some titles I have found useful in this respect or choose one of the many alternatives available.

One of the best methods of achieving the above is to have one's own birth chart constructed and analysed. This can be of great benefit in the unfoldment and development of the Tarot Therapist to which they should be always paying some attention for the effective and progressive delivery of their own work. Please see Appendix 2 for an address that offers such a service, but do look in your own area for a reputable astrologer offering a one-to-one service, taking it over and above that of the computer generated horoscope.

Meditations on the Tarot have been included in previous Exercises, as preliminaries and preparations to actual meditations on the cards. Have a go at a meditation journey back to the Temple of the Major Arcana. This time, step inside whichever card seems to draw you or that you have chosen to enter consciously beforehand. Follow the same procedure as with the earlier meditations, taking each stage carefully before proceeding. Tarot meditations are surprisingly powerful and care should be taken.

When it comes to stepping into the card, this is best done by visualising the card before you, life-size. Draw close to the card and simply step into it. However, if it helps you, you may imagine effects such that you are being taken along some king of time tunnel, akin to special effects seen in films nowadays. When you finish the trip, you arrive gently at the scene of the card.

Events are now best left to unfold as they will. Treat card figures with respect, they are ancient beings full of knowledge of their particular realm. Address them as you would any elder, but not falsely. Be yourself, be genuine, honest and polite and they will help you. Never forget to thank them before leaving or you may find them not so willing next time.

You may find on entering a card that you have become the figure or chief player in its scene. This is an indication that at the time of your meditation you are resonating deeply with the card in some form, be it in a purely energetic form, physically, emotionally, mentally or spiritually. Events should again be left to unfold. Trust what comes to you intuitively and do and say what you feel is appropriate. It may be that you have nothing to do but as Justice for example, only sit in the throne and lift your scales of Justice and Sword of Truth.

When it seems correct to do so, give your thanks and return from the card to the Temple the way you entered. Once back in the temple, adjust yourself to your surroundings. Pause here and see if anything has changed and ensure you have brought with you what you have experienced and learned. When you feel ready, return from the Temple and out of the meditation following the same procedure as before.

This kind of meditation should not be done too often, usually no more than once per moon cycle, giving chance for the energy caused by the exercise to flow, to settle and take effect. You may then move on to another card as is appropriate in your studies.

Have a go at creating some stories as a practise exercise by yourself. You may choose to write these down, or perhaps and preferably speak them aloud on to tape. You may use any of the methods outlined in this Chapter, selecting deliberately or at random. Having written or recorded your stories, leave them long enough to have forgotten their content and then review what is said. Be open to impressions as you review them, seeing if they have anything to tell you of a therapeutic nature. If there is nothing that strikes you, do not be disappointed, since it is often the act of creating the story itself that is the therapy. Therapy can occur without our knowing at a conscious level.

If you are in a suitable group situation, try to organise a role-playing exercise or enact a small piece of drama. Do not set your sights too high or ambitiously and the results may be surprising in their power. For guidance as to what to do here, re-read this section in this Chapter.

At the next suitable Festival time, either construct a ritual based on the Tarot table in this Chapter or undertake a meditation journey to the card or cards for this Festival.

There is a great deal of work that can be done in this area, as indicated in the Chapter, requiring some preparation. Determine to yourself to follow the Festival pattern through a year and observe the effects meditation and ritual has upon you.

AFTERWORD

Even as humanity moves into a new millennium and a new age in its evolution, the Tarot stands poised, ready to guide, to offer of its wisdom and its experience. Wise words and ways are not always followed, as our history shows, but truth endures despite and apart from practical action. What is required for humanity now is a means of living in harmony with each other and a way of living that allows our planet to recover its health and fulfil its maternal role of caring for us all in her ample provision.

In order to do this, humanity must look to the basics truths it has learnt. The constancy of the teachings of the Tarot will outlive the cards themselves, for they are made from the very stuff of life. For humanity to find what it needs the individuals that make up this whole must each find what they need within themselves. This requires many souls at the forefront of new teaching and learning methods as pioneers, able to withstand the ridicule that will be displayed by the majority until the tide of opinion turns by mass open hearts and minds.

Such souls are those that brave the demons we each drag with us and in so doing deserve respect and admiration. The discoveries made by these people will assist those of us who lurk in the safety of their shadows. What can be done to assist those people on their brave quest is to attempt to guide them and administer to them as best we may. To enable this to be done, the therapists and healers that do so must avail themselves of what tools they may, suited to their task. If the goal is to address and heal the whole person, the therapy must be rooted in this same philosophy.

The Tarot is only one such therapeutic method among many, but has the virtue of having been adapted to the ever changing needs of humanity as it has itself evolved. In being derived from the very substance and structure of Earthly life, it finds a natural home in the new therapy of the Aquarian Age. The Tarot has for a long time been seen only as a form of prediction, relegated to a sad position of the peeling paint of seafront piers. With its recognition as a therapy it can retain it rightful place once more, in the sanctity of the consultation room, created for this purpose.

This volume has sought to expound the theory of the Tarot as a therapy, attempting to explain the cards in this sacred light. Volumes 2 and 3 of this series will dissect the body of the Tarot, conducting exploratory surgery to the Major and Minor Arcana respectively. These books will feature an in-depth examination of each card in the pack and show how the symbols on each one form a coherent whole in a therapeutic context.

It is my sincere hope and wish that the hearts and minds of those shining souls seeking to push back the boundaries of our medicine and healing are illuminated by the new light of Tarot Therapy. May the Tarot ever be your guide, from darkness into light.

APPENDIX 1 - VARIETIES OF TAROT

ARTISTIC

With the technological advancements we have seen in recent years, it has become possible to faithfully reproduce some stunning effects on Tarot cards, which have been exploited to the full by the wide range of artists working in different mediums with the Tarot. Many of the packs listed here, as well as many that aren't, are of interest for their artistic content alone. Collecting Tarot packs can also become an exercise in art history, since the cards have fascinated artists from different genres for a long time.

Mention can be made here of some packs that are produced in black and white outline, leaving the individual to colour them as they see fit, such as The Druid Tarot (see Esoteric packs). This tendency does provide some element of what is truly required for the Tarot to be used in its most effective way. This is for individuality of interpretation. For this to be pure and carried through to its conclusion, each person using the Tarot must therefore design and construct their own pack, as would no doubt historically have been the case. Most of us however, have not the inclination, time or wherewithal to do this and so we must settle for the mediocrity of the modern, mass produced 'unit'.

Aquarian Tarot	David Mario Palladini, US Games Systems, 1970 (art deco),
William Blake Tarot	Ed Buryn, Harper Collins, 1996
Dali Universal Tarot	Salvador Dali, Salem House, 1985
Elemental Tarot	Caroline Smith, Viking, 1988 (Modern, stylised artwork)
The Haindl Tarot	H & E Haindl, Droemersche Verlagsanstalt, 1988
Sacred Rose Tarot	J. Gargiulo-Sherman, US Games Systems, 1982 (stained glass window designs)

| Voyager Tarot | James Wanless & Ken Knutson, Merrill-West Publishing, 1984 |
| Yeager Tarot | Marty Yeager, (surrealist). |

CULTURAL

The ancient tribal and historical cultures of the world seem to lend themselves perfectly to adaptation to the Tarot and thus we have many packs each based on a different culture across the world. These tribal existences are now historical, their way of life having been exterminated by the march of modernity, as their lands and rights have been systematically invaded. It is interesting to note that there is currently great interest in these cultures - hence the appearance of the Tarot decks listed below. It becomes clear that the values and practises of the tribal approach to life have a great deal to teach us, as we move into a new millennium. I have listed the packs in their respective cultural groups, in no order of preference or importance.

AFRICAN - Two packs, by Anna Branche (Aquarian) and Maria Romito (US Games Systems) respectively

CELTIC - The Arthurian Tarot Caitlin & John Matthews, Aquarian, 1990
The Celtic Tarot, Helena Paterson, Aquarian, 1990
The Merlin Tarot, R.J. Stewart, 1988
The Greenwood Tarot, Mark Ryan & Chesca Potter, Thorsons, 1996

EGYPTIAN - The Tarot of Transition, US Games Systems, 1983
The Ancient Egyptian Tarot - Clive Barrett, Thorsons, 1996

GREEK - The Mythic Tarot, Juliet Sharman-Burke, Rider, 989

MAYAN - The Xultan Tarot, Peter Balin, Arcana Publishing, 1976

NATIVE AMERICAN - The Native American Tarot, M.W. &
J.A. Gonzalez, US Games
Systems, 1990
The Medicine Woman Tarot, Carol
Bridges, US Games Systems, 1987
Tarot of the Southwest Sacred
Tribes, Violeta Monreal, US Games
Systems Inc. 1998
NORSE - The Norse Tarot, Clive Barrett, Aquarian 1989
ROMANY - Zigeuner Tarot, Walter Wegmuller, A.G. Muller,
1982
Tarot Tzigane, Tchalai, J.M. Simon-France
Cartes, 1984

ESOTERIC

Builders of the Adytum Tarot, Paul Foster Case, 1947
The Druid Tarot, Philip Shallcrass, British Druid Order, 1997
Gareth Knight Tarot, US Games Systems, 1984
Golden Dawn Tarot, Robert Wang, US Games Systems,
1977
Magickal Tarot, Tony Willis, Aquarian, 1986
Mandala Astrological Tarot, AT Mann.
Servants of the Light Tarot, Dolores Ashcroft-Nowicki,
Aquarian, 1989
Tarot of the Spirit, Pamela Eakins, Samuel Weisner Inc.
1992
Thoth Tarot, Aliester Crowley, US Games Systems 1969
Witches Tarot, Ellen Cannon Reed/Martin Cannon,
Llewellyn, 1989
Oswald Wirth Tarot - US Games Systems, 1975

FANTASY

Hanson-Roberts Tarot, US Games Systems, 1984, (fairy tale
style artwork)
Lord of the Rings Tarot, Terry Donaldson/Peter Pracownik,
US Games Systems, 1996 (Based
on Tolkein's book, doubling as a
game)

Tarot of the Cat People, Karen Kuykendall, US Games Systems, 1984

TRADITIONAL

Cosmic Tarot, Norbert Losche, FX Schmid, 1988

IJJ Swiss Tarot, AG Muller & Co, 1970

Morgan Greer, Susan Gerulskis-Estes, Morgan & Morgan Inc. 1981

Prediction Tarot, Bernard Stringer, Aquarian Press, 1985

Rider Waite Tarot, A.E. Waite, Rider & Co, 1910 (classic, 'standard' pack)

Robin Wood Tarot, Robin Wood, Llewellyn, 1991

Tarot Classic, AG Muller & Co, 1972

Tarot of the Old Path, Howard Rodway, Urania Verlags AG, 1990

Tarot of the Witches, Fergus Hall/Stuart Kaplan, US Games Systems, 1973 (as used in the James Bond film 'Live and Let Die').

GODDESS

Daughters of the Moon Tarot, Ffiona Morgan, 1984 (round cards)

Goddess Tarot, Kris Waldherr, US Games Systems, 1998

Motherpeace Tarot, Vicki Noble, Motherpeace, 1981, (round cards)

HEALING

Herbal Tarot, Michael Tierra/Candice Cantin, US Games Systems, 1988 (Ascribes a herb and its therapeutic properties to each card)

HISTORICAL

Visconti-Sforza Tarot - the earliest Tarot known to exist, made for two great Italian families of the 15th Centuries. There are many derivative packs (e.g. Cary Yale Visconti-Sforza Tarot and so on) from the above. The originals cards exist in three separate museums and collections, with four cards sadly lost. There are also a great many other historical cards in existence. The British Museum in London has many which it will show you, on request.

Other historical packs include:

Gringonneur Cards
Rothschild Cards
Court de Gebelin Tarot
Etteilla Tarot
French Revolutionary Tarot
Piedmontese Tarot.

NOVELTY

H.J. Heinz Tarot - Wes Michel, 1972. This is nine cards that were on the front of the 1972 Annual Report for the Heinz company! Each card featured some of Heinz's products: tomato ketchup, vinegar and so on. Why they did this is unknown, but one would have expected them to have produced more cards - around 57!

Opera and Operetta Tarot - C. Titze & Schinkay, 1860. Specifically this is a Tarock pack, which is a variation on Tarot, designed for game playing, but worth mentioning as the cards are all scenes from various operas.

Pop/Rock Tarot Calendar - Julia Noonan, Scholastic Book Service, 1972. This pack contains card titles from rock music of the 60's and 70's that relates to the card meanings.(i.e. The Magician - 'Pinball Wizard', Temperance - 'Let it Be'.) Proverb Tarock - Another Tarock deck, with each card featuring a well-known proverb, which gives some interesting adjectives to interpretation.

Shakespearean Tarot - Dolores Ashcroft-Nowicki, Aquarian, 1993

Mention must also be made here of the Gnomes Tarot, a pack that was the size of postage stamps - specially for use by Gnomes of course!

PSYCHOLOGICAL

Jungian Tarot, Robert Wang, Urania Verlags AG, 1988

There are more Tarot packs being issued all the time, each offering something to the evolution of the cards. Some seem to restate what has been done previously while others provide innovative new ways of viewing the cards. I look forward to the introduction of those cards which will carry of knowledge and view of the Tarot forward.

APPENDIX 2 - USEFUL ADDRESSES

AROMATHERAPIST
Aromatherapy Organisations Council, PO Box 355,
Croydon, CR9 2QP
Tel: 0181 251 7912

BACH FLOWER REMEDIES
These are obtainable, along with a list of qualified therapists,
from:
The Dr. Edward Bach Foundation, Mount Vernon, Sotwell,
Wallingford, Oxon, OX10 0PZ, Tel: 01491 834678

BOXES FOR CARDS
These are best found in the local craft shop, costing only a
few pounds and decorated yourself. Oxfam charity shops
often stock a range of wooden boxes that are a good size for
Tarot cards and not expensive, having the added benefit of
being an ethically positive purchase. Antique and 'junk'
shops also provide a good source, as do general gift shops.

CLOTH
Your Tarot cloth can be purchased in your local material
shop. It is best purchased and then sewn by you, giving you
the chance to add your own unique embroidery or perhaps
design with fabric pen. Cost will vary greatly dependent on
where you shop and the type of material you decide to use.

COLOUR THERAPY
The Colour Therapy Association, PO Box 16756, London,
SW20 8ZW,
Tel: 0181 540 3540

COUNSELLING
British Association for Counselling, 1 Regent Place, Rugby,
Warwickshire, CV21 2PJ, Tel: 01788 550899

HEALING

The Confederation of Healing Organisations, 113 High Street, Berkhamtsead, Herts, HP4 2DJ (Please send s.a.e)

HERBALIST
National Institute of Medical Herbalists, 56 Longbrook Street, Exeter, Devon, EX4 6AH, Tel: 01392 426022

INCENSE/SMUDGE/CANDLES
Star Child, The Courtyard, 2-4 High Street, Glastonbury, Somerset, BA6 9DU
Tel: 01458 834663, Fax: 01458 8311096, Email: http://www.isleofavalon.co.uk
Hand blended incense and ready made smudge, together with hand made candles are all available here, by mail order or in person in a wonderful shop, well worth a visit. There is also an excellent range of essential oils and herbs.

For a supply of Incense sticks, the best I have found can be obtained from:
The Bombay Incense Company, PO Box 2016, London, E11 1TJ.
Their incenses are widely available in shops and include a range made from organic ingredients.

MUSIC
There is a great deal of music available, of varying quality. An excellent selection, perfectly suited to the Tarot Therapy environment is available from:
Eventide Music, PO Box 27, Baldock, Herts, SG7 6UH, Tel: 01462 893995, email:
http://members.aol.com/eventidmus

TAROT CARDS
One of the widest and well-priced selections available can be found at this excellent shop: Watkins Books, 19 Cecil Court, London, WC2N 4EZ
Tel: 0171 836 2182 Fax: 0171 836 6700,
Internet: www.watkinsbooks.com
Email: service@watkinsbooks.com

BIBLIOGRAPHY

ASTROLOGY
Cunningham, Donna - *An Astrological Guide to Self Awareness* (CRCS Publications 1978)

Hashrouck, Muriel Bruce - *Tarot and Astrology* (Aquarian 1986)

Huntley, Janis - *The Elements of Astrology* (Element 1990)

March, Marion D. & McEvers, Joan - *The Only way to Learn Astrology* (ACS Publications Inc. 1981)

Mayo, Jeff - *Teach Yourself Astrology* (Hodder and Stoughton 1964)

Mayo, Jeff - *The Planets and Human Behaviour* (CRCS Publications 1985)

COLOUR
Lacy, Marie-Louise - *Know Yourself Through Colour* (Aquarian 1989)

Ouseley, S.G.J. - *Colour Meditations* (L.N. Fowler & Co. Ltd. 1949)

Wilson, Ann & Bek, Lilla - *What Colour Are You?* (Aquarian 1981)

ESOTERIC
Bailey, Alice A - *A Treatise on White Magic* (Lucis Trust 1951)

Bailey, Alice A - *Esoteric Healing* (Lucis Trust 1953)

Blavatsky, H.P., from the writings of - *Foundations of Esoteric Philosophy* (The Theosophical Publishing House Ltd. 1990)

Bloom, William - *Sacred Times, A New Approach to the Festivals* (Findhorn Press 1990)

Carr-Gomm, Philip - *The Elements of the Druid Tradition* (Element 1991)

Cooper, D. Jason - *Understanding Numerology* (Aquarian 1990)

Cowan, Tom - *Fire in the Head* (Harper Collins 1991)

Crawford, Ina - *A Guide to the Mysteries* (Lucis Trust 1990)

Fortune, Dion - *Psychic Self-Defence* (Society of the Inner Light 1957)

Green, Marian - *The Gentle Arts of Aquarian Magic* (Aquarian 1987)

Green, Marian - *The Path Through the Labyrinth* (Element 1988)

Green, Marian - *The Elements of Natural Magic* (Element 1989)

Green, Marian - *The Elements of Ritual Magic* (Element 1990)

Green, Marian - *A Witch Alone* (Aquarian 1991)

Hartley, Christine - *The Western Mystery Tradition* (Aquarian 1986)

Hounsome, Steve - *Taming the Wolf: Full Moon Meditation* (Capall Bann 1996)

Hounsome, Steve - *Practical Spirituality* (Capall Bann 1998)

Hope, Murry - *Practical Celtic Magic* (Aquarian 1987)

Matthews, Caitlin & John - *The Western Way, Vols. 1 and 2* (Arkana 1985)

Matthews, John - *The Celtic Shaman* (Element 1991)

Matthews, Caitlin - *Singing the Soul Back Home* (Element 1995)

Schimmel, Annemarie - *The Mystery of Numbers* (Oxford University Press 1993)

Stewart, R. J. - *The Underworld Initiation* (Aquarian 1985)

White, Ruth - *Working with your Chakras* (Piatkus 1993)

HEALING

Barnard, Julian - *A Guide to the Bach Flower Remedies* (C.W. Daniel Co. Ltd. 1979)

Bek, Lilla & Philippa, Pullar - *The Seven Levels of Healing* (Century 1986)

Bradshaw, John - *Homecoming: Reclaiming and Championing your Inner Child* (Piatkus 1990)

Chopra M.D., Deepak - *Quantum Healing* (Bantam Books 1989)

Davis, Patricia - *Aromatherapy, an A-Z* (C. W. Daniel C. Ltd. 1988)

Gawain, Shakti - *Creative Visualisation* (New World Library 1978)

Gawain, Shakti - *Living in the Light* (Eden Grove Editions 1986)

Hay, Louise L. - *You Can Heal Your Life* (Eden Grove Editions 1984)

Hoffman, David - *The Holistic Herbal* (Element 1983)

Hounsome, Steve - *Practical Meditation* (Capall Bann 1997)

Ingerman, Sandra - *Soul Retrieval* (Harper Collins 1991)

Jampolsky, Gerald G. - *Love is Letting Go Of Fear* (Celestial Arts 1979)

Kennedy, Eugene & Charles, M.D., Sara C. Charles - *On Becoming a Counsellor: A Basic Guide for Non-Professional Counsellors* (Gill & Macmillan 1977)

Krystal, Phyllis - *Cutting the Ties That Bind* (Element 1982)

Salmon, Philip & Jeoffroy, Anna - *The Bach Remedies and the Chakras* (Energy Works 1996)

Tierra, Michael & Cantin, Candis - *The Spirit of Herbs: A Guide to the Herbal Tarot* (U.S. Games Systems Inc. 1993)

Worwood, Valerie Ann - *The Fragrant Pharmacy* (Bantam Books 1990)

MYTHOLOGY

Carlyon, R - *A Guide to the Gods* (Heinemann 1981)

Graves, Robert - *The White Goddess* (Faber & Faber 1961)

Hope, Murry - *Practical Atlantean Magic* (Aquarian 1991)

Hall, Manly P. - *Atlantis, an impression* (Philosophical Research Society 1976

SCIENCE

Capra, Fritjof - *The Tao of Physics* (Flamingo 1976)

Davidson, John - *Subtle Energy* (C.W. Daniel Company Ltd. 1987)

Hawking, Stephen - *A Brief History of Time* (Bantam Books 1995)
Roney-Dougal, Serena - *Where Science and Magic Meet* (Element 1991)

STORYTELLING
Mellon, Nancy - *Storytelling and the Art of Imagination* (Element 1992)
Stewart, R.J. - *Magical Tales, The Story-Telling Tradition* (Aquarian 1990)

SYMBOLISM
Chetwynd, Tom - *A Dictionary of Symbols* (Paladin 1982)
Cirlot, J.E. - *A Dictionary of Symbols* (Routledge 1971)
Jung, Carl - *Man and his Symbols* (Picador 1964)
Jung, Carl - *Psychology and the Occult* (ARK Paperbacks 1982)

TAROT
Ashcroft-Nowicki, Dolores - *Inner Landscapes* (Aquarian 1989)
Ashcroft-Nowicki, Dolores - *The Shakespearian Tarot* (Aquarian 1993)
Barrett, Clive - *The Norse Tarot* (Aquarian 1989)
Bridges, Carol - *The Medicine Woman Inner Guidebook* (U.S. Games Systems Inc. 1991)
Cannon-Reed, Eileen - *The Witches Tarot* (Llewellyn 1989)
Case, Paul Foster - *The Tarot, A Key to the Wisdom of the Ages* (Builders of the Adytum Ltd. 1990)
Chamberlain, Mary Susan - *The Millenium Tarot* (Published by the author 1984)
Clarson, Laura G. - *The Tarot Unveiled* (U.S. Games Systems Inc. 1988)
Crowley, Aleister - *The Book of Thoth (Egyptian Tarot)* (Samuel Weiser Inc. 1974)
Douglas, Alfred - *The Tarot* (Penguin 1972)
Dummett, Michael - *Twelve Tarot Games* (Duckworth 1980)
Dummett, Michael - *The Visconti-Sforza Tarot Cards* (George Barzillier Inc. 1986)

Eakins, Ph.D., Pamela - *The Tarot of the Spirit* (Samuel Weiser Inc. 1992)

Gad, Dr. Irene - *Tarot and Individuation* (Samuel Weiser Inc. 1994)

Gardner, Richard - *The Tarot Speaks* (Tandem 1974)

Gerulskis-Estes, Susan - *The Book of Tarot* (Morgan & Morgan 1981)

Gonzalez, Magda Weck. & J.A. - *Star Spider Speaks: The Teachings of the Native American Tarot* (U.S. Games Systems Inc. 1990)

Greer, Mary K. - *The Essence of Magic, Tarot, Ritual & Aromatherapy* (Newcastle Publishing 1993)

Hager, Gunter & Wascher, Hansrudi - *The Arcus Arcanum Tarot* (AGMuller)

Hall, Manly P. - *The Tarot* (Philosophical Research Society 1978)

Huson, Paul - *The Devils Picturebook* (Abacus 1972)

Jayanti, Amber - *Living the Tarot* (Llewellyn 1993)

Kaplan, Stuart R. - *The Encyclopædia of Tarot Volume 1* (U.S. Games Systems Inc. 1978)

Kaplan, Stuart R. - *The Tarot of the Witches Book* (U.S. Games Systems Inc. 1973)

Knight, Gareth - *The Treasure House of Images* (Aquarian 1986)

Knight, Gareth - *The Magical World of the Tarot* (Aquarian 1991)

Lerner, Isha & Mark - *Inner Child Cards* (Bear & Co. 1992)

MacGregor-Mathers, S.L. - *The Tarot* (Unicorn Bookshop)

Matthews, Caitlin & John - *Hallowquest* (Aquarian 1990)

Matthews, Caitlin - *The Arthurian Tarot Course* (Thorsons 1993)

Nichols, Sally - *Jung and Tarot* (Samuel Weiser 1980)

Ozaniec, Naomi - *The Element Tarot Workbook* (Element 1994)

Ouspensky, P.D. - *The Symbolism of the Tarot* (Universal Books Ltd. 1985)

Papus - *The Tarot of the Bohemians* (Wilshire Book Co.)

Paterson, Helena - *The Celtic Tarot* (Aquarian 1990)

Peach, Emily - *The Tarot Workbook* (Guild Publishing Ltd. 1984)

Pollack, Rachel - *The New Tarot* (Aquarian 1991)

Pollack, Rachel - *Salvador Dali's Tarot* (Salem House 1985)

Pollack, Rachel - *Seventy Eight Degrees of Wisdom Vols 1 & 2* (Aquarian 1988)

Renee, Janina - *Tarot Spells* (Llewellyn 1990)

Rodway, Howard - *Tarot of the Old Path* (Urania Verlags 1990)

Ryan, Mark & Potter, Chesca - *The Greenwood Tarot* (Aquarian 1996)

Sharman-Burke, Juliet - *The Mythic Tarot Workbook* (Rider 1989)

Shepard, John - *The Tarot Trumps* (Aquarian 1985)

Sherman, Johanna - *The Sacred Rose Tarot* (U.S. Games Systems Inc. 1982)

Smith, Caroline & Astrop, John - *Elemental Tarot* (Dolphin Doubleday 1988)

Stewart, R.J. - *The Merlin Tarot* (Aquarian 1988)

Summers, Catherine & Vayne, Julian - *The Inner Space Workbook,* (Capall Bann 1994)

Summers, Catherine & Vayne, Julian - *Self Development with the Tarot* (Foulsham 1992)

Suster, Gerald - *The Truth About the Tarot* (Skoob Books Publishing Ltd. 1990)

Tierra, Michael & Cantin, Candis - *The Herbal Tarot Deck* (U.S. Games Systems Inc. 1988)

Unknown - *The Tarot of Transition* (U.S. Games Systems Inc. 1983)

Waite, Arthur Edward - The Key to the Tarot (Rider 1910)

Waldherr, Kris - *The Goddess Tarot* (U.S. Games Systems Inc. 1997)

Walker, Ann - *The Living Tarot* (Capall Bann 1994)

Wang, Robert - *Tarot Psychology* (Urania Verlags 1988)

Willis, Tony - *Magick and the Tarot* (Aquarian 1988)

Willis, Tony - *The Magickal Tarot* (Aquarian 1992)

Wirth, Oswald - *The Tarot of the Magicians* (Samuel Weiser Inc. 1985)

Woudhuysen, Jan - *Tarotmania* (David Westnedge Ltd. 1979)

Ziegler, Herd - *Tarot, Mirror of the Soul* (Aquarian 1989)

BIOGRAPHY

Steve Hounsome has been involved in this field for over thirty years and has completed a wide variety of studies and activities in this time.

Steve holds qualifications in the following subjects –

* *Progressive Healing*
* *Psychic Studies*
* *Esoteric Soul Healing*
* *Tarot*
* *Bach Flower Remedies*
* *Basic Counselling Skills*

The training Steve has completed is as follows –

* *One year Progressive Healing, Sanctuary of Progress*
* *One year Psychic Studies, Sanctuary of Progress*
* *Meditation - 2 years, private tutor*
* *Natural Magic, 1 year, Marian Green*
* *Ritual Magic, 1 year, The London Group*
* *Esoteric Soul Healing, 2 years, Isle of Avalon Foundation*
* *Bach Flower Remedies - Foundation Level Certificate*
* *Order of Bards, Ovates and Druids - 12 years, now initiated Druid member*

Steve has also attended lectures and workshops too numerous to mention over the years and continues to add to his knowledge and experience by attending events as they occur and maintaining his own regular sacred practices in Meditation, Yoga and Chi Kung.

Steve has had articles published in many magazines, on a variety of the subjects he works in. These include Positive Health and Pagan Dawn, as well as many of the smaller titles produced in the Pagan and holistic communities.

Steve has appeared on TV, twice alongside Derek Acorah on Granada TV's show 'Psychic Livetime' and acted as examiner on the Living TV series 'Jane Goldman Investigates', overseeing the work of Michelle Knight who taught the Tarot to Jane.

Steve acted as advisor and consultant for the New World 'Music of the Tarot' CD, for which he also wrote the accompanying booklet.

Steve has had eight books published –

* *Taming the Wolf: Full Moon Meditations*
* *Practical Meditation*
* *Practical Spirituality*
* *How To Be A Telephone Psychic*
* *Tarot Therapy Vol. 1: Tarot for the New Millenium*
* *Tarot Therapy Vol 2: Major Arcana, The Seekers Quest*
* *Tarot Therapy Vol. 3: Minor Arcana, The Map of the Quest*
* *The Tarot Therapy Deck*

Steve has also produced his own unique card sets –

* *The Tarot Therapy Cards*
* *Chakra Affirmation Cards*
* *Tarot Therapy Affirmation Cards*

Steve has also produced a range of 15 highly-acclaimed Meditation and Development CD's, which you can see full details of in the Shop on this website.

Steve is currently working on his own 'Tarot Therapy' deck and plans to produce a major new workbook, called 'Sacred Living'.

Steve has taught in person across the South of England and by distance learning internationally. Apart from his own private events, Steve has taught at Adult Education Centres in Hampshire and was tutor of the 2-year Tarot course at the prestigious 'Isle of Avalon Foundation' in Glastonbury, Somerset. Steve has tested and trained psychic readers for some of the leading telephone psychic companies in the UK, working across the world.

Steve was a Founder Member and Secretary of the Professional Tarot Society and was also Secretary of the British Psychic Registration Board, although both these organisations are no longer in existence. Steve is now a member of the following organisations –

* Order of Bards, Ovates and Druids (Steve acts as mentor for those following their training programme)
* *Spiritual Workers Association*
* *Tarot Association of the British Isles*
* *British Astrologers and Psychics Society*
* *Tarot Professionals*

Though a member of these Groups, Steve's approach to spirituality is an eclectic one, as he feels that every path has something to offer. He reads widely on spiritual subjects and incorporates what he learns into his teaching, in its various forms. Steve feels that a sense of the sacred for each individual is vital to the maintenance of health and well-being and for the fulfilment of our potential, development and life purpose. More personally, Steve has a deep love of many forms of music, runs long-distance and cycles. He enjoys visiting sacred and natural sites, plays tennis, attends his local gym regularly as well as watching football, remaining loyal to his origins by supporting his home-town team, Brighton & Hove Albion. He is the father of two children, Dakota and Amber.

TAROT THERAPY PRODUCTS

Steve Hounsome produces a range of products and services, which are detailed below –

TAROT THERAPY TRAINING
There are three courses available, for those wishing to train as a Tarot Therapist –

- **INTRODUCTION** – For the complete beginner
- **CERTIFICATE** – For those wanting to read professionally for others
- **DIPLOMA** - For those wanting to develop their existing knowledge and ability

TAROT THERAPY READINGS
Steve is available for readings either in person in Dorset, England, by 'phone or by email.

PERSONAL, PSYCHIC & SPIRITUAL DEVELOPMENT
Steve has produced a range of meditations and exercises for personal, psychic and spiritual development. These are available as cd's or as downloads from the website.

MEDITATION, PSYCHIC DEVELOPMENT & TAROT STUDY GROUPS
Steve runs groups in all the above subjects, as well as holding a series of workshops throughout the year, in Dorset, England,

Full details of all the above are available at Steve's website –

www.tarottherapy.co.uk

You can also email Steve at –

steve@tarottherapy.co.uk

Made in the USA
Las Vegas, NV
20 August 2021